Unearthing Your Latent Potentials

ALSO BY OGBONNAYA AGOM-EZE

Acorns of the Soul

Unearthing Your Latent Potentials

DISCOVERING THE GEMS OF YOUR SUBLIMINAL-SELF

OGBONNAYA AGOM-EZE

OUNOIAE BOOKS

Ounoiae Books
27177 185th Ave SE, STE 111-182,
Covington, WA 98042-8419, United States

Originally published in paperback in the United States by
Ounoiae Books, LLC.

LIBRARY OF CONGRESS CATALOGING-IN-PUBLICATION DATA
Names: Agom-Eze, Ogbonnaya, author.
Title: Unearthing Your Latent Potentials: Discovering the Gems of Your Subliminal-Self/Ogbonnaya Agom-Eze
Description: Covington: Ounoiae Books, [2019]. |
Includes index and mini-workbook
Identifiers: LCCN 2019917954 | ISBN 9781734215205 | ISBN 9781734215212 (eBook) |
Subjects: Nonfiction: Self-Help: Motivational & Inspirational | Personal Growth: General
Classification:

Trade paperback edition: 978-1-7342152-0-5
eBook : 978-1-7342152-1-2

First Paperback Edition

Printed in the United States of America

Ounoiaebooks.com

Book designed by Amnet-Systems

For Kelchi

Don't die old, die empty. That's the goal of life. Go to the cemetery and disappoint the graveyard.

—Myles Munroe

Table of Contents

Preface

—~—

Seventeenth-century England was a seething cauldron of many uncertainties that made life in those times quite unsettling, and not desiring better or more would have been an absolute blunder. The several disruptions of English life due to erratic leadership, overpopulation, and civil and religious disturbances—these were the foreboding characteristics of the times. It was an upsetting time in England under the unimaginative leadership of the Stuart monarch James I, King, and the son of Mary, Queen of Scots. The disconcerting times became the catalysts that stirred the crew of the *Mayflower,* the Pilgrims—102 souls in all—to undertake the maiden voyage across the Atlantic to the New World, North America.

To these pilgrims, it was an act of faith to embrace the passage. Despite the many known and unknown qualms concerning the expedition, the die was already cast regarding their quest for change. They trusted their brazen instincts that whatever they were bound to encounter would be better than the *status quo* of the then England. With the spirit of adventure and faith as their best acquaintances, they set sail from Plymouth, a city on the south coast of current-day Devon, England, braving the rough seas and storms, traveling about 2,750 miles in sixty-six days, and arriving at Cape Cod, Massachusetts, in the fall of 1620. It was there that they set up the Plymouth colony, an English settlement, second only to Sir Walter Raleigh's Roanoke Island colony off the North Carolina coast in 1587, in what is now the body-politic, the United States of America.

The Plymouth colony settlers, voyagers of the *Mayflower,* were in search of *new possibilities*—a fresh start and a new page to write a new story. They were in search of a *tabula rasa*-slate and state of mind—unaffected by experiences and impressions of their turbulent life in England—to write a new Puritan story of unadulterated faith in God. A lot had precipitated into their ears from the propagandist rhapsodies of Richard Hakluyt, the English writer, in his book that prodded the idea of North America and the New World, titled *Divers Voyages Touching the Discoverie of America,* published in 1582, and from the hypes and mockery of Humphrey Gilbert and Walter Raleigh that the Spaniards had laid claims to North America. All this became the catalyst that moved them to undertake the voyage in the allegorical pursuit of *the golden fleece of new possibilities.*

The same prospects for *new options* in the New World also led Giovanni Verrazano, Italian explorer of North America in the service of King Francis I of France, to scope almost the whole coast from Spanish Florida all the way to Nova Scotia, a current-day Canadian peninsula. It was the pursuance of *new possibilities* that made the French, in 1608, following up on earlier travels by Samuel de Champlain, French explorer and cartographer of the New World in the 1600s, to grasp a firm hold on the site of present-day Quebec, a current-day province of Canada. The pursuit of the *New World Dream—the dream of becoming more than you currently are*—remains the heart of what draws everyone to these lands.

The quest for North America is still on the minds of many across the globe. The desire to journey particularly to North America from then up until now has not diminished through the years—the pursuit of possibilities is still the main reason for the upward surge of interest to come to North America. The United States of America is known to all as *the land of opportunity*. It is a land where possibilities come to bear. Here, anyone can achieve anything they set their minds on. It is the land where dreams and aspirations come to life. The superstructure of the American Dream rests on the underpinnings of the Declaration of Independence. It declares that "all men are created equal" with the freedom to "life, liberty and the pursuit of happiness."[1] These declarations capture the ideals of the American Dream.

The American Dream is a metaphorical magnet that draws millions to the United States of America. The ideals of democracy, a land of rights, a place of liberty, a crucible of opportunity, and the champion of equality are the fields of attraction that draw people *en masse* into the United States of America. This nation is a cauldron—the melting pot of *possibilities,* the epicenter of global diversity and inclusion. The fact that peoples from various countries of the world come together to embrace the hopes that society avails; under the canopy and aegis of the United States of America, the idea of "one Nation under God, indivisible, with liberty and justice for all"[2] is the factor that makes America great.

---

1 The excerpt was obtained from *The United States Constitution.* (Reference: U.S. Const. amend. XXVII. Retrieved from https://www.uscis.gov/sites/default/files/USCIS/Office%20of%20Citizenship/Citizenship%20Resource%20Center%20Site/Publications/PDFs/M-654.pdf).

2 The excerpt was obtained from *The United States of America Pledge of Allegiance.* (Reference: The Pledge of Allegiance. (n.d.). The pledge of allegiance. Retrieved from https://usconstitution.net/pledge.html).

Whether then or now, the United States has remained a land that daily draws people from across the globe to its shores. The United States, for many decades, has stood as the land of *liberty, enlightenment,* and *iconic new opportunities,* an expanse seeded with the possibilities of a more opulent and fuller way of life for everyone—the symbol of an inclusive and diverse state. A land where what stands between you and the practical realization of your dreams and the maximum utility of your talents is your *energy, perseverance,* and *your sheer will to just try.* That is the *potential* that still draws many—through *push* or *pull factors*—to the United States of America. The numbers don't lie. In 1850, the number of immigrants and their share of the total U.S. population was 2,244,600, as opposed to 44,525,900 in 2017.[3] The growth and heterogeneity of the United States is its greatness. *America is potential.*

Coming to the United States of America was a thrill for me. I was excited about coming to the proverbial land of opportunities. I was eager to explore this great country—via my studies and travels—my two foremost passions. My *Coming to America* story was an educational pilgrimage or *hegira* to the land that I consider to be one of the Holy Lands of all erudition. I came to the United States with the vision of becoming the best version of myself. I, too, saw, and still see, the United States of America as the *land of opportunity.* If there was any place where I could see my dreams come true, it was here. Here I was, and here I

---

3 The United States immigrant population continues to grow. This study reflects an in-depth data analysis that surrounds the various immigration factors of the United States of America. Zong, J., Batalova, J., & Burrows, M. (2019, March 14). Frequently requested statistics on immigrants and immigration in the United States. Retrieved from https://www.migrationpolicy.org/article/frequently-requested-statistics-immigrants-and-immigration-united-states#Now).

still am, walking on the soils of possibility. A land where *dreams, hopes, aspirations, gifts, crafts,* and *depths* all come to embrace every success. *America is—possibility, and my life and story attest to this very fact.*

The American society, past and present, was and still is chock-full of opportunities. The societal gaps I experienced growing up in Nigeria are pretty much non-existent here in the United States of America. These are the things many people here may take for granted, through no fault of their own. That is the benefit of living in a land of opportunity, a place filled with many advantages. Things like constant electric power supply, potable water, an appealing and hygienic landscape, functional and accessible road networks, security, numerous modes of transportation, relatively affordable internet access, diverse mobile communication, a healthcare system that is bar none compared to what is obtainable in many nations of the world, good food, socio-cultural stability and tolerance, a society that works, just to mention but a few. The country is teeming with so much advancement, development, and possibilities.

Seeing all these civil positives that exceed the amenities and lifestyles most nations of the world provide made me question myself extensively. I pondered on how I could leverage the possibilities and advantages that the American society offers to become the best version of myself yet. Introspecting, looking back to those years, I truly believed that I could become more, and I still do entertain such views. Like the immigrant settlers of the Americas who saw the *possibilities* of the New World, I too see the opportunities in the United States. If there was anywhere in the world that my *dreams, hopes, ambitions, potentials, gifts, crafts,* and *depths* could ever become a reality—then destiny has me smack in the *eye* of that place. Now, the onus is on me to unravel these gems from the depths of my subconscious and become my best self ever.

The title of this book, *Unearthing Your Latent Potentials,* first came to me several months after I arrived here in the United States of America. It happened in the fall of 2002 while I was nestled in my humble apartment on Harrison Street in Oakland, California. It was here that my mind became most expectant. It was here that the many musings of *What more can I become?* amplified most intensely. I passionately believed that I had the capacity then, and still have the faculties to become more—that is, the best version of myself. I had made it to the land of many potentials, then I asked myself, *What more could I become?* It was there that I started journaling my thoughts about the *depths* I possessed that could distinguish me and cause me to become celebrated. I started penning down my thoughts from then and until now. I also began taking actions toward making my dreams, aspirations, and possibilities happen. In January 2019, I decided to take that plunge in setting down, in ink and paper, all my thoughts and tacit knowledge gained through the years into this title, *Unearthing Your Latent Potentials.*

Still dwelling on this line of thought, I kept on asking myself, *What more could I become?* I went on to tackle my dreams, one after the other. Whether it was writing my *first* book, *Acorns of the Soul,* a poetry compendium, my first job and the subsequent organizational leadership opportunities with Fortune 500 companies (e.g., Walmart and Amazon) that came down the road, my faith walk, marriage, the birth of my kids, educational pursuits, starting a couple of businesses, writing this book, *Unearthing Your Latent Potentials: Discovering the Gems of Your Subliminal-Self,* which you are now reading, etc. It all boils down to one thing—this is *my journey into discovering my possibilities and the best I could ever become.* I am most thankful to God for these possibilities, however little or big. All I can say is that *I'm just getting started on my options. I am still a W.I.P. (i.e., a work in progress). I am nowhere near done.*

I wrote this book to promote individual self-awareness and the personal discovery of one's abilities. Many people are oblivious to who they really are. Many people struggle with the questions that probe into who they really are, such as, *Who am I? Why am I here? What was I created to do? How do I go about doing what I was created to do?* and the like. You will be quite surprised at the number of people who do not have a clue about these kinds of questions or what they can do. *Could the reason be that many people are not deliberate in thinking about their latent (i.e., hidden, underlying, or possible) capacities? Could it be that people don't just understand what their different faculties are?* Hence, their hesitation toward wanting to even search themselves. I want people to become action-oriented toward unearthing (i.e., finding, discovering, uncovering, unraveling, or learning) their innate abilities. Therefore, this book is my attempt to apply a systemic structure to the process of self-discovery.

I wrote this book to give those seeking answers about themselves a clarity of purpose. When it comes to the question of *purpose,* many people are often confused and directionless. This book is poised to give its readers direction when it comes to the question of their purpose. Via self-discovery, they can eliminate the confusion that not knowing their *first use* can breed. By giving people clarity and direction, I want them to be inspired. I want them to aspire to become more than they currently are. I don't want my readers to expire or quench the flames of wanting to know more about themselves or the thought that they could be more. Thus, this book is a catalyst to motivate you into action regarding self-discovery. It is a spur to think outside the box or an innovation spark igniter, so to say. It nudges you toward greater self-achievement so that you can become more fulfilled. Finally, this book is my attempt to help you expunge the notion of *fatalism* (i.e., the acceptance of all things and events as inevitable, or submission to fate) from the lexicon of your thinking.

People across the world need to engage in more *self-reflection.* I want people to look deeper within themselves and pinpoint the attributes that make them most exceptional. I want people all over to see the benefits of expending their energy in building up their depths and transforming their lives for the better. I want people across the globe to develop an *explorative* or *investigative* mindset thinking toward what they can do. I want this kind of mindset to become the proverbial elephant in the room that will help foster a conversation about self-awareness and self-discovery regarding possibilities or abilities. Developing an *explorative* or *investigative* mindset opens the portals of the encephalon to discovery. I want the world to *dream, create,* and *innovate. Dreaming* gives you access to *becoming.* It is time for the world to leave the familiar by suspending their limiting thinking models and embrace the unfamiliar through deep subliminal-self-discoveries. The details outlined above are the reasons why the world needs *Unearthing Your Latent Potentials: Discovering the Gems of Your Subliminal-Self.* It is a new *perspective* of looking at self-awareness and the discovery of one's abilities.

What *new world* awaits your discoveries? Look to the horizons yonder, and just ponder. You can never know until you embark on the voyage toward unraveling the *possibilities* that lie ahead. They will remain *impossibilities* until you dare to take the first step unto the upper decks of the aphoristic *Mayflower* of your mind. The maiden voyage of discoveries awaits. Hoist your masts—your foremasts of forward-thinking, your main masts of absolute resolve, your mizzen masts of awareness—as you catch the winds of opportunities and prepare to navigate the uncertain waters of the vast seas of the subconscious, ready to crush the distance of lore, and embrace the possibilities of every discovery.

Bon voyage!

O.A.E.

MAPLE VALLEY, WASHINGTON
August 2019

INTRODUCTION:

Unearth Latent Potentials

—ɯ—

un·earth \ ˌən-ˈərth\ *verb*
1: to dig up out of or as if out of the earth
2: to make known or public: bring to light

la·tent \ ˈlā-tᵊnt\ *adjective*
1: present and capable of emerging or developing but not now visible, obvious, active, or symptomatic

po·ten·tial \ pə-ˈten(t)-shəl *adjective*
1: existing in possibility: capable of development into actuality
2: expressing possibility; specifically: of, relating to, or constituting a verb phrase expressing possibility, liberty, or power by the use of an auxiliary with the infinitive of the verb

—ɯ—

Everyone wants to *become something.* Apart from wanting to just become something, people want to move up a notch in *becoming more* than their *status quo.* We all carry a hidden power within us that is literally crying out for expression. We are all capable of doing something. We all have the *inner strength* to exist in possibility. Whatever this *hidden-inner-power* may be, we can express it; we can develop it into actuality.

Now, this *hidden-inner-power* is what makes us *dream* of shifting ourselves into that very *aspiration.* We desire to *become,* in reality, the subject of our purpose. To grow into our design, we begin to dig deeper into our subconscious. Our subliminal-search, taken up a nick, gravitates toward actions or making efforts (i.e., unearthing) toward seeing our latent (i.e., hidden) inner powers or possibilities (i.e., potential) a reality.

Potential can be likened to a small fetus developing in the womb that later grows to become a baby, then a toddler, and eventually an adult. As humans, we carry within us the potential for growth, as the very nature of life is built on us becoming something more and entering the fullness of what we are truly capable of becoming. A brick becomes a home; a seed becomes a tree; ingredients become a meal; a painting becomes art, and so on.

Before I get down to the brass tacks of delving deeper into this self-exploration book, let me start by laying the groundwork to help you understand the contents of this seminal opus. By the way, may I remind you that *you've got potential in you.*

If, up to now, you have erroneously believed otherwise, I dare to say it is high time you had a hard rethink. You may have failed at things you set out to do in life. You may have disappointed the people who believed in you. You may have lived in a cycle of endless failures, capable of rupturing your self-confidence; leaving you with the assumption that there's very little left in you to offer to the world. Yet, I still dare to say that there is still so much in you to make a meaningful and long-lasting contribution to the good of mankind. You were made for more.

However, if you are at the end of the spectrum where you know and believe that *you've got potentials,* but you're still struggling to figure out how to unearth or uncover them—look no further. This book has been written for you too. I want to take you on the journey of discovering your latent or hidden potential(s). However, I need you to stay committed to the process of digging out the truths set in the pages of this book.

As we go through different stages of life, we are constantly confronted with proof that we all have potential in us, in one form or the other. It is quite evident around us. You see it everywhere—in a toddler trying to take his or her first step, an entry-level employee in an organization filling a leadership role quite effectively, or in the tiniest of acorns growing to become an oak tree. Everything around us has in them the ability to blossom, the capacity to become uncommon, the strength to become extraordinary. The true potential of all can come to fruition only if they are given the right attention and not left dormant and unattended.

How often have you thought about some people who had the opportunity to make something meaningful with their lives but never did? I am sure you know that one individual within your circle of friends, who made quite a lot of unpopular and careless choices with life and has gone ahead to squander many opportunities that came along the way. Wouldn't you tag that as a waste, to say the very least? Isn't it disappointing how some of us don't take advantage of all the resources that are inherent within us?

Even if you are that one person who has squandered opportunities, that one person who has become an expert at wrecking their lives via perpetual practice, you have made the right choice of picking up this book to learn about your capacities. The truth is that there is still hope for you. The information contained in the pages of this book will become that scent of water that will revive that seemingly withered sapling. Don't write yourself off just yet—stick with me through this self-discovery expedition. It will be worth your while. May I remind you once again that *you've got potential in you.*

Time is a precious commodity. I do not make light of it, nor do I take it for granted. I personally value my time and yours. As a result, I always make a concerted effort not to waste it. Time is the only resource in this life that can never be replenished. Once spent, that's it. It is gone. So, the onus lies on you to spend it frugally with wisdom. I say all that to say this, *I appreciate the fact that you are looking at this book. I appreciate the fact that you are considering purchasing it, or you have already done so. My commitment to you is that the time you will spend, interacting with this book, will be nothing more but an investment in a productive, meaningful unearthing of your purpose as you discover your hidden potentials.*

So, join me on this *potential* unearthing journey.

Also, as it turns out, potentials are not always synonymous with privileges. Our inner gifts do not exist only for those born with silver spoons. They are available to everyone, given to each person according to their capacity. What you choose to do with your abilities is what makes you stand out in the limelight or remain in the dimness of obscurity. These intrinsic qualities, buried in the depths of our subconscious, have power in them. They are seeds, potent with possibilities, able to replicate and infuse growth and change. Our innate abilities could be anything from positive to negative. Everyone wants to be remembered for having expressed positive traits; however, some people walk through this life basking in the euphoria of their negative potentials—hopefully, not my readers.

For instance, the infamous Adolf Hitler had the potential to become a revolutionary leader, given the level of influence he wielded in Germany. Contained within that sphere of sway was the inherent ability to inspire togetherness and a kind of worldwide unity. However, the history books are a testament to the destruction of millions of people that was the result of his abilities. Hitler became the grand architect of the Jewish Holocaust. That was his legacy—his epitaph—that stipulates what he is remembered for. He had potential, but he chose to unleash it toward a malicious cause. Therefore, how we decide to harness and use our potentials is what makes the difference. Positive or negative—the onus lies on us.

When you have potential, you have possibility nestled firmly within you as *strengths, dreams, aspirations,* and *visions* that are yet to be birthed and manifested, but ready to be dredged up from the depths of your subconscious. What I want to do with this book is to activate your hidden potentials. I want to help you discover and express your hidden inner possibilities. To help you turn each potential you carry, into action-oriented abilities that are performing in full capacity. To show you that you have hidden gems in you, and to take you through a process of unearthing your greatness.

You won't get the best out of this book if you insist on believing that you have no potential, or if your mind is closed. *Open sesame!* Open your mind-portals and give the facts that are presented in this book a chance to work in your life and bring about the desired end that you wish for. A sealed-off subconscious hardly ever learns. Therefore, I want you to keep an open mind to the facts in these pages.

The process of *unearthing* involves unraveling bit-by-bit, layer-by-layer, that, which has been concealed. It consists of taking away excesses to make room for the essence and reaching for the substance of significant value. It is a process of digging, exploring, and peeling off layers to extract hidden gems. It takes effort and time to unearth. So, when I talk of discovering our potentials, I am referring to the process of removing excesses to reveal the kernel of your latent inner abilities. It is the process of looking deep within—a productive introspection that yields a life-shifting, life-shaping, and life-reshaping value. It involves reaching for the hidden talents that can elevate us in a given endeavor.

You could liken the process of unearthing your potentials to the method of mining for minerals. After studying the geology of an area, geologists conduct preliminary tests to confirm the presence of natural resources (e.g., precious stones, metals, or even crude oil). This is a process that can sometimes last for a couple of months or even several years. This testing determines, to a large extent, if the mine is rich enough in said minerals to justify a further search. If the results are satisfactory, then mining exploration begins in full swing.

Diamonds are one of the many varieties of gems that undergo the explorative process. They are formed and hidden deep within Mother Earth's ripe belly at up to 93.21 miles or 150 km under enormous pressure and heat. However, in time, the diamonds tend to move closer to the surface through tectonic movements. Therefore, thankfully, miners do not have to reach the core of the earth to find them. During exploration, a lot of digging still must be done. The subsequent mining process yields diamonds of various quality and caratage.

After these diamonds have been mined, they are then transformed into jewelry but remember that when diamonds are initially found, they are nothing like the beautiful jewels you admire when you walk into your favorite jewelry store. In fact, if you didn't know what they were, and you found them lying carelessly on the floor, you could easily mistake them for stones or a piece of broken glass shard. In their raw state, rough and untreated diamonds look like stone; it takes someone with a keen perception to recognize the difference. Once the rough diamonds have been extracted, they are cut, refined, polished, and shaped into finished jewelry of different kinds. It is after this process that the diamonds become really pleasing to the eyes. By this time, their price skyrockets, making them unaffordable for many people.

Diamond, subterranean in nature, require the process of searching, digging, refining, processing, and polishing to reveal its true beauty. The same goes for our potential—it also requires searching, digging, refining, processing, and polishing to bring out its true worth. In their raw and unprocessed states, they don't mean very much or look very appealing to all to say the very least. Recognizing the inherent value of potentials and investing the time needed to nurture them to maturation, they start to become invaluable to you and to the world in general. If there were no notion of the intrinsic value of diamonds, no one would bother to test their genuineness or confirm its availability. Their rarity and beauty characterize their worth.

Also, if nobody took the chance to uncover what lies beneath the earth, then diamonds would remain entirely concealed without any knowledge of their existence, value, or usefulness. We are often utterly oblivious to the presence of potentials of great value buried in our subconscious. Sometimes, we do not even give room to think about the fact that we possess life-changing gems within us, thereby shutting the door on what could lead us to success and a lifetime of abundance.

Unearthing one's latent potential—just like the process of mining and refining raw diamonds—requires hard work, time, focused attention, pristine precision, and tact. Connecting with the right people is another bedrock factor that directly relates to the discovery of the invaluable ability-gems stored up in you. Surrounding yourself with the right people, at the right place, and at the right time can make the process of self-discovery easier. The right people around you can become catalysts that speed up the exploration process. Solo-self-mining can be arduous at times; however, with the help of others, the process can become more efficient and effortless, to say the very least.

Another analogy I'd like to use to explain potentials is the process involved in the exploration of crude oil. As you might already know, crude oil is the largest source of global energy today, contributing some 2%–3% of the world's Gross Domestic Product (GDP). Pretty much every country depends on crude oil and its by-products like plastics, jet fuel, gasoline, kerosene, diesel, and many more. Crude oil is the world's black gold. Nations across the globe compete fiercely to lay their hands on the coveted black gold, willing to gamble everything for the chance to shore up their supplies of this source of energy. Some are even ready to go to war with other nations over it. It's a finite treasure of immense value, and the rush for it hot and steady.

The formation of crude oil is a slow process that happens over eons. It is constituted from the remains of once-living animals and plants (i.e., biomass). Over a prolonged period, this biomass is covered by several beds of mud, silt, and sand that form stratifications that eventually become sedimentary rock formations. The geologic heat and pressure of the overlying rocks change this biomass into a hydrocarbon-flush liquid ooze called crude oil, which seeps into porous rock stratifications called reservoirs. When crude oil is found in these underground reserves, they usually contain some impurities in them. When a discovery has been made, an exploration is carried out and then drilling begins until the oil is reached—generally to depths of up to 5,000 feet or more.

Once that has been done, and the crude oil is found, it is then refined through the fractional distillation process, by heating and separating into various products and by-products. During this process, the impurities are also removed. Products like Liquefied Natural Gas (LNG) (i.e., predominantly methane, CH_4, with some mixture of ethane, C_2H_6), found just above the crude oil reserve because of its which is lighter nature, is also tapped and used as fuel for large over-the-road haulage trucks, high-torque engines, maritime applications, etc. Hence, sometimes during the process of exploration and unearthing, the deeper you dig, the more you find beyond what you set out to look for.

—∿∿—

Your potentials do not merely exist; they are there to help change lives and help others find the inspiration they need to be their best. The pitfalls of leaving your potentials untapped are greater than you can ever imagine. While you might believe that it does no harm to anyone, you forget to put into consideration factors beyond you as an individual. The discovery of your potential can become the birthing crucible for new abilities in others. New job opportunities could be created because of your potentials. People may be inspired because of your potentials that are unearthed. Your process of self-discovery can have a domino effect that sets in motion the birth of new potentials in other people—a chain reaction of some sort.

Let us assume that you had an idea for a business that you somehow talked yourself out of starting. Because of that decision, others who could have been employed by you may go without a job. Your inaction to unearth your potentials can become a limiting factor to the birth of others' abilities. People's lives that could have been transformed become non-existent. Communities that could have been created remain in the *could-have-been* realm. Your inaction toward unearthing your hidden potentials could spawn socio-psychological obstacles that send out negative ripple effect into the time continuum of existence. In other words, inaction in exploring one's latent possibilities could lead to a plethora of other non-discoveries.

But what if you started that business? Just think about the positive ripple effect and energy that you would unleash on life. Think about the possibilities that will be borne in the form of others unleashing their own potentials because of your action. Think about those you would empower by your response to this call to unearth your latent abilities. Your effort to heed this call is a chain reaction that would lead to more positives. People whose success or progress are somehow linked to your ability and willingness to unlock the potential you carry within yourself will blossom.

If your excuse of not acting is that someone else will do it, I wonder what that person is also saying to themselves. Maybe just like you, they too are convinced that they are not the right person to act on those dreams. Therefore, the world is left destitute of uncommon achievers who are willing to take that first step of unraveling their gifts, but full of those who never get the chance to discover their potentials, all because we all failed to act on ours.

This is one of the primary reasons why you cannot afford to keep your potentials hidden. It is not just about you—it is for all the people whose lives will be changed because of your action rather than inaction. That is my core reason for writing this book: *To move you from the place of inaction to a place where you are discovering the hidden gems of your subliminal-self.* I don't want you to only find your potentials, I want you to maximize them for your utmost benefit. I want you to become a potent force that will make a maximum impact on society. I want you to become an instrument of change.

Through the various chapters of this book, I will take you on a transformational journey that will change the landscapes of your thinking faculties concerning how to unearth your potentials. In a nutshell, you will discover what potentials are. You will understand why many people leave their inner possibilities latent. Through detailed steps, you will learn how to unearth, refine, and make the most of your abilities. By the end, you will grasp how you can sustain the process of unearthing and maximizing those potentials so that you don't slide back to your former limiting habits.

Chapter 1 of the book is an exclusive look at what potential is. They are compared to the skills or abilities we acquire and utilize. We look at this through various examples of successful individuals who have discovered and revealed their potentials.

Chapter 2 is an elaborate answer to the question, *Why are potentials latent or hidden?* We will see the roles that *fear, self-doubt, procrastination, giving up prematurely,* and *laziness* play in keeping potentials latent.

Chapter 3 prepares the reader for the self-exploratory expedition and unearthing processes in the chapters that follow via certain pre-activities. The preparatory activities that we will look at include the *art of journaling, noting your patterns,* and *drawing up a vision of your life.*

Chapter 4–7 extensively elucidate my strategic self-analysis tool of choice—the SWOT Analysis Matrix—for identifying your potentials. We will begin in **Chapter 4** by looking at how to identify your Strengths (**S**). **Chapter 5** looks at how to recognize your Weaknesses (**W**). **Chapter 6** surveys how to find your Opportunities (**O**). **Chapter 7** looks at how to identify your Threats (**T**).

Chapter 8 highlights how the reader can practically answer the question, *How do you unearth your latent potentials?* To do so, we explore the use of the four-step model for carrying out change, the PDCA (i.e., **P**lan–**D**o–**C**heck–**A**ct) cycle.

Chapter 9 talks more about how we can polish or refine the potentials we discover. The analogies of the process of refining gold and crude oil are used as comparisons. We look at the process of extraction, distillation, and refining through the lens of inimitable principles.

Chapter 10 covers how we identify the outputs (i.e., *products and by-products*) of our potentials after the refining process. We will see that some of the by-products of our newfound abilities can be *skill experience, confidence, competence, passion, enthusiasm, valuable network,* and *service.*

Chapter 11 addresses how we can trade the outputs of our potentials. To do so, we will look at the concepts of *branding, product development, publicizing* or *advertisement, training, entrepreneurship, volunteering,* and *adding value as an employee.*

Chapter 12 focuses on the need to enjoy the rewards that your newfound potentials present to you. When you trade the outputs of your abilities, you will profit from them. As you do so, enjoy it while you are at it.

Chapter 13 is a call for a sustaining or preserving the successes and profits that ensue from discovering your latent potentials.

We will look at various sustainability bits or nuggets on how to achieve this goal.

Chapter 14 is a call to the readers to begin the self-exploratory expedition. Several warnings are also laid out regarding the dangers of procrastination in reference to acting on the information garnered here. Especially after learning and journeying through the page-landscapes of this *magnum opus.*

Chapter 15 is my envoi—my last hurrah—to, first, call you to action one final time, then to say, *Congratulations,* in advance for the discoveries you have made on this epic self-exploratory journey, and lastly, to say, *Thank you,* for staying with me till now.

My advice is that as you read the pages of this book, please ensure you approach it with the understanding that you are not merely unearthing your latent potentials for yourself but also for the people whose lives could be significantly impacted by your decision not to live under the umbrella of your limitations. In other words, interact with this book. Act on the series of introspective inquiries that you will encounter as you read through its pages. Write down thoughts that come to you as you go through this self-explorative journey. Already, the *art of journaling* and *noting patterns* should be instinctive by now, so do record your lessons, should you need to recall them on a future date. That is the only way to move toward the goal of becoming the best version of yourself.

Your move toward becoming the best version of yourself as you explore your innate abilities is for the betterment of humanity. It is for the improvement of all those you influence toward making better decisions for themselves as they emulate your examples of continuous improvement and positive achievement. The discovery and maximization of your potentials make them believe in the seemingly impossible. Because of this, they likewise launch themselves toward maximizing their own possibilities. It becomes a sustainable cycle of the unearthing of potentials. I hope that you inspire, nurture, educate, and elevate yourself, one page at a time, as you read through this work and unearth your latent potentials.

CHAPTER 1

What Are Potentials?

—ᨓ—

LIFE, AT TIMES, CAN BE a paradox. It can be full of contradictions that make us pull back and just think, as we get into a *tête-à-tête* with our subconscious. The things that can produce positive results could also produce contrary outcomes. The determinant of what becomes positive or negative stems from the options we choose to exercise. The clear differentiator in the paradox of life is the *choice* we make. In this book, we will be talking about how to unearth latent potentials or abilities in our lives for a positive impact.

Think of the most recent skill you acquired. Say you learned how to play an instrument, or you learned a new method of organizing your desk—don't get me started on the various ways that you can 5S your table and make everything have its place. It could be that you embraced a new custom of cleaning or reorganizing your home by going the *KonMari Way* (i.e., the Marie Kondo—the Japanese organizing consultant and author—way of organizing spaces). It doesn't have to be anything complex at all. It could be something as simple as learning to boil an egg or fixing a leak.

Before acquiring the said skill, the important fact remains that you may not have previously known how to address such a challenge beforehand. However, after learning the art or process, you know how to tackle it. Now, whenever you are presented with that specific challenge, you can address it without much effort. So, where previously you couldn't boil an egg, you now know how to do so without much thought after you have acquired the skill to do so. Therefore, by obtaining the knowledge of the craft, you can now address the challenge without much thought.

Potentials (i.e., skill, ability, craft, talent, gifting, or art, etc.) are like the skills mentioned above. On most occasions, they may not blossom in a day, nor are they always fully formed in an instant. Often, they require an aging process through repetitive usage to become fully functional in its use. Before realizing your potentials, it may seem like a walk in the dark—you grope and mope, you fumble and stumble, getting up oft. Your path is froth with many unknowns until you come to the light of realization at the end of the tunnel. However, unearthing the abilities in you comes with a refreshing appeal—the things which once intimidated or even overwhelmed you would faze you no longer.

Every human being has abilities they have never put to work. Take the instance of the person who newly learns to boil an egg—literally, the assumption is that anyone can boil an egg. As simple as the skill may be, not everyone has it, until they learn the simple process. You could be the shortest or the tallest person in a room, you could be the smartest or even the busiest person in a group and have never been in a kitchen before, and still learn to boil an egg in a day! Why? The reason is simple. You put yourself up to *learn*. The process of learning helps us to search broader, dig deeper, refine, process, and polish our abilities. The exploratory journey to understand what your potentials are is a continuous learning process.

Unearthing latent potentials is *a process of discovery*. It is discovering how to do things and coming to the realization that you can do the things you really want to do, after all. You could argue that some talents are innate, but it doesn't rule out the fact that constant practice is what eventually leads to expertise in a craft. You didn't learn how to write the first time you held a pen, did you? Oh, no. It took years of learning to adequately handle your pen. It took learning how to form your thoughts and learning how to spell correctly. It is a combination of different types of things that makes up the rudimentary gist of effective and efficient handwriting and penmanship. It wasn't instantaneous. It was a process of gaining a step-by-step process that brought you closer to the due expertise with each up-step.

After work has been done to unearth potentials, what ensues is the derivation and delivery of value that spawns from those possibilities. The goal of every unearthed ability is the value that *it* consequently delivers. Just as the purpose of mining is to see what is buried underground (i.e., a precious stone or metal of value, or some valuable natural resource) that yields the result of proffering profits, our potentials as individuals in similar vein also deliver results and produce value in the process.

There are many stories about how skills, abilities, crafts, art, etc. (i.e., potentials) have been discovered, uncovered, and put into valuable use. There are the stories of people you have heard and watched rise to the limelight because of their potentials. There are also stories of people, who because of their resilience, have turned their lives around. In their stories, we see unquestionable and uncommon outcomes that provide credence to the power of potentials at work. Let us consider some of these stories that portray discovered golden and value-adding possibilities remarkably at work.

Consider the story of Jack Ma, the Chinese bureaucrat, business magnate, investor, and philanthropist, and popularly known for being the co-founder and executive chairman of the multinational technology conglomerate, *Alibaba Group*. Jack Ma heard about the internet and was introduced to it by friends in 1995. Three years earlier, the web had been made public in the United States with just 600 websites live and online. At the time, China was merely catching up with the internet buzz, and you could hardly find information about the Republic online. Because of this, Jack Ma decided to start a website where such information would be made available.

The internet, although still in its infancy then, was already is a goldmine of potentials. Even after having advanced over the years, it remains a quarry of opportunities waiting to be unearthed by the next genius-cipher. Its advent brought people to the realization that, with a network of computers, they could store and retrieve loads of data. Not only that, with this network of computers, people in different geographic locations could easily be connected at a whim. This marked the dawn of the information age, and more people were going to their computers to search for information. The coming of the internet paved a new allegorical Appian Way of communicating, socializing, doing business, etc., forming the foundation of a whole different way of living, making the world more of an interconnected global village.

Jack Ma himself could only guess the extent of the impact that the internet would have—all he had to work with was the fact that there was hardly any information about his country on the World Wide Web. The population of his country was a significant number, and he had heard about how valuable the internet was becoming. Clinging onto that knowledge, Jack Ma started *China Pages,* where he worked with Chinese businesses to create an online presence through website creation. All this he achieved without knowing how to code or even having extensive experience with the web. However, his idea was the potential that drove him toward discovery. By 2013, two of Alibaba's websites made $240 billion in sales—twice the size of Amazon, and thrice that of eBay—taking Jack Ma to the position of the richest man in China (NB. As of August 2019, and at the time of this writing, he still retains that top spot as the richest man in China).

Before any of these successes with Alibaba, Jack Ma was met with failures of varying degrees. He failed at various levels of education (e.g., in elementary school and in college), got rejected after several job applications (e.g., up to thirty jobs), got rejected ten times at the famed Harvard Business School, even failing at the first two business ventures he started, just to mention a few of his failures in life. His is a classic never-giver-upper story. Despite all the failures that he faced, he never gave up, and he kept on pushing forward until his story took a positive turn. He was determined to become the next rags-to-riches story. He did not allow his failures to become a stumbling block toward unearthing his potentials, but instead, they became the stepping stones that he used to ascend to greater heights of success. He did not let the disappointments he faced cloud his judgment toward becoming the very best version of himself. A lot of people would have cowered after suffering just a few of what he went through—not Jack Ma. He was a man mad with the frenzy, zeal, and hunger to succeed. He refused to be dispirited at the throes that his failures must have brought. He armed himself with the *quitters never win, and winners never quit* mindset. As we see in his story, his attitude molded his eventual altitude in life.

The potential that brought him to the limelight of extraordinary success, however, lay in the ascent of the internet and its capacity to reach a growing number of people. Jack Ma saw a need, and he filled it. He saw the need that existed in China at that time—the lack of information on the internet about China—and he started China Pages, a directory of various Chinese companies looking for customers abroad, to fill that need. Despite China Pages being a flop, it was his first stab on launching an internet business. That was his *Eureka!* moment. China Pages gave him the *oomph* to take a second stab at the internet business, creating Alibaba, his second company. Jack Ma was in the circus of life for the winning. He hit that opportunity high striker with the mallet of determination and with all the power he could muster, which has landed him on the 21st spot on the Forbes list of Billionaires (at the time of this writing,) with a net worth in the high thirty-plus billions of dollars as of August 2019. Who knows what the future will hold for him. Only time will continue to tell his story.

The premise of potentials is that whatever lies hidden could become more exceptional than our initial conception of it. A little idea of today could become a vast company of tomorrow with an international presence. A short song written by an unknown and uncelebrated musician and sang in a moment of inspiration could become a hit song that tops the various billboard charts across the globe, with the young and old belting it out of their bellies every chance they get. A new writer of today can become the best-selling author of tomorrow. A genius code writer, nerd, and cipher of today can become another Facebook or Google of tomorrow. A dancer showing off their moves on

Instagram or YouTube could become an A-List dance choreographer tomorrow.

Speaking of A-List dance choreographers, consider the story of Sherrie Silver—the young twenty-something-old Rwandan dancer who started showing off her dance moves on Instagram and YouTube just a few years back. Today, she has been credited for being the choreographer for Childish Gambino's *This Is America* (NB. The YouTube video has approximately 583 million views and counting at the time of this writing). She has also been credited for being on NBC's Saturday Night Live (SNL) and has worked with Rita Ora, Victoria Secret Fashion Show, Nike, etc. She is the perfect epitome of a discovered and blooming potential. Do look her up. Her story is inspirational. The possibilities of potentials are endless across many circles.

Back to our Jack Ma story, the truth is that he only had a slight inkling of what started out as a failure in the Tech world could eventually become. The more Jack Ma explored, the broader became his understanding of the spectrum of the potential. The more he dug deeper into the possibility, the more he unraveled. To his awe and the utter amazement of all, his findings and small beginnings grew astronomically in no time. The more he peeled off the chances of the potentials that he had discovered, the better he was able to lead Alibaba to the successes it now enjoys. The basis of his possibilities had become more exceptional than his initial conception of it.

The story of Jack Ma is an illustration of the process of unearthing the potential of a business idea. There are possibilities in various spheres of life waiting for discovery—potentials (i.e., skill, ability, craft, or art, etc.) come in different forms—you just must try to find them. Consider the case of the top-performing United States women tennis player, Serena Williams. She is widely acknowledged to be the most prominent women's tennis player of all time, as well as being the most dominant and iconic. Among many other accolades, the Women's Tennis Association (WTA) listed her as No. 1 in singles at eight different instances between 2002 and 2017.

The possibility of tennis started with Serena's father, Richard Williams, another *Eureka!* moment. He had seen a professional female tennis player, Virginia Ruzici from Romania, play a winning game and picking up a $40,000 check after the performance during the 1978 French Open Championship tournament. This inspired him to decide to raise his daughters to become top-performing tennis players they are today. He had started a security agency but after this revelation would teach himself and his family how to play tennis. Before this, he had no experience with the game. Talk about the infusion of potential via deliberate education in a craft.

Virginia Ruzici's tennis adroitness and stardom inspired Mr. Williams to unearth the tennis sports' potential in himself and his daughters. Youngest of five sisters, Serena at the age of five started playing tennis at the public courts in Compton, California. At the age of eighteen, she was playing full time, having gone professional by the age of fourteen. Her dad had taught himself how to play tennis by watching videos, coaching his girls with the help of his wife, Oracene Price, subsequently with a reported two-hour daily practice time. Now, *can we call this the grafting of a potential?* It might as well be. Could this be an affirmation to Malcolm Gladwell's *10,000 Hours rule to attain greatness?* If she practiced two hours a day, before the age of eighteen, she would have honed her skills to perfection. Anyway, the fact is that the Williams *sought broader, dug deeper, refined, processed,* and *polished* their tennis craft to stardom status.

Committed to unearthing every latent potential in her, Serena Williams has gone on to win twenty-three grand slam titles and took the entrepreneurial route in 2018 by starting her fashion line, *Serena.* Married to Reddit co-founder, Alexis Ohanian, she is also a proud mother to her daughter, Alexis Olympia Ohanian, Jr. However, without the vision and guidance of her father who recognized what was possible, Serena Williams would probably never have developed an interest in playing tennis. In understanding what potential is, *recognition of possibilities is a critical factor.*

So far, having seen Jack Ma's and Serena Williams' potential discovery and potential-in-action stories, I hope that you can now appreciate that the ability to learn whatever skill you admire is attainable. It is possible to achieve the success you wish for. They are only an effort-reach away. To be the person, you would very much love to become is feasible. That potential to become your best version ever is available—it is inside of you—waiting for a full expression; waiting for you to discover it by searching, digging, refining, processing, and polishing that specific potential (i.e., skill, ability, craft, or art, etc.) to reveal its genuine worth in you.

Potentials can be *innate* and native to a person. Also, as we have seen, it can be *acquired* by shared will and deliberate practice. Achieving any *inherent* or *acquired* potential is possible. It requires grit and an unflinching drive toward making it a reality. Unearthing a latent potential does not apply only to just human beings as we have seen in the above examples—pretty much anything and everything has some kind of latent (i.e., inherent, innate, internal, fixed, or natural) potential or capacity to become much more. For instance, the internet is one of the ways the power of potential has been leveraged—in this instance, to reach millions of people.

An instance of leveraging the power of the internet is *Facebook,* the online social media giant and social networking service that was founded by Mark Zuckerberg, in conjunction with his fellow Harvard College students and roommates Eduardo Saverin, Andrew McCollum, Dustin Moskovitz, and Chris Hughes. As of December 2018, Facebook, having taken hold of the power of the internet, now boasts of 2.3 billion monthly active users, averaging about 1.4 billion active daily users.

The Facebook idea, which got its very first start as a tool for students at Harvard, was initially conceived as *Facemash,* with the intent of letting students judge their attractiveness and create a ranking system out of it. Within the first few hours of the platform launch, *Facemash* received 22,000 photo views, creating a buzz on campus—so much so that the school authorities got wind of it. Not long after that, Facebook was founded in 2004 for people with Harvard email addresses, opening to the public in 2006. By October 2007, Facebook had reached fifty million users and had already attracted the attention of investors who would invest more than $10 million into the company. Its growth trajectory *was* and still *is* in hyper-drive.

Despite the backlash that the company faced in the Cambridge Analytica Scandal that seemingly dragged its reputation through the proverbial mud of the mainstream media regarding the 2016 United States Presidential Election, Facebook's annual revenue has continued to grow exponentially. According to Statista, its revenue in 2018 was $55.8 billion, up from $40.6 billion in 2017, with the major source of its income stemming from digital advertising. Excluding the countries where Facebook is banned, the social media giant can be accessed from anywhere with a connection to the internet. By tapping the power of connectivity that the internet offers, Facebook sits regally on the throne as the biggest social network worldwide.

The building up of biomass that eventually becomes crude oil starts *small* and progressively grows over a long period. The same goes for potentials, on most occasions, they often begin *small,* like the tiny acorn that becomes a giant oak tree. In the process of time, more and more, they grow gradually and then balloons to epic proportions. As the Good Book says, "do not despise the days of small beginnings." An instance is Facebook, which started from the college dorm room of Mark Zuckerberg and his colleagues. It's not that it couldn't have started differently. It certainly could have. However, the process of formation and growth had to take its full course. The unearthing of the full potential of Facebook, then Facemash, required due diligence. Several missteps and course corrections had to happen during its infancy stages before it could take flight and command the attention of the plethora of users as it now does.

Every individual has a *spark* or *wow* factor, which is why we are exploring the notion of potentials. As we have seen from the stories in this chapter, it is not a mere theory that is relegated to the pages of a book. The notion of *potentials* or *possibilities* is an attainable practical experience, and that is why we are delving into it. We are dissecting the concept from all angles to find out how we are to seek it out, how to *prospect* it, and how to *refine, process,* and *polish* it. When you recognize something about you that pops—your potential—something about you that could reach myriads of people, the first thing to do is taking baby steps to gradually unravel the idea where you are, just like Zuckerberg did with his colleagues in bearing Facebook. You will notice that Facebook did not start as a business idea. It was just something college students used to keep in touch. It's like peeling an onion—one layer at a time.

"Familiarity," they say, "breeds contempt," meaning that *if you know someone or something very well, you can quickly become bored with them and stop treating them with respect.* We often apply the facts and truth of this idiom when we are dealing with others. Have you ever thought to employ this idiom on yourself? Let's look at this from the lens of potentials. Being too familiar with yourself, or the potential(s) that come easy to you is a pitfall that many people fall into. The *first* reason is that you often don't recognize the innate potency of potentials and the weight of impact they carry when maximized. The *second* reason is that you could become too familiar with yourself that even when the best comes out of you, you neither recognize it nor respect it because you've not taught yourself to value the depths of your being.

Beyond just being the thing you can do better than others, potentials also form the bedrock of greater things you can inherently achieve, deeper-seeded within the core and inner *sanctum sanctorum* of yourself. These greater things embedded in you are *seeds*—potent with life—waiting to sprout into greater prominence. The *strengths* and *interests* you possess are the couriers of *seeds of potentials.* Inside these are the traits of more *powers* and *profits* that you are yet to discover. Facebook saw the potential in something *ordinary* and made it *extraordinary.* They took the organization of networking events to a higher dimension. Instead of having twenty people at a networking mixer, Facebook brought the mixer to the whole world through the power of the internet. Because of this, Facebook has allowed everyone to socially mingling in the matrix of the World Wide Web. The result of maximizing the potential of connectivity has been outstanding on scales of astronomical proportions. Talk about the maximization of potential.

—⁂—

Simply put, *potential is undiscovered or unattained greatness.* It is an architectural blueprint on paper that has not become a concrete building that people can admire, live, or work in. The idea of potentials, *latent* or *acquired,* in the embryonic stage, can readily be doubted. Why is that? Because people like to believe what they can see, and without proof, accepting a notion becomes more of an arduous chore.

Potential is the gem buried underground. Whether the people who live in that area recognize what they have or not doesn't change the fact that the stretch is laden with wealth-blossoming potential. Discovering such an expanse would make the founding explorers wealthy beyond proportion and make the place an attraction, like the Kimberley mine of South Africa, or the Mir mine in Russia, which had held diamonds long before their discovery.

As with these mines, you must learn to recognize your own value now before you become the person that commands much more. Your potentials are your *dreams,* your *goals,* your *ideas,* your *talents,* the new *skills* you picked up, and the ones you admire in other people. Take the first step in unlocking those potentials in yourself by making the commitment to getting better at them, and you might be unbarring the world's next best invention or innovation bar none.

CHAPTER 2

Why Are Potentials Latent?

—∞—

WHEN SOMETHING IS *LATENT,* IT means it is present but not immediately visible, apparent, or actualized. You are cognizant of its existence but its full capacity is unrealized. For instance, gems like diamonds, precious stones, other metals, and natural resources of worth must be dug up from underneath the earth to reveal their true essence, beauty, and value. Similarly, something latent is *concealed, underground, veiled, contained, passive, sleeping,* and merely existing as *potential,* until it is tapped and revealed. Most *potentials* are often *hidden,* requiring seekers to discover them, put them to use, and then maximize them efficiently.

Occasionally, there is the possibility of perceiving the value of something *latent.* However, we are often tepid or uninterested about it. Why is that? *Could it be because it is in its raw state and unattractive?* More often than not, that line of thought is right on the money. In many instances, valuable things in their crude form—before they undergo any kind of refinement—are not always very appealing or inviting. It is only the keen eye, with deep perceptiveness and foresight, that can see its latent potential in that state. Hence, such a person can celebrate it for what it is *then,* and most importantly, what it can *become.*

Take a seed, for instance. As small and insignificant as it may appear, that seed holds within it the capacity to become a tree. On its own, a seed is uninteresting. An orange seed is nothing like an orange tree or, more precisely, *the fruit.* There is no likeness when we compare them, not even from the looks. The promise of sweetness in the orange seed is manifested in *the fruit.* The fruit cannot exist without the seed. The essence of the fruit is embedded in the innate traits of the seed that gives it its value as an orange. Similarly, all that we can become cannot come to full realization without manifesting the potential we have in ourselves. Consequently, *the essence of our becoming is inherent in the traits of our potentials.*

The General Sherman Tree, the Giant Sequoia tree that is in the Sequoia National Park in California is considered as the world's most massive tree by volume. According to facts provided by the United States National Park Service and the web, it is about 52,500 cubic feet (1,487 cubic meters) in volume, which is equal to more than half the size of an Olympic-size swimming pool. Despite being the *largest* known tree in the world, Giant Sequoia seeds are diminutive. They are usually 4–5 mm (0.16–0.20 in) in length, and 1 mm (0.04 in) broad, with a 1 mm (0.04 in) width. These seeds are minuscule compared to what the trees eventually become—case in point, the General Sherman Tree. Synonymously, what is in you—*your inherent potential*—may seem so minuscule, almost invisible, or literally latent. However, the Herculean magnitude of what you can become is hidden within the essence of that small or seemingly insignificant potential.

The potential that you carry may be seemingly unattractive and underdeveloped. It may have no similitude or likeness to what it could eventually become from the onset. Your potential could look so microscopic to the point of being seemingly invisible. The fact is not whether your innate attributes qualify as pleasant or whether it is big or small; the truth is in *the code of what it carries* and *what it could become.* Michelangelo's David is revered as one of the best—if not the best—marble sculpture ever made. Standing at 17-feet tall, it is literally larger than life—plainly three times the size of the average man. However, would you have guessed that this magnificent statue was borne out of the potential hidden in a block of marble that two sculptors (Agostino di Duccio and Antonio Rossellino) discarded as trash? Why was that? All because it was hard to crack and work with before Michelangelo picked it up and worked it into the masterpiece it now is. In the same way, that which you consider *latent, hidden,* or *insignificant* could be the core of your eventual distinction.

Notwithstanding whether you believe it or not, the fact remains that we all carry potential(s) within us—the untapped strength and dormant ability, if awoken, could take us from obscurity to a place of prominence in life. You probably look at successful people as being endowed with some ethereal quality that somehow makes success just a little easier for them than it is for you. The reality is that they could be only working to unlock their potential bit-by-bit, discovering their strengths and capacities as they go along. The difference between *them* and those who don't succeed in finding and expressing their hidden abilities is that they dared to take the initial step of discovering their talents in the first place. They tried, and it yielded results. No one is born fully formed. That is, no one is born with all their inherent and acquired potentials functioning at full capacity. We discover and deploy them one-at-a-time or in batches—depending on how much our will can carry.

The thing with potential, as with most things, is that you can have it, but you remain oblivious of its existence. A lot of people could even be staring at it dead in the face and stay blind to that distinguishing trait it carries that could make them shine. Potentials are usually inert, requiring discovery and drive to set it in motion. Too many people walk about, not cognizant of what they carry within themselves. They consequently live the rest of their lives with undiscovered potentials, dying *full* rather than *empty*, and where there could have been a discovery, the world experiences a gap, a *void* that should have been *filled* with *innovation, creativity,* and *possibilities* of what could have been. All because of people failing to discover their potential, believing that they are currently all they could ever be—the philosophy of *fatalism* (more on this later) in action.

We all have strengths and talents that remain unused and untapped. We could also become numb to the ability to make our dreams a reality. The concept of our preferred realities of what we want in life is not farfetched. The fact that we can conceptualize a thought in our dreams means that we have the potential to do it. The brilliance of unearthing your potential is that as you discover new strengths that you possess, you gain the capacity for more. This offers an explanation to why super successful people seem to be able to skillfully manage different projects at the same time. It's not so much as their ability to multi-task, but their ability to grow effectively through the different roles they play. Hence, it wouldn't be wrong to say that discovered *working potentials* have the innate capacity to *multiply*.

I've been thinking, *Why do very few people achieve the success they desire in life? What are the factors at play that help shape the realities that people experience? Is it because of some hardwired genetic makeup? Could it be their background? Could it the environment that they grow up in? Could it be a factor of economics—maybe, resting on the pylons of the fact that they are born into wealth, and can stand on the wealth amassed by their predecessors to succeed?*

I am always ruminating on these questions to ascertain why only a *few* attain the successes they desire. We could posit a lot of speculations concerning what molds extraordinary experiences, however, *I am inclined to say it is a factor of* ***time, chance,*** *and* ***making the most of the opportunities*** *that life throws at us despite the framing factors that surround our realities.* That is my position regarding the above introspective questions. I can say that a lot of it rests on the *decisions* we make in life.

For instance, Miuccia Prada of Prada, an Italian billionaire heiress who, born into wealth, became a part of the family fashion business, after which she launched her own line, *Miu Miu,* further expanding the reins of her success. We can stipulate that the economy of her heritage played a massive role in her process of becoming a super successful fashion heiress. However, someone like Howard Schultz, who was born into dire poverty but went on to lead Starbucks Coffee Company as the Chairman and Chief Executive Officer from 1986 to 2000, and then again 2008 to 2017—is also capable of great success. Like these two, there are many other polar examples of background that results in success—rich or poor notwithstanding. Indicating that what matters ultimately is not so much what you are born into. Instead, your ability to *unearth* those *latent* (i.e., hidden) potentials inside of you.

Privileges differ, but the availability of potentials is not limited to a select group of people. However, there is a general privilege that we all share in life—*Time.* It is the only commodity that everyone has the fundamental customary concession of sharing—it levels the playing field. There are around 31,536,000 seconds in a year (non-leap year), available to all. What differentiates us all is how we choose to invest this common privilege. The possibility of becoming the best version of yourself depends on how much potential you decide to unearth within yourself in the *limited time* that you have here on earth. Despite the commonality of the time privilege, many people still fail to excavate and maximize their potentials. Why? In this chapter, we will explore some of the reasons why people's potential(s) remain hidden despite all the things they can become, as well as the need for uncovering those potentials.

Before we continue, have you ever pondered on why gemstones are so valuable? Have you ever wondered about the fact that the things that are most valuable world-over are not always standard or copious in amount? From gems to high-level skills, inventions, and so on, the adjective that usually qualifies them is the word *scarce*. These things of value are in limited quantities—insufficient to satisfy the need or demand. Their availability, or lack thereof, depends on accessibility—they are often hard to access. *Scarcity* announces the *inherent value* of something, which is precisely the case of the potentials within us. Different kinds of abilities, unique to an individual, are available for discovery and access. However, not everyone discovers and uses their distinguishing trait. Why is that? Despite the value and availability of these skills in people, not many are willing to put in the required work needed to discover and access their innate abilities. Hence, it becomes remarkably crucial to expend the effort to *unearth* those unique attributes that are hidden in us.

One may wonder, *why are potentials hidden at all? Why does one have to make so much efforts to discover them? What makes them special and different from the rest?* It is valid to say that in the absence of scarcity, potentials become like everything else—*cheap*. Rarity increases the value of things. For instance, that is why organizations seek out *rare* talent to join their teams, to improve the cumulative worth of their talent pool and human capital. They bring exceptional know-how to the table that distinguishes them as they add unique value to the organization. The more distinct the talent, the more value is placed on it. A golden example is the value that a talented player like LeBron James instantly brings to a team in the NBA league—his skills and record in the NBA are bar none, increasing his value to the team. The same goes for our potentials. There is distinctiveness and individuality that being different offers, which explains why the rarity of gems make them valuable.

We hide gifts by wrapping them to surprise the recipients. Consider a time when you were presented with a wrapped gift on some special occasion. Can you recount the medley of feelings that raced through your mind as you guessed from corner to post what the present could possibly be? Say the gift was unexpected, but it was given to you by someone dear to your heart. If you know anything about the thrill of unboxing a gift, then you know that the process of unwrapping elicits a deep sense of excitement and expectation for something pleasant—the anterior pituitary gland is on overdrive producing endorphins, or *Happy Hormones,* to mark the occasion. A smile forms at the corner of your lips, but you try to downplay the bubbly emotions because you're trying to be cool. But it's there, that joyful expectation you can't just unhinge—a typical analogy of what it feels like to unravel our latent potential.

It's almost like, "Sweet Christmas!" channeling my inner Luke Cage. Imagine yourself as a giddy young kid with exploding anticipation to unwrap your gift under the Christmas tree. Except if you are Superman, Kal-El, or Super Girl, Kara Zor-El, of the planet Krypton that has x-ray vision, perhaps. Your wrapped gift in hand, you absolutely have no clue of what is under the wrapping material, but your curiosity compels you to keep unraveling the package as you unwrap it layer after layer. You are fully invested in the process, as you become shrouded in the euphoria of the possibility of what you could find. Not only is it rewarding after unboxing to discover something exceedingly worthwhile but also the buildup to that moment is everything. It prepares you for what is to come. If the process is that significant to unboxing a wrapped gift, what is to say that it wouldn't be just as vital in the unearthing of your latent potentials, something with the ability to transform your life and usher you into a whole new world of worth, significance, and impact.

Discovery is what makes us. It is an appraiser of our self-worth and value. The effort and the time that elapses to find out our potential multiplies our value factor. If we could be all that we can become in just a flash, without the process of discovery, the value factor that we derive from that process will be lost. In a way, it cheapens potentials, as it now becomes banal, and people would no longer take it seriously. Life doesn't just happen in many cases as a flash, although Barry Allen, the Flash, would beg to differ. That is why it is imperative to dedicate yourself to reveal your innate potential. In unraveling what is hidden within, we not only develop an appreciation for life but also for ourselves, because in going through the process, we discover the real value of what is hidden within us. The discovery process is a course of self-illumination. Hence, unearthing your latent potentials can be said to be a process of self-discovery.

Potentials are available, yet quite a few of them lie dormant in the alcoves of people's subconscious, unused throughout the lifetime of the carrier. The late Dr. Myles Munroe rightly observed the grave to be the most opulent place on earth. Why? Because the cemeteries are replete with many *could-have-been(s)*. No longer living, all the people that have gone six-feet under can no longer be the best they were created to become. Those are all lost possibilities now. Their talents or gifts have become *forgone opportunities*—never discovered, never celebrated—*the unsung heroes of Mother Earth.* They are gone, never to walk the face of the earth as we who are alive currently do.

In the graves, as Dr. Myles Munroe further explains, are many *possibilities* that now remains *impossible* to ever achieve. In the graves are books that were never written, songs never sang, inventions that never materialized, scientific discoveries never made, art masterpieces never crafted, athletes never discovered, unique culinary delicacies never created, just to mention but a few. These are people laden with a lot of potentials, individuals who *could have done* great things in the world but died with their ideas and their possibilities, robbing the world of these gifts.

"Don't die old, die empty. That's the goal of life. Go to the cemetery and disappoint the graveyard."

So, tell me, *What will your story be after reading this?* The ball is entirely on your court to hit and unearth the potentials hidden in the depths of your subliminal-self.

Potentials never promised to be dressed in fancy suits and ties. Most times, potentials come clad in the four-lettered word, *W-O-R-K,* often in that guise for the discerning to decipher. No wonder it often seems unpleasant or unattractive—a lot of people recoil from having to work hard or even smart, often shying away from it. That very fact is the nucleus of why many people leave this earth still full of the many possibilities that they could have unleashed.

How many people would impose themselves to the hard work of introspectively searching within themselves to discover their innate abilities? The work does not stop at just finding your potentials. You must then process, refine, and polish them to bring out their true worth. However, many people don't have the will power to subject themselves to such discipline. That is the reason why a lot of people die with all their potentials. Colonel Sanders, who in his lifetime worked different jobs in different industries before finally succeeding with Kentucky Fried Chicken said, "There is no reason to be the richest man in the cemetery. You can't do any business from there."

The aim of the book you have in hand gives you the schematics of how you can commence your journey of *self-awareness* and *self-discovery* with regard to your potentials. The greatest gift, as Dr. Myles Munroe noted, is to deliver what you came on earth for, and you cannot go in expecting a finished product from something you haven't tried to polish. Part of the process of unearthing is *finding, digging, cutting, buffing,* and *shaping* the potentials in us for the fabulous life that you have been called to live. There's a false expectation that *potential is everything*—that's not true. Unless potential is recognized through keen perception, most will wake up with their *skills* or *abilities,* but never go any further in their quest to *refine, reshape,* and *reorder* them for purpose.

Being so conscious of this reality, *Why then do potentials remain untapped?* If truly everyone has potential in them waiting to be tapped, *Why do so many people live unfulfilled lives, giving less than their very best to the world?* Among many other factors, here are some of the reasons that I have chosen to share on why I think a lot of people fail to reach the depths of their potential. They are—*fear, self-doubt, procrastination, giving up prematurely,* and *laziness.* Let us discover some things about these limiters and learn how we can curb, eschew, or preferably eliminate them, shall we?

Fear

Assume you entered a room and found a snake in it. You don't have any details about the kind of snake it is, or how big it is. In this instance, *what would you do, if you had a phobia of snakes?* Also, *what if you then realized it was a non-venomous species and couldn't do you any harm. Would that make you feel relaxed?* If you honestly answered the questions, it wouldn't matter whether it was *poisonous* or *not.* The mythical fangs of Phobos would dig into your flesh at an instant, giving you the jitters, Right? However, the question then would be, *Was there a real threat in this scenario or an imagined one?*

While a certain level of fear (i.e., caution) is necessary for a balanced reaction to life, too often, we give too much control to little worries, exaggerating them beyond what they are because we have taught ourselves to anticipate the worst—making mountains out of molehills. In so doing, it cripples our will to want to achieve anything. We become nauseatingly *risk-averse,* incapacitating our determination, preventing us from trying new things. Stop always anticipating the worst. In the words of a Helen Keller, "No pessimist ever discovered the secret of the stars, or sailed to an uncharted land, or opened a new doorway for the human spirit." Steadily having a negative perspective due to fear will damn all possibilities of you ever discovering your potential.

Fear is one of the most acute reasons for unrealized potentials. Think about the things you most fear that inherently holds no danger in them: the fear of public speaking, of intimacy, heights, ants, and the list goes on. Fear is a very natural human instinct that allows us to respond to danger. However, where the danger lies is to dwell perpetually under the canopy of fears cover. But I ask, *what is the risk of reaching out to things that can change your life as well as the world?* Fear will usher you into the catacombs of pessimism—an abyss devoid of accomplishments and hope. In the words of an unknown author, "Pessimism is an investment in nothing; but optimism is an investment in hope." So, what will it be? *Would you rather invest in nothing than in hope?* You tell me.

You have this ability to become all these great things, yet you hold back because of fear that you are not good enough. You *assume* that you do not deserve the successes you've earned and fear that people are thinking so. Now, *don't you think you have become the judge and executioner of your dreams and aspirations for far too long? Why base your life on unfounded assumptions?* You may have even persuaded yourself that you don't have much to give the world anyway, letting your strengths lie dormant. The world is eagerly waiting for the exhibition of your pure and innate essence. Fear will perpetually shroud your dazzle. Indulging in fear is like being an uncut and rough diamond, whose beauty is not known because it has not been refined. Hence, you embrace mediocrity and obscurity, never giving yourself the chance to be all that you could ever be. Give faith an opportunity and not fear. Have some ounce of self-confidence as you move forward to unearth your potentials.

The challenge is this—because we are acquainted with our potentials in their crude state, and have not developed the capacity to refine them, we don't know what to do with them. Should the opportunity avail itself and come up with ideas of what you could do with them, you're too paralyzed by fear to do anything worthwhile about it. *Fear asphyxiates potentials*—the same way a lethal dose of the Botulinum Toxin (BTX) Type H (2 nanograms) can kill an adult human. But, *what if the larva was too scared to become a butterfly? What if, through some bizarre twist of nature, the seed decided it was too frightened to become a new plant that bears brand-new fruits? Wouldn't that be weird, right?* Don't let fear cripple your potentials. In the words of Franklin Delano Roosevelt, "The only thing we have to fear is fear itself."

The fact with fear is its power is more of intimidation than an actual attack. At the root of it, it stems from the mind, buoyed by environmental conditioning, repeated negative thoughts, and reiterated glum self-talk. Fear will operate by attacking you at your weakest, like a lion preys on vulnerable its vulnerable victims. For instance, *you're scared of public speaking? Well, how about you sit quietly in the dimness of inaction while the message you have for the world gathers dust and cobwebs?* Or, *are you just afraid of embarrassing yourself and becoming a laughingstock should you attempt to step into the ambiance of your innate potentials?* Well, fear will only succeed in keeping you from going for outstanding opportunities that could conceivably turn your life around. In the words of an Edmund Burke, "No passion so effectually robs the mind of all its powers of acting as fear." Don't let fear blind you to the possibilities of your potentials.

However, the funny thing with fear is that we know the truth about it. Some of the things we fear that eventually cripple our will to unearth our potentials are not real and pose no immediate danger to us or anyone around us. Don't get me wrong, there are legitimate fears—whether real or imagined. Fear is the human emotion aroused by impending danger, evil, pain, etc. It is a primordial instinct that gets the adrenaline pumping when we are in danger. It is understandable to be afraid if you are being chased by a ferocious-looking rottweiler, or if someone is threatening with a firearm aimed at you with an intent to cause you harm. We can say that these instances are legitimate fears, all things being equal.

Usually, the things we fear are well within our control, but we still give in to that feeling as if that will somehow make that situation less threatening. For instance, every public speaker is aware that the people in the audience do not bite. Now, *what's the worst thing that could happen while you are up there on the stage?* You could get booed by the audience, should you go there and fumble. Or, you could get *George-Bushed.* Remember on December 14, 2008, when the Iraqi journalist Muntadhar al-Zaidi threw both his shoes at the United States President, George W. Bush, during an Iraqi press conference. President Bush had some quick reflexes there, as he was able to duck quickly, evading either of the shoes. If you don't have rapid reflexes, should you get *George-Bushed,* then you would be way out of luck because whatever is thrown at you will make an unpleasing contact. However, *should this bar you from your ambitions of becoming a compelling public speaker?* I don't think so. Don't let your fears justify your hesitation. Just do it.

Even in instances when the voice of fear is louder than that of a possibility, action despite general apprehension should be the goal that propels you forward. Remember, you are what you teach yourself to be—we become what we celebrate. If we celebrate fear, then we will become fearful. I don't deny that there are factors that have contributed to your fears. You might indeed have had a traumatic experience. Still, no matter how real the things that caused your anxieties are, you need to understand that, *courage,* not fear, is what the world applauds and celebrates. In the words of Samuel Langhorne Clemens, better known by his pen name, Mark Twain, "Courage is resistance to fear, mastery of fear, not absence of fear." Learn to master your fears, and don't let it master you or your potentials.

Rather than holding you back, your fears should be the motivation that launches you forward in the quest to discover and unleash your latent potentials. Every time you are assailed by the thoughts of how unpleasant things could go, you must also remind yourself just how well they can go. Think positively. I couldn't resist not sharing this quote from an unknown author who said that "Faith, belief, positive thinking makes better people and a better world since the outer world shapes itself to our intuitive thinking. Quit thinking and talking about war, poverty, hard times. Think and talk about peace, health, plenty, success to help bring them about. Guard your thoughts against negatives as you would your house against thieves." Think about the man whose life might be dependent on your courage and let that motivate you to act. Your fear benefits no one but your courage profits all.

Marianne Williamson's quote is so befitting at this point in the book. She said that "Our deepest fear is not that we are inadequate. Our deepest fear is that we are powerful beyond measure. It is our light, not our darkness, that most frightens us . . . " Now, after reading this quote, I want you to honestly answer the question—*What are you most scared of? Of failing, or of succeeding?*

Master your fears, unearth your innate potentials, and become the shining star that you were made to be.

Self-Doubt

Right beside fear is *self-doubt* which, if unaddressed in its infancy, can spiral out of control into a cycle of deception that leads nowhere. Self-doubt is the lack of confidence in the reliability of one's own motives, personality, thought, etc. Everyone questions themselves, intermittently but it becomes a problem when people become pre-programmed to question themselves at every moment, in every case, creating a habit of inaction that truncates one's vision to become. It is a state where you are constantly second-guessing yourself. You have no faith in yourself nor in your ability to achieve anything meaningful. Like fear, self-doubt can smother your potentials and good intentions until there is no more life left in them.

When you live with self-doubt, you fall into the trap of believing you do not have potential, perhaps because of a series of wrong decisions you have made in the past and not living up to your own expectation of yourself. Self-doubt sows and nurtures the seeds of nervousness, insecurity, and discouragement. Self-doubt makes you an overly skeptical person. You doubt everything, and it leads you into the paths of failure. Self-doubt makes you a chronic self-critic. You criticize yourself to the point of inaction. Whatever it is, let it go. You become what you think, you become what you celebrate. What you tolerate takes root in your subconscious and becomes your reality. You are only as good as how you perceive yourself.

We already established the fact that every seed can be a tree. Likewise, every human being can become a nation. However, allowing self-doubt to overtake your consciousness will constrict your ability to explore that which is hidden inside of you. An unearthed potential could become the king in the macrocosmic jungle of possibilities. However, if you allow yourself to be overcome by the mental boa of self-doubt, it will constrict the life out of your king-size potentials, killing your will to achieve them, squeezing and crushing you under its weight, and swallowing you whole. In the words of Bill Clinton, "It's heartbreaking to see so many people trapped in a web of enforced idleness, deep debt, and gnawing self-doubt." Don't let self-doubt constrict the possibilities that await discovery. Don't get caught up in the web of self-doubt. Free yourself.

When you struggle to believe in yourself, you will not take the first step toward the life you desire, much less the things that you can become, all because the thoughts in your mind are very limiting. Self-doubt is a straitjacket that will bind your potentials. It restrains your ability to unearth your strengths. Self-doubt urges you to steadily affirm over and over again, fatalistically, your own perceived lack of value. It holds you back from embracing opportunities when they are presented to you. It limits your growth potential. Orison Swett Marden once said, "Discouragement, fear, doubt, lack of self-confidence, are the germs which have killed the prosperity and happiness of tens of thousands of people." Don't allow the virulence of self-doubt to infect your will to unearth the innate potentials that are in you. Overcome it with self-confidence as you discover yourself.

You should know that every time you let yourself reach for the latent potentials within you, you give room to discover more of your depths or strengths, develop the capacity to take on more, and be efficient at execution. Thereafter, you begin to trust yourself more, you become assertive, people start to trust you to get the job done, and before you know it, your opinion is required before vital decisions are made. Your potentials create a whole new world of opportunities and possibilities. So, why would you allow self-doubt to truncate your upward rise to become? Boost your emotional well-being and refined immunity with the eclair of self-acknowledgment. This will help you muster the fortitude you need to set yourself free from the shackles of the past as you ascend above fear, doubt, or resignation.

Having gotten that out of the way, we can move on to address the root of self-doubt as it relates to potentials. Firstly, self-doubt and fear are entwined. A fearful person is someone who steadily anticipates the worst and doubting their ability to achieve. Someone who doubts themselves is scared, either of failing or even succeeding. Secondly, you must be aware that self-doubt is self-inflicted, it's straightforward. The same way fear is mostly a construct of the mind, self-doubt also is chiefly connected to the kind of dialogue that transpires in our heads. It is impossible to talk about unearthing your latent potentials without addressing that dynamite of self-doubt in the mineshaft of your mind.

If your mind is filled with negative thoughts, it is almost near to impossible for anything positive to create a positive impact in your life. Your competitive advantage is lost inside the confusion, and the vision of getting ahead in life takes a cliff-drop plunge. It's almost like wheat fighting for survival in a field overrun by tares. You must declutter your mind and get rid of all the non-essential clutter (e.g., self-doubt, fear, and the like) that is clouding your judgment. You must have an introspective conversation with your subconscious, as you place a demand on yourself to be the kind of person you will accept—the version of you that is destined for excellence. As an instance, it is the reason why a lot of people who win lotteries go broke after the win. Often, they become worse than the average earner. Why? Because, as much as their physical circumstances changed because of the gain, their minds did not.

You have to address the things you think and say to yourself. Understandably, self-doubt plagues us all when we're doing something we've never done before. However, there is absolutely no justification in holding on to it for long; the time has come for you to ditch it and begin your exploratory journey toward unearthing your potentials. Preliminary naiveté could be allowed at some point, for instance, if you are a novice in a career field. Self-doubt could also be an expectation when you hang around a circle of new acquaintances. However, as you continue to spend time in these situations, it is only realistic that you begin to get comfortable. Become a quick study in order to become a part of that system, or flow better with the new friends that you have. You cannot continue to bask in the euphoria of self-doubt. You must intentionally give yourself space to grow.

So far, we have seen that fear can bar you from unearthing your hidden abilities. Next, we have seen that self-doubt is a close sibling to fear and they both carry the same consequences of stopping you on your tracks from unraveling the profits of your innate potentials and must be eschewed at all cost. Thus far, there is a clear notion that you possess one form of potential or the other. On this note, I have two questions for you:

One, do you believe it?

Two, what will you do with it?

As Victória Fyódorovna Azárenka, the Belarusian professional tennis player, once said that "I had to battle the doubts and fears for a while, but I committed to making sure that my strongest emotion was self-belief. Once I did that, I knew I would be okay." If you must be that one person who will discover and unearth their latent potentials, like Ms. Azárenka, you must fuel your self-belief. Stop giving self-doubt so much reign over your life. Tell yourself what you need to hear to motivate yourself. Better still, allow the words of this book to spur you into action toward changing your *status quo* through the discovery of your hidden abilities. It is time for some tough self-love to get you on the right tracks of self-discovery. Believe that you can unearth the best version of yourself that the world will cherish and celebrate. This is the only way you will begin to see the results that you want to experience in your life.

Procrastination

In addition to fear and self-doubt, potentials can also remain hidden because you procrastinate. A lot of people fail to achieve the very best because they continue deferring required actions that they need to take today for tomorrow. The sad thing that happens in most cases is that the tomorrow they anticipate never comes, and opportunities are lost. Many of us may have heard the proverbial saying by the English poet and dramatist, Edward Young, "Procrastination is the thief of time." Hence, if you keep putting things off, you will ultimately achieve very little in life. If explorers did not go out to find mines, and importantly, dig them out, nothing would have been found. The potentials will remain rich underground, and no one will bother with them.

In procrastinating, your actions could be driven by either *fear* or *self-doubt.* The potentials are there, you have an idea about what they are, but don't find it urgent enough to begin the unearthing process. You have all the things you recognize you can be. You realize how good you are at sales, writing, speaking, singing, or some unique talent you have that is quite evident, but you keep telling yourself you are not quite ready to take the first step toward actualizing it. While you already have the things you need to create the life you want to be embedded within you, because it's in its crude state, you don't appreciate it enough to explore it further.

I'm going to be brutally honest with you—the truth is that you procrastinate because you are just outright lazy. It is a hard pill to swallow, but that is the truth. You are putting things off for tomorrow because you have chosen to dine with *Aergia,* the Greek mythology deity of sloth, idleness, indolence, and laziness. You may already know or may not know what gems that lie within the labyrinths of your subconscious being, but you are just too lazy to dig, to explore, to unearth yourself. Becoming is not easy work. It is hard work, and you are unwilling to pay the steep price that is required to release the value buried in those potentials. To access pleasures at times requires some painstaking effort, but laziness has a hold on you. To triumph and become requires you to go through some tests or trials, but you are scared, besieged by self-doubt, and crippled by laziness. So, you just put it off by giving yourself excuses why you can't do it. Quite simply, *you are dastardly lazy.*

Now, the question is, *will you continue to embrace laziness?* Or *will you now get up and start digging? Stand up and commence your discovery process? Get up and become.* Pay the price to find and put to work those potentials that make you exclusive. Pay the price of those sleepless nights needed to discover the hidden gems that are inside of you. Pay the price of investing those sixty to eighty-hour workweeks that might be necessitated in the early days of unearthing those latent potentials that are innate in you. Pay the cost of severing yourself from relationships that are a deterrent toward your becoming. If you pay the price, you will reap the reward when you become an extraordinary success in your chosen endeavor. Remember, if you don't pay the price, and choose to procrastinate, you will remain a pauper because your potentials will remain dormant within you. Do not be envious of those who have paid the price and are now reaping the rewards of their labors. Stop procrastinating and get to work.

Procrastination might seem like a quick-fix now to get off the hook from putting in the required work needed to be your best self ever; as you're thinking to yourself that now isn't quite the time to unearth your potentials. The two-horned detractor's best tool is persuading and tricking you is to put things off—to procrastinate. Outsmart him. Do it now. Stop telling yourself that you have all these roles you are filling that has taken much of your time. Stop making excuses by saying you're a boss, a parent, an employee, a volunteer, and in between all these roles that you juggle, that you don't have enough time. Time is the greatest leveler—everyone is given the same amount of time. What you do with yours is what counts. Make time to get it done. Stop giving yourself the lame excuse of not having the needed urgency to discover anything that is currently covered in the depths of your subliminal-self. The best time to have unearthed your latent potentials was yesterday. The next best time to do so is *now.* Don't put it off till tomorrow. That is already too late. Now is the time to *dig,* to *process,* to *refine,* and to *polish* your abilities.

When you uncover your latent potentials, one of the benefits is that your life gains a new momentum. You reach new levels of traction as things around you begin to be more seamless with less friction. You start to live with less stress because you have gone through the pressure of the toils and tasks to get to your current *status quo.* Not only do you now operate wholly in your strengths, but you also begin to prioritize your time, as you avoid the non-essential time-wasting elements that formerly plagued your ephemeral walk. Your life begins to have a better structure, vision, and purpose. However, when you keep procrastinating, these strengths that could distinguish you remain just potential that is nice to have, but not urgent enough to pursue.

Seeing that potentials are in a raw state majority of the times before they are unearthed, and do not come fully formed, pushing the process of discovery to an unspecified future date seems like the easiest thing to do. Anything to opt-out of the hard work required to do the *digging, processing, refining,* and *polishing* of your potentials always become more appealing and an easy way out of effort you needed to put into. For instance, suppose you set a goal to learn a new language, say Spanish. However, you then start to rationalize that you don't need to use it every day, which might be a valid assertion. Because of that, you consciously or unconsciously become lukewarm about your goal, pushing it off to the next day, the next week, the next month, and then the next month, until you lose the desire altogether. If you would fear anything, fear procrastination. It will smother all your good intentions and stifle your dreams.

Fear procrastination. Why? It is like cancer that slowly metastasizes until it becomes malignant and eats away at the tissues of your willingness to become anything meaningful. It will kill your potentials. Procrastination is a virulent disease waiting to attack your success and happiness. It is a limiter to your efforts at becoming a pro. If you must unearth your hidden abilities, you must also ban procrastination from your life. Courting procrastination will only land you in a world of regrets. Procrastination is a fire that burns everything in its wake. Don't let it assassinate the opportunities that life presents to you. Start digging, start processing, start refining, and start polishing your innate abilities. Denzel Washington couldn't have said it any better when he said, "I'd be more frightened by not using whatever abilities I'd been given. I'd be more frightened by procrastination and laziness." Be afraid of not unearthing your innate potentials. "Be afraid of procrastination and laziness," as he says. Run far from its grip before it incapacitates your will to unravel the best you ever.

Until you commit to learning that language of getting it done right now, you will always find reasons to shillyshally around starting. Hesitation is as bad as procrastination. In the words of Robert J. Shiller, the American economist, academic, and bestselling author, "Hesitation is often like procrastination. One may have vague doubts and feel a need to mull things over; meanwhile, other issues intrude on thought, and no decision is taken. Ask people why they procrastinate, and you probably won't get a crisp answer." Hence, hesitation is synonymous with procrastination. Start working on discovering your potentials right now. Until you commit to the process of *recognizing, digging, processing, refining,* and *polishing* your *skills, talents,* and *abilities,* you will not unearth anything. Sadly, some people get to the end of their lives, having lost the desire and energy to make any more discoveries. Will this be your story?

Giving Up Prematurely

The next factor that we will consider is the act of *giving up prematurely.*

Giving up prematurely means yielding control or possession early in the process of making efforts to accomplish a task. There is a plethora of reasons that explain why people give up so easily. *First,* they do so when they place the cart before the horse. They focus primarily on the outcome of their pursuit, instead of immersing themselves in the process of their exploration. They fail to maximize their *Now* by gaining mastery of the skill(s) they have found. Because of this, when they hit a roadblock in their dig, they give up so easily. The process is in the *Now.* Focus on the *Now,* and that will take care of the future outcome.

Second, they give up prematurely because of fear they are afraid of what people will say about them should they not succeed. One thing in life is sure—people will always talk. Whether you succeed or fail, they will always have something to say, good or bad. Why shape your existence on the opinions of others?

Don't focus on what people will say, pay attention to the process of your exploration. Focus on your *Now.*

Third, people give up prematurely when they are too rigid. They fail to be flexible enough to accept change and innovation. They fail to adapt to the changing conditions of the equilibrium in the process of exploring and maximizing their innate potentials. In the face of challenges that require adaptability, their unchanging mindset causes them to ditch the whole process rashly.

Fourth, they give up prematurely because they have not cultivated the discipline needed to evolve into the new versions of themselves in the pursuit of their innate skills. In the words of an unknown author, "Discipline is the hidden ingredient that turns nobodies into somebodies." Discipline is fortitude and the cultivation of the art of self-mastery. If you don't pay the price, you will not gain the prize. Paying the price is all about sacrifice. It's about sacrificing the time and effort needed to unearth your potentials on the altar of daily routine, master it, and achieve distinction through its deployment.

Fifth, people give up prematurely in the discovery of their potentials because they are too consumed by matters that don't concern them. Instead of paying attention to their dig—their process, their refinement, and the polishing of their potentials—they choose first to pay attention to what other people are doing in their own journeys. Their loss of focus causes them to make a blunder of their dig, leading them to give up the whole process impulsively.

Sixth, they give up prematurely on the exploration of their potentials because they don't have the belief that they can succeed in the process, through thick and thin, no matter the cost. These individuals are plagued by self-doubt, which constricts their faith in the power to unravel their hidden skill set or talent.

An unknown author once said, "Doubt sees the obstacles, faith sees the way; doubt sees the blackest night, faith sees the day; doubt dreads to take the step, faith soars on high; doubt questions, 'Who believes?' Faith answers, 'I!'" Once again, as earlier mentioned in the preceding paragraphs, *will you allow self-doubt to constrict your innate ability to become the best version of yourself ever?* Your choice.

An analogy of giving up prematurely can be seen in, for instance, a marathon runner, who starts the race with gusto, but quickly drops out of the race after burning out just before going the distance in the race. That athlete drops out early in the race, giving up prematurely because they did not strategize their run. Going back to our recurring mining analogies, diamonds are formed at up to 93.21 miles or 150 km below the earth surface, after which they reach closer to the surface through specific volcanic eruptions and tectonic movements. Despite shifting upward from those depths, miners must still dig up to depths of approximately 1.5 miles or 2.4 km below the earth surface to find them. Imagine if they stopped searching at the 0.7 miles or 1 km mark? They would be way out of luck, and no discoveries would be made by them. It would be a lost effort, only to the gain of any other explorer who pays the price to reach the right distance.

Exploration involves actively searching for information or resources. It is a process we are hardwired for, as human beings. The human is a curious being by nature. We are wired to travel through familiar or unfamiliar territories armed with the purpose of an objective. It was this drive that drove the early settlers to the Americas as we saw in the *Preface*. We want to investigate and discover new things. We are naturally inclined to embrace adventures. We do it for the thrill. We do it for growth, and to expand our territories. We do it to discover the next new, exciting thing. We also do it for profit. For example, exploration is what began the California Gold Rush that started on January 24, 1848, with the discovery of gold by James W. Marshall at Sutter's Mill in the surrounds of Coloma, California. This, in turn, led to an inrush of about 300,000 prospectors, adventurers, and explorers to California in the quest for gold. Man has a constant hunger for more—a better life, better relationships, and a better self—which, without actively searching for it, will come to null.

Your potentials may be buried, but until there is focused attention on the discovery process, there is a high tendency to give up easily with every hurdle you encounter on your path. You are likely to give up readily after any discouragement. It takes a dedication of steel to find rare diamonds. That is why diamond mining companies expend all the resources necessary in their diamond prospecting and mining processes. For instance, in a De Beers Group Mining 2013 Snapshot Report, the company stipulated that since the year 2000 to 2013, the diamond mining industry spent almost US$7 billion on exploration, sparing no effort toward the search for these rare gems by all diamond companies across the globe. That is a shared dedication put forward by all these companies (e.g., De Beers, Alrosa, Rio Tinto, Debswana, Dominion Diamond Corporation, etc.) in their search for these gems of worth. Similarly, you must dedicate yourself to the process of searching for the hidden strengths that you possess until you unravel them.

There is a toll that hits your psyche, should you invest too much time in a project and it doesn't pan out as expected. There is no way you would be termed a loser if you poured your heart into an endeavor toward the discovery of your potential and found nothing in that angle. The loser is the person that did not even take a step into the mineshaft of their subconscious. Losing is not attempting to explore your potentials at all. Don't be too willing to give up. Don't be in too much of a rush to throw in your towel when you face challenges in your exploration process. Staying the course is the key to a successful search. Remember the moral of the story in the Aesop Fable series, *The Hare and the Tortoise?* Slow and steady wins the race. Always remember, *Winners never quit, and quitters never win.* Become a never-giver-upper. Always remember that whoever perseveres eventually succeeds. Most people who give up too early in their exploration to discover their potential barely go the distance and decide to give up their quest, and nothing guarantees a find like a search.

The exploration process is a journey of discovery. The deeper you go, the more you learn about yourself. With every layer that you find underneath as you make progress in your dig, you discover something new, something valuable in and about yourself. Unearthing your latent potentials is a continuous improvement process. You unveil a new piece of yourself with every stratum you unearth. You begin to realize the uniqueness of your subconscious makeup. You start to recognize that you are one-of-a-kind wonder in what makes you who you are. Your self-perception takes a new turn, and you start to really believe in everything that you could become. But none of this could have transpired if you never gave it a shot, or if you gave up prematurely—and not just a haphazard shot that merely grazes the surface, but actually going all the way.

Have you ever wondered what would have happened if Thomas A. Edison gave up on his light bulb experiment at the 2nd, 10th, or even 999th trial? Every failure presented an opportunity for Mr. Edison to throw in the towel prematurely. However, he persisted with an unflinching determination in his experiments. Granted, someone else would have made the discovery, but what would happen if everyone decided that the 10th trial was as good as it could get? What if he became discouraged, deciding by himself that nothing could possibly take that many actions to find? Then, there would be no light bulb, which Mr. Edison discovered after 1,000 unsuccessful attempts, nor would there be electricity as we know it today. He persisted and did not consider himself a failure, despite all his failed attempts. Mr. Edison was resolved to accomplish his set goal. In his words, he said, "I have not failed. I've just found 10,000 ways that won't work." His attitude paved the way for further technological discoveries and innovations. If he could, then others could also do the same and more.

The world is better today because of the persistence of people who, despite the initial challenges, insisted that the potential of their ideas must become tangible. From the Pre-Paleolithic times to the present day, there have been many mind-blowing inventions that have altered how we live—from Philo of Byzantium (c. 280-220 BC) with the water wheel, the Han Dynasty (202 BC-AD 220) court eunuch Cai Lun with the paper, Hans Stopler with the Revolver, James Watt with the steam engine, the Wright brothers with the airplane, Auguste and Louis Lumière who pioneered the Cinema, Ray Tomlinson with the Email, to Steve Jobs and Steve Wozniak with the Apple-1. The list of those who made life-changing inventions that have transformed our everyday living is extensive. Without the persistence of these people, much of the comforts of the modern world will not be in existence.

Sir Thomas Edison would himself attest to that, saying, "It is not that I am so smart. It's just that I stay with problems longer." Persistence is what kept him going, despite the failures.

Persistence is the result of a compelling vision. The reality of what lies underneath the mass of our subconscious should excite you enough to keep digging and digging until you reach your potential because it *is* there. There is a lot of potential(s) within you, waiting to be discovered. Therefore, you must keep seeking until you find those essential gems in yourself, and don't give up your search prematurely. This is the reason diamonds miners will not give up at the first few levels of exploration when mining for diamonds. They will expend all necessary resources toward various exploration projects.

Take a cue from this and dedicate yourself to the process of unearthing your latent potentials. Stay the course, however long it takes—a day, a week, a month, a couple of years. Whatever and however long it takes, just stay the course. There will be roadblocks, challenges, and tough times that could make you give in prematurely. My advice is to plug away and be a never-giver-upper. Give your latent potential search some time. Trust the process. Focus on taking care of your *Now,* and your *Now* will take care of your tomorrow.

Don't give up. Keep pushing until you discover your hidden skills, strengths, and abilities. Pay your due diligence and give the process what it requires, and you won't regret that you did.

Laziness

We have established that the process of unearthing your hidden potentials requires digging until your hidden abilities are *found, processed, refined,* and *polished.* Hence, every stage of the process is crucial and requires dedicated work. However, we have seen that several factors (e.g., fear, self-doubt, procrastination, and giving up prematurely) are responsible for keeping your innate potentials undiscovered, untapped, and unexplored. We need to be cognizant of these factors and ensure that we do all this in our power to eschew, curb, or preferably eliminate them so that they don't hinder our quest to find all the treasures of distinguishing abilities that are hidden in us.

Laziness is another reason why potentials remain latent. It is a severe aversion or disinclination to work, activity, or exertion. To be lazy is to be idle. Jules Renard, the French author and member of the Académie Goncourt, couldn't have said it any better about what laziness is. According to him, "Laziness is nothing more than the habit of resting before you get tired." *Indolence* is a sibling to *fear, self-doubt, procrastination,* and *giving up prematurely.* These factors are the five fingers of the hand of destitution that will keep your potentials hidden if you allow them to have a firm grip on you. To have your skills uncovered, you will be required to work actively by yourself. Therefore, if you are not passionate enough about revealing your skills and abilities, your potentials will remain latent due to lethargy. Eschew laziness and idleness at all cost.

Idleness is the Devil's Workshop, Inc. Mr. Beel Z. Bob is the longstanding Chairman and Chief Executive Officer (CEO) of this global corporation. The products of this company are *poverty, slavery, destruction,* and *hunger.* The associates work here are called the *Idles.* The currency of payment for the Idles is *Ruin* or *Ru* for short. The *Idles* are also awarded a copious amount of the products of this corporation. The CEO of this corporation allows its associates free rein on the shares of the corporation as part of its asset sharing plan incentive. Hence, the *Idles* are opulent in *poverty, slavery, destruction,* and *hunger.* By the way, this corporation is always hiring associates at all levels, and their pay is pretty good—just being facetious. The first step in the hiring process is having extensive experience in the *Art of Couch-Potatoness.* Become a Couch Potato and do precisely nothing, and you will get a call from their recruiters in no time. Are you already working for this corporation? You know if you are. Would you want to work for this company? Yeah, right. Thanks, but no thanks.

Your potential is yours to unlock, and you are responsible for what it eventually becomes—that is if it will become anything at all. Laziness is not limited to just physical work alone. As you may well know, the digging that is required in the process of unearthing your hidden potentials is more figurative than literal. You probably pride yourself on exerting your physical strength to work. As admirable as it is to see what we can achieve with our bare hands as we work hard in an endeavor, there's another crucial part of the work to be done that you might, in fact, be lazy about. This is the more unseen part of the potential unearthing process, which is mental and more internal than external. Hence, you could be physically or mentally lazy at the same time, which would be a double whammy on the journey to becoming the best version of yourself yet. In the exploration and discovery of your inherent potential, physical and mental hard work are a crucial and unavoidable part of the process.

It is one thing to be lazy in terms of putting the physical work needed to be done, and another to be lazy about *thinking, planning,* and *ideating.* Physical work probably comes more natural to most than mental work. Unearthing our potentials will require that we exert ourselves physically—sleepless nights, long hours of work, multitasking, commuting, etc. These requirements are upfront. With cerebral or mental work, you need to think deep and more precisely. Thinking takes a different manner of work, and if you are not used to it, it can quickly become a daunting and possibly draining task. In the words of Savion Glover, American actor, tap dancer, and choreographer, "Great athletes last because they let the mental do all the work. What we do as hoofers is not so much a physical strain as everybody thinks. It's more of a mental stretch." So, to last the stretch of the way in the process of unearthing your inner abilities, you need to let your brain do significant work. Because of this, many opt for the lazy path, not willing to pay the required price to uncover their innate skills.

My reference to mental work does not allude to the bouts of anxiety that stems from worrying or distressing ourselves over the goals at hand. This is also a mental exercise but lacks a positive connotation and hence is not productive work. Cerebral work in this context is proffering working solutions to the challenges you face, and your immediate environment as well. It is worthwhile to put your mental resources to work toward building the life you want to build and becoming the person you want to be. Unearthing your latent potentials requires a copious amount of cerebral work, which should give no room to mental laziness.

Laziness can stem from being overwhelmed by the thought of the work to be done. This is a negative self-image that projects slothfulness, encouraging less work in the direction of discovering your innate abilities. Hence, the onus lies on you to break free from physical and mental laziness, as these will prevent your essential skills or abilities from being manifested. Embracing inertia, *physical* or *mental,* is the pathway toward poverty, slavery, and destruction. In the words of Philip Dormer Stanhope, 4th Earl of Chesterfield, the British statesman, and man of letters, "Know the true value of time; snatch, seize, and enjoy every moment of it. No idleness, no laziness, no procrastination: never put off till tomorrow what you can do today."

Keep the joy of discovery in front of you and commit to giving your very best self to unearthing your latent potentials.

—w—

The first step in solving a problem is to recognize that you have a problem in the first place. Several factors are at war to ensure your hidden abilities remain under the bedrock of your subconscious. In this chapter, we have seen five agents that will ensure that your potentials remain under and they are *fear, self-doubt, procrastination, giving up prematurely,* and *laziness.* These negative factors that we have studied are all somewhat interconnected. You can never be fully productive if you allow these factors to prevail within you. You must strive to take steps to rebuff them and expunge them from your lives.

At this stage in the book, I want to reiterate the fact that unearthing your latent potentials is not optional for those who want to ensure they make the most of their lives. Reading this book shows that *you want to become more.* You want to discover your potentials and maximize them. Many hopes and dreams are hanging on you unearthing your possibilities. Remember the man whose livelihood and families are dependent on the jobs you create by discovering and maximizing your abilities? The fact is that Small and Medium-Sized Enterprises (SMEs) provide jobs on average to up to five people. Those are five people whose livelihoods are dependent on you—five families, five marriages, and several children involved. Destiny is waiting for you to unearth your potentials that have a replicating function. Your maximized potentials will lead to others discovering their skills and abilities too.

For instance, your potential could be the creation of soulful tunes with compelling depth and meaning, music that mends worlds and changes lives. Maybe there could be a message in the lyrics of your songs for broken people who need healing, such that every time your song is heard, it disseminates a restorative effect in the hearts of its hearers. Don't let them down by dismissing that potential. Yes, your first few songs may not be great, or anything even close to what that potential can deliver, but they hold the potential for more, just like the diamond that is mined rough and the iron ore encumbered with loads of impurities. In your practice, you are purifying your skills and perfecting your craft. Through deliberate practice, you are cementing your strengths and becoming more of the gem you are on the inside. The same goes for all potentials. Discover them. Process them. Refine them. Polish them. Then, profit by them. You may be surprised at what gems you will discover in the process of your exploration and self-discovery.

You owe it to yourself, and to the world, to unearth those latent potentials. It is not just about you. It stopped being about you a long time ago. So, start digging into the very fiber of your being and begin to unearth those nuggets of abilities, competencies, and strengths that you have. Start expressing yourself to the world. Start inspiring and begin awakening the potentials in your path that have otherwise been long buried.

It is time you start asking yourself some questions.

What are my latent potentials? What skills do I have that I can begin to process, refine, and polish to make me a distinguished personality in the Commonwealth of nations? What abilities can I hone? What are my crafts and gifts that I can develop?

Let us continue our explorative journey to answer these pertinent questions.

CHAPTER 3

Self-Exploration Pre-Activities

—~—

WHEN GEMS, PRECIOUS STONES, SUB-EARTH natural resources are to be mined or extracted, the miners and prospectors *know* what to search for. They have knowledge of what they are looking for and have done all necessary calculations and preparations before embarking on the journey to unravel the hidden resources. To gain this knowledge, mining companies usually carry out feasibility studies. Three things makeup feasibility studies, and they are as follows: *order of magnitude, pre-feasibility,* and *feasibility.*[1]

In a mining project, the feasibility study is a knowledge gathering or a fact-finding mission and process. A mining project

1 The *first* part of a Feasibility Study in the Mining process is the *Order of Magnitude* or *Scoping Studies.* They are designed to define the scope of a potential project, plus it itemizes approximate estimates of possible production values and costs. Here, a preliminary mine plan is also drawn up. The *second* part of the study is a *Preliminary* or *Pre-Feasibility Studies,* and it includes a further exploration drilling program for a more precise knowledge about the target ore body and the adoption of a more detailed mine plan plus mining methods for the actual exploration that is cost effective and time bound. The *third* part is the *Feasibility Study.* This is the final step; and, its objective is to determine if the mine is viable. It is a cost-intensive process when compared to the other two. (Reference: Peláez, J. (n.d.). Starting a mine: Pre-feasibility and feasibility studies. Retrieved from https://www.geologyforinvestors.com/starting-a-mine/).

can only commence with the knowledge of the extent and value of the mineral deposit. It would be futile to go into the process of excavation without prior knowledge of what is being sought after. The exploration process has several pre-activities that precede the actual mining process. Some of these mining pre-activities include but are not limited to surveys, field studies, drilling test boreholes, and other exploratory excavations.[2] The core of the feasibility study is *knowledge*. You learn about what you are seeking and explore the various avenues available to you to establish how to get it.

I have been taking you on an expedition to teach you how you can explore and unearth the latent potentials that are hidden in you. The whole process is comparable to what those in the geo-industrial fields of mining go through. They pre-learn, they learn, and they execute the knowledge of their findings when exploring to unearth whatever the *metals* or *materials* of their specialties may be. These *metals* or *materials* (e.g., copper, diamond, nickel, cobalt, gold, silver, lead, zinc, molybdenum, platinum, or even crude oil, just to mention but a few) could be used to typify *potentials* in human beings. Now, the question that we posit is this: *Beyond available strengths and talents that we may know of, what makes for potentials in human beings?* Gaining that knowledge, mastery, and the recognition of your natural talents could be quite complicated and can take a while at times to understand before

---

2 There are various phases of a mining project. They are as follows: exploration, development, active mining; disposal or overburden, and waste rock; ore extraction, beneficiation, tailings disposal, and site reclamation and closure. The one that picks my interest is the *exploration* phase, which is where most or all the pre-activity processes are taking place. (Reference: Guidebook for Evaluating Mining Project EIAs. (n.d.). Overview of mining and its impacts. Retrieved from https://www.elaw.org/files/mining-eia-guidebook/Chapter1.pdf).

the inception of self-prospecting. So, the resounding question is, *How do you recognize what you need to unearth in yourself?*

Let's go on a journey to gain some understanding of how we could recognize our hidden abilities, skills, strengths, and talents.

The fact is that there is no one set of definitions that could do absolute justice in elucidating every essence of the word *potential.* When we attempt to put a set of words, synonymous to *potentials,* we drift into several paths to explain them for what they are. So far in our journey, I have expressed potential as analogous to gems, precious stones, and sub-earth natural resources. I have also previously compared it to a seed that becomes a tree, a fetus that becomes a baby, and so on. However, I must express that all these analogies, as descriptive as they may be, are all limited in the way they convey the essence of potentials. The possibilities of what potentials could be ascribed to remain very vast and tend more toward infinity.

Everything that exists is laden with potentials. If you let your mind run wild for a minute, everything that crosses your mind, everything that exists holds the possibility of becoming more than it currently is. Hence, in defining potentials as it relates to you, I would not want to box you in and say the potential you carry is just *one* thing because it isn't. Doing that would be unfair to the other parts of yourself that have gone unexplored. You are replete with many possibilities. Your potentials hinge on your ability to explore the next frontiers of the above-ordinary innate strengths buried in the depths of your subliminal-self. It depends on your ability to beam yourself into the unexplored mantle, outer core, and inner core, buried within the depths of your subconscious self. Here, you will find the body of skills, talents, abilities, etc., waiting to be reached, tapped, and unearthed.

Potentials that will make you discover the *better-to-best* version of yourself. The possibilities could be endless, hence a deep-calling-to-deep self-space-introspection into the subliminal realms of self-curiosity to determine your potentials is crucial.

To get to your depths then, you will have to carry out an introspective self-analysis, and self-subliminal deep-space exploration that reaches to as many areas of your life as possible. It is not just a limited search of the skills that you have an inkling of and are present in your life. It is an extensive self-search that explores the various substrata of your inherent possibilities. A shallow search may not reveal much. It must be as deep as possible to reach the core labyrinths of your unknowns. The search is akin to the actions of geologists when they carry out pre-feasibility and feasibility studies or tests in an area to determine the presence of minerals or other subterranean natural resources. The analysis they carry out is not limited to the specific metal or ore they are looking for and nothing else. Often, it would include an extensive search of the topography, the intrusive rocks that exist underground, and seismic surveys to better understand the area to be tested.

The last thing they want is to discover an unexpected presence of some unforeseen naturally occurring or man-made subterranean objects or things that might jeopardize the safety of the miners or the environment. All these preliminary tests help them to prepare for the possible challenges and opportunities that will be encountered during the exploration process. The pre-tests to know what they are looking for are extensive. It is not a superficial process to be taken lightly. It is comparable to an Apache Helicopter's Dillon M134D Gatling Guns of detail barreling at full blast. Unearthing your latent potentials, in the same vein, can also be challenging. You may confront some mental or subliminal barriers (e.g., a low self-awareness, a weak motivation, a faulted focus on the wrong qualities, mental fatigue, etc.) as you work to unravel your innate skills. This discovery is not meant to discourage you, but rather encourage you to plow through them as you push for gold. Your pre-test and the actual process must be saturated with detail.

In working with you to unearth your latent potentials, we will look at some of these preliminary tests by employing some self-analysis tools. We will look at some pre-activities and precursors that we will need to help us as we start to explore and learn about our different potentials. Analogous to the feasibility and pre-feasibility studies that mining companies go through as we saw earlier in the preceding paragraphs, these antecedents will help us learn more about how to use the SWOT Analysis tool for self-exploration in the next chapter. These pre-activities are vanguards to the unraveling process. Doing them gets you into a matrix-frame-of-mind for deploying the Self SWOT Analysis Assessment tool in the discovery of the *you* in *you,* or *the best version of yourself yet.* They are not new by any means, but if you want to get the best out of them, do not hesitate to use them. As you may or may not know, it is not the things you know that bring you results. What produces outcomes in your life are the things you know and apply. The pre-activities we will consider here are the *Art of Journaling, Noting Your Patterns,* and *Drawing up a Vision for Your Life.*

The Art of Journaling

Anyone who knows me on a personal level will know about my passion for journaling. *Journaling is a process of recording or keeping track of your thoughts daily or periodically as they come to you.* You could do so mechanically through writing by hand, or you could journal digitally by using your computer or other mobile devices. There are a lot of times when you could be hit by a thought or idea. These thoughts come in flashes during the hustle-and-bustle of the day. Failure to record the impression through whatever method you choose—mechanical or digitally—could mean losing that thought or idea. Recording that idea could be pivotal to a life-transformational experience.

The art of journaling has become an ingrained habit that I cultivated, honed, processed, refined, and polished for over thirty-seven years—yes, that long. As a kid, I loved recording everything by writing in notebooks and journals. I took this habit into elementary school, middle school, high school, all the way through college until now. The fun thing about it is that I collect actual journals—notebooks, papers with my writings, napkins with my scripts, leather journals. Oh! I really love those well-crafted Italian Leather-Bound Journals. Those are my favorite. And, with the advent of digital technology, I began journaling extensively using applications like Evernote, OneNote, my iPhone Notes, etc. As ideas and thoughts come to me, I write them down somehow and anyhow—even on Starbucks napkins. As a matter of fact, the building of the chapter synopsis for the book you are reading right now is a core product of my journaling endeavors. Talk about a platinum tool for unearthing hidden potentials.

Okay, I admit I am a journaling aficionado, but I am not saying you should become one unless you wish to make it a hobby like I did. All I am trying to draw out is that if you could cultivate the habit of journaling—the art of writing down your thoughts, visions, and ideas—you could be recording world-changing and destiny-transforming notable thoughts that could revolutionize your life. It is a precursor art toward effectively unearthing those hidden gems that will make you a high flyer in the affairs of life. However, *junkie-journaling*, if I could call it that, may not be everyone's forte. All I am asking is for you to put down on ink—on paper or digitally—ideas as they come to you, and thoughts as they are blown your way. Don't ignore them or let them fly by without you capturing it unless you are a walking human-computer who can remember everything. If you are, I envy your ability. If you are not, record those ideas that could help you in the discovery of your innate potentials. Embrace the art of journaling.

For this explorative process, you will need a journal that you keep with you for self-reflection and introspection. The type of journal you decide to use is a matter of preference. There is no hard and fast rule to the method you select. You could physically write by hand in a journal booklet, or make entries in a digital journal, as thoughts and ideas come to you. However, we live in a digital age, and there are many computer applications tailored to Mac, Windows, iOS, Android, and the web that people could deploy at their beck and call in the art of journaling. These apps tend to offer more than just marshaling ink on paper. I have mentioned my preferences in the preceding paragraphs and am not in any way endorsing one method or application over the other. However, at the time of this writing, there are many different digital journaling applications available (e.g., Day One, Diarium, Glimpses, Journey, Penzu, Dabble.me, Momento, Grid Diary, Five Minute Journal, etc.). Our first focus is not to explore the various apps out there. Our goal is to develop a habit that builds us a tool for capturing elements of our hidden potentials. The art of journaling gives you the competitive advantage of capturing moments as they roll by in your life. In these moments could lie hidden gold nuggets that could distinguish you immensely when unearthed.

Mine drillers don't just drill when they feel like it, right? Or, should I say that you don't just go to work when you feel like it, right? Just like any endeavor, they (i.e., miners) must have a set structure in their approach to their prospecting and explorative expeditions. Likewise, the process of self-discovery should not be left to chance—to moments when you feel like it. There must be some level of discipline to the process to get the most from it. Technically, there is no set time for you to dedicate to journaling. It all depends on when the ideas come to you, and it is entirely subjective. Some people choose to randomize the process of their journal entries. However, those given to structure—just like mine drillers or establishments in a professional setting—prefer to be more methodical in their approach and set aside a specific time daily or weekly for journaling. It is, however, imperative that you try to do this as often as is possible—daily would be best if you could find the time. In the words of Jim Rohn, a business philosopher and author, "If you're serious about becoming a wealthy, powerful, sophisticated, healthy, influential, cultured, and unique individual, keep a journal." Know that *ideas captured are ideas treasured. Ideas treasured could become the potentials to be unraveled tomorrow.*

The art of journaling is not as easy as people portray. It requires a lot of discipline. Like every other habit, it will require repetition to make it regular. However, it is all a function of perception. Look at it as a tool that will help you record nuggets that could help you discover your innate abilities and skills. The inculcation of the journaling habit is like a journey—an introspective adventure into your subconscious targeted at self-discovery. And like the Proverb stipulated by the Chinese philosopher Lao-Tzu, "A journey of a thousand miles begins with a single step."

Start with the first step by writing your first page. Do it repeatedly until it becomes a habit. In the words of Charles Reade, the English novelist and dramatist, "Sow an act, and you reap a habit. Sow a habit, and you reap a character. Sow a character, and you reap a destiny."

Make journaling a habit. In the journaling journey, you will document the discoveries you make about yourself. You will be recording things that you have found yourself to excel at, patterns that seem to form your personality and the compliments you receive. Now, this isn't meant to promote narcissism. Taking note of the things people most compliment you for could be a pointer to the hidden potentials you have been missing.

In summary, as we earlier established, the art of journaling *could* give you a competitive advantage in your journey toward discovering your hidden potentials, if you put it to work in your explorative journey. You could go traditional (i.e., writing by hand on paper), or you could deploy the use of a digital journal or application. Whatever the method, the core of the process is to ensure you are documenting flashes of ideas and thoughts as they spear out of your subconscious. Write! Write! Write! The content of your reflective journal will cover a wide range of topics and themes you want to explore concerning your life. It should be more of a multicolored image of your innate self on the canvas of your psyche transcribed deliberately into the pages of your journal entries. These could include everything ranging from your beliefs on spirituality to relationships, abilities, future, just to mention a few. Nothing is off-limits. Remember, the deeper you reach with the questions, the better your chances of unearthing gems of surpassing worth from within yourself. (NB. To encourage you in the *Art of Journaling*,

I have provided a mini-journal in the *Appendix* of this book. Use it. Write down your thoughts. It will be worth your while).

Note Your Patterns

Following closely behind *reflective* or *reflexive* journaling is the need to observe and *note your patterns.* Patterns are all around us. We can recognize them in nature, weather, music, mathematics, behavior, just to mention but a few. Life is a mosaic of patterns coming together as a whole from different angles and perspectives of being. Patterns are guides or models that direct us in action born in the matrix of repetition. They could be disadvantageous when ingrained models lead us ineffectiveness, inefficiencies, and waste, and advantageous when they assist us in avoiding deviations that lead to waste, invariably making us more effective and efficient. Patterns form the foundation of uniformity that could be appropriate or inappropriate and beneficial or detrimental, respectively.

When patterns are appropriate, the resultant characteristics are positive and beneficial. These patterns are to be honed and perfected to unravel their maximum capacity. However, when patterns are inappropriate, they become detrimental harbingers of diversions that create a crater of disadvantages. The martial arts legend, Bruce Lee, once said, "All fixed set patterns are incapable of adaptability or pliability. The truth is outside of all fixed patterns." Hence, when models become obsolete, there should be some room for adaptability for them to morph into a better state. Consequently, noting your patterns is crucial for what you want to unearth as your patterns help you understand who you really are or who you have become.

Every human being is a gestalt—an organized form or pattern—of sequentially learned behaviors that spring from the aquifers of our subconscious. Humans are a gestalt of thoughts that become words, words that become woven into the tapestry of deeds, deeds that transform themselves into habits, habits that seep into our character, and character that becomes our destiny. We are gestalts of our actions that transform into the unified whole of who we finally become through our daily experiences. In concord with the human-gestalt-concept, Stephen Covey, renowned American author, affirms that "Our character is basically a composite of our habits. Because they are consistent, often unconscious patterns, they constantly, daily, express our character."

There are many mosaics of instances that necessitate the need to note our patterns. For example, you may be moved by politics and have a great understanding of current affairs, but you recoil into your rhetoric shell because of the partisan nature of the political landscape. Or, maybe you are prone to react passionately to topics that others don't pay much attention to. Or, perhaps you are just creatively inquisitive. Or, you see that you are particularly adept in understanding musical notes, with a quick knack at learning musical instruments. Or, you don't know how to be physically or mentally productive after a specific time of the day. The scenarios can go on *ad infinitum*, but the fact is that there is a clear pattern to it all. There is a transparent model to the characterization of our actions that transforms us into the unified whole of who we become through our daily experiences. I encourage you to understand and note the patterns that define your life. These patterns are milestones that show you more than you would expect.

There are geological indicators that direct us toward the presence of various subterranean natural resources. For instance, some repeated subsurface indicators of the possible presence of gold are the following: color changes in bleached area rocks, iron staining and gossans (i.e., a rust-colored deposit of mineral matter at the outcrop of a vein or ore body containing iron-bearing materials), quartz vein matter accumulations, productive rock types, etc. Prospectors of diamonds believe a possible indicator of an area that has diamonds is to locate the rocks called kimberlites (NB. Kimberlites are a variety of micaceous peridotite, i.e., a coarsely granular igneous rock composed chiefly of olivine with an admixture of various other minerals, low in silica content and high in magnesium content, in which diamonds are formed.). Similarly, patterns are indicators that lead us toward the hidden potentials that we have in our lives. These potentials, as we have seen, have the possibility of changing our lives for the best if unearthed, processed, refined, and polished.

Patterns are born out of repetition. These models are the governors of our moments—our days, our weeks, our years, and our lifetime. The repetition of patterns can best be seen in *personal habits* that we internalize. These habits are the vanguards of structure, whether positive or negative. Good habits give us good structure, and bad habits destroy any form of sound structures we may have. In the words of Robert Fulghum, the American author, and Unitarian Universalist minister, "Structure gives us a sense of security. And that sense of security is the ground of meaning." Good patterns—born out of repetition—support the traits of the potent force for change. In the words of Nina Hagen, the German singer, "We can change the world if we change ourselves. We just need to get hold of the old patterns of thinking and dealing with things and start listening to our inner voices and trusting our own superpowers." We have our hidden talents, our innate superpower qualities, waiting to be unearthed. Start taking note of these positive patterns.

In summary, we have seen that patterns are all around us. Positive exemplars that are adaptable become beneficial to us when honed, refined, and polished. We have seen that every human being is a gestalt of sequentially learned behaviors that spring from the aquifers of our subconscious. Patterns, like geological indicators of natural resources of worth, point us toward our hidden potentials. Patterns such as personal habits are products of repetition. Your patterns are the most effective way to identify your strengths and weaknesses. Put your journaling to work and begin noting down all the patterns that you see in your life, whatever they may be.

Taking note of your patterns is also a great way to take stock of your routine if you have one. Doing so will give you better visibility, which would, in turn, help you draw up a vision for your life, so if there is any way you can increase productivity, you will see it clearly, and then strategize on how to adjust your time to make that to happen.

Draw Up A Vision for Your Life

So far, we have looked at two pre-activities before we delve into using the SWOT Analysis Assessment to measure ourselves as we work toward finding out what our latent potentials are. We have looked at the *art of journaling* and *taking note of our patterns*—the two being somewhat interconnected.

We have seen that *every human being is a gestalt of sequentially learned behaviors that funnel up from the springs of our subconscious.* In a nutshell, we can take note of our gestalt—our patterns—by recording them using our paper journals or digitally. These patterns help us to start forging a mental picture—a vision of who we are—by giving us marking indicators of the potentials that we need to unearth.

What does it mean to mean to *draw up a vision for your life?* What does it mean to have a vision? A vision (i.e., insight, intuition, foresight, penetration, etc.) is a mental conception or picture of the innate self that drives us toward itself as it matures to become our aim, goals, and objectives. Vision gives sight to our subconscious. It allows you to say, *I was blind . . . I now see.* An unknown author once said, "The subconscious mind tends to actualize what we visualize. So even when the roof is caving in, picture yourself as an immense success." Vision answers the questions of, first, *Who do you want to become through this process of unearthing your innate skills, abilities, talents, etc.?* and second, *What qualities are most real and noble about the person you hope to transition to, that is, your future self?*

Having no vision is a state of mental bankruptcy. It is a state of blindness, devoid of the light of purpose and meaning, where people are pigeonholed by the stumbling and staggering of hopelessness. *Drawing up a vision for your life* is like transferring—by journaling or taking note of exemplars—that mental vision from your subconscious to print. Write the vision (i.e., idea, concept, image, thought, or fantasy, etc.) down and make it visible to motivate yourself to start unearthing them.

Vision gives you sight. When you see, you don't stumble. You have a sense of direction. You become a vector quantity, far from anything scalar, moving with intention and purpose. That is why organizations have a *vision* that becomes the guiding mantra that drives them forward with the full aim and attention to achieve the goal. For instance, the vision of De Beers Group, the diamond exploration juggernaut, is "Pursuing Brilliance." For Rio Tinto Diamonds, an Anglo-Australian multinational and one of the world's most extensive metals and mining corporations, high on the list of diamond exploration, "Continuing to pioneer progress for a better future," is their driving vision. Some other companies and their compelling *objectives* and *visions* are as follows:

Microsoft, "Empowers every person and every organization on the planet to achieve more."

Amazon, "We strive to offer our customers the lowest possible prices, the best available selection, and the utmost convenience."

Facebook, "To give people the power to share and make the world more open and connected."

Tesla, "To accelerate the world's transition to sustainable energy."

Disney, "To make people happy."

Sony, "To be a company that inspires and fulfills your curiosity."

At the base of all these *Vision Statements* and more are these two words: *Vision guides.*

Companies are guided by their compelling vision. It becomes the foundation of their goals and objectives. It guides them toward becoming that picture and goal on the canvas of their aspirations of what they plan to be at the end of the day. Similarly, for the individual, the vision you spell out will, among other things, guide your search. As you begin unearthing who you want to become, notating your vision will guide you along the journey as you begin the process of excavating your talents. As you dig through the subterranean stratum of your subconscious, make the image of that person you are pushing to uncover from the depths of the shadows plain—*write it down.* What does that look like? What matters to you as a person? What does success look like? How confident are you? What part of your contribution will add value to your immediate environment? The world? From the preceding paragraph, we saw that companies can't exist without a vision, which is *a clear understanding of where it is going and how it wants to get there.* Likewise, never go on without a clear vision of your destination. As you begin the process of self-discovery by unearthing your latent potentials, have a vision.

Admittedly, visions (i.e., a self-stipulating mental picture) don't always come fully formed. However, there is a finality to them that keeps you grounded on a clear path. Vision is a guide. It is the foundation of your mission. Hence, to be visionless is almost tantamount to being foundationless. Vision is like the whorls that constitute the fingerprints of your subliminal-self. It distinguishes you, and it makes you uniquely you. In the words of Neil Gaiman, the English Fantasy Writer, "The one thing that you have that nobody else has is you. Your voice, your mind, your story, your vision. So, write and draw and build and play and dance and live as only you can."

Hence, record the patterns that define you. These patterns form the psychic signature of your subconscious self—your unique vision. Once your life's *vision* is clear, *noted,* and *recorded,* we can move on with the process of unearthing.

—ꟿ—

We have looked at the three related precursor activities that will prepare you toward using the SWOT Analysis assessment to reveal what your hidden skills are. *First,* learn to record your thoughts and ideas through the *Art of Journaling.* By writing, you can capture moments *exactly* as they happen. In the words of Francis Bacon, the English philosopher, statesman, scientist, jurist, and author, "Reading maketh a full man; conference a ready man; and writing an exact man." You are giving yourself no room to forget what you have in mind of putting down as a note. The core of it all is writing down that thought. *Write! Write! Write!* Remember the Medieval proverb, *The pen is mightier than the sword.* Develop the *Art of Journaling,* as it is your pathway to exactness and sureness.

By cultivating the *Art of Journaling,* you will be able to *capture your patterns,* our *second* precursor activity. These patterns are reoccurring themes that could serve as clear indicators to the gems that are hidden inside of you. They are born out of the *matrix of repetitions in the inner portions of routines or habits.*

Finally, the *third* antecedent was *drawing up a vision for your life.* As you make the recording of your thoughts, ideas, and patterns a habit, you will begin to forge a mental picture of the future version of yourself—this is your *vision.* This simply put, gives you an aim as you begin to self-excavate and explore your innate potentials hidden in the subterranean stratum of your subconscious. Let us now progress forward as we start delving into the various portions of the SWOT Analysis Tool as we explore ourselves, beginning with the question, *What are your strengths?*

CHAPTER 4

Self-Exploration I: What Are Your Strengths?

—~—

ORGANIZATIONS LOOKING TO MAKE A decisive impression in their sphere need to be more strategic in discovering what they are adept at, where they are weak at, their opportunities (i.e., chances or prospects), and the threats on their paths of progress, should they not correct their inherent obstacles. Organizations conduct a *SWOT (Strengths, Weaknesses, Opportunities, Threats) Analysis Assessment* to make them more robust in accomplishing their goals and objectives. In my opinion, this evaluation tool should not be limited only to corporations. I believe that *individuals* could deploy this strategic tool, amongst others (e.g., SCORE Analysis, SOAR Analysis, NOISE Analysis, etc.)[3], for

3 There are other tools comparable to the *SWOT Analysis* that we will not cover in this book but could also be alternatives for self-exploration. We will just mention them here with their meanings. However, for more on these strategic tools, the reference has been provided for more exploration should you choose to. *First,* is the *SCORE Analysis.* The acronym stands for *Strengths, Challenges, Options, Responses,* and *Effectiveness. Second,* is the *SOAR Analysis.* The acronym stands for *Strengths, Opportunities, Aspirations,* and *Results. Third,* is the *NOISE Analysis.* The acronym stands for *Needs, Opportunities, Improvements, Strengths,* and *Exceptions.* They all have their attendant *Pros* and *Cons,* including the *SWOT Analysis* itself; use it's all a matter of preference. (Reference:

self-assessment and introspective. As you progress in this section, I will introduce you to this strategic planning tool that will help you—as an individual—in the process of unearthing your latent potential(s). Albeit used by organizations, this self-assessment tool can help you identify your strengths, weaknesses, opportunities, and threats that surround your life, acting as a propellant toward the life you envision for yourself.

The SWOT Analysis strategic assessment tool (See Figure 4.1) has been used for years by companies to drive productivity and increase organizational efficiency, effectiveness, and profitability. It is an introspective tool that allows the organization to look inwards stipulating its *status quo* characteristics. This strategic tool made its debut in the seminal opus by Edmund P. Learned, C. Roland Christensen, Kenneth Andrews, and William D. Brook in the 1960s, so it has been around for a while. What does the tool do? *First,* it allows your company to overcome challenges as it determined new leads to pursue. *Second,* it gives organizations the full knowledge of all the minute constituents involved in a decision. Therefore, this tool can be strategically used in the process of self-discovering and the unearthing of latent potentials in an individual. How? *First,* a planned introspection is necessary to discover your hidden abilities that allow you to overcome the challenges of your *status quo* and forge a new path. *Second,* this discovery hinges on being fully aware of all the granular factors involved when you decide to explore your innate self.

Durden, O. (2019, March 16). Alternatives to SWOT analysis. Retrieved from https://smallbusiness.chron.com/alternatives-swot-analysis-64967.html).

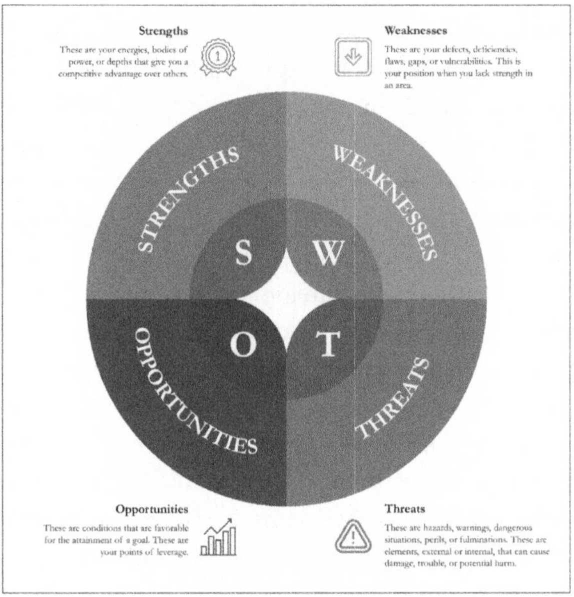

FIGURE 4.1 SWOT Analysis Matrix Tool

In businesses, the SWOT Analysis tool helps them map their future. It is used to evaluate the enterprise when acting on strategic decisions, embracing new initiatives, revamping internal organizational policies, improving operational efficiency, pivoting, capitalizing on strengths to eliminate weaknesses, etc. Likewise, as you start mapping and evaluating your explorative process of self-discovery, the SWOT Analysis tool can help you understand what your *Strengths* (**S**), *Weaknesses* (**W**), *Opportunities* (**O**), and *Threats* (**T**) are. In organizations, the **S** and **W** are internal factors (e.g., financial, physical, human, and natural resources, current processes, etc.). The **O** and **T** are usually external factors (e.g., market trends, economic trends, funding, demographics, etc.). Customarily, the tool is presented in a table, split into *four* *columns* or *quadrants*, with each element in each of the quadrants (i.e., **S** and **W** on top two quadrants, and **O** and **T** on the bottom two quadrants (See Figure 4.1)). This explorative tool allows businesses to x-ray their organizations to get an in-depth look into the various aspects of the company. Understanding the internal and external factors enables firms to have a full view of their organization, allowing them to adjust accordingly to maintain organizational equilibrium by eliminating obstacles for better effectiveness, efficiency, and productivity.

Hence, with this tool, you are looking at both the positives and negatives. You are looking introspectively at the internal factors *(i.e., Strengths* and *Weaknesses)*. You are evaluating ways to leverage your strengths by understanding what they are, to make them stronger, and to use them to compensate for your weaknesses. You are also anticipating the external factors *(Opportunities* and *Threats)* in your way and preparing yourself to handle them so they do not overwhelm you or halt your explorative process.

In the mining industry, companies evaluate threats that arise during prospecting and the actual mining process. The last thing any mining company wants is to ignore warnings and cause a catastrophe. I refer to the SWOT analysis as a self-explorative tool because it can x-ray your subconscious to unearth the hidden talents (i.e., your strengths). It gives you a broader perspective into your weaknesses so that you can strategize on how to mitigate them, or preferably, eliminate them. It gives you an insight into your opportunities so that you can find ways to leverage and exploit them. It makes you aware of your threats so that you can tread cautiously and not allow them to destroy your purpose and aspirations. It is a very engaging tool that employs questions to discover latent potentials in organizations, and, as we will see in this book, in a person.

Let us jump right in and look at the various aspects of the SWOT Analysis tool and understand the nitty-gritty of how we can use it to x-ray our lives to understand our hidden potential(s). Before we begin, I would encourage you to put the art of journaling to work. (NB. Mini-journal provided in the *Appendix*). As you learn how to use the SWOT Analysis tool to x-ray your subliminal-self, you need to start taking notes of your findings. You will start discovering certain things about yourself that will be worth noting down in this self-exploration process. What you unravel will help you draw up a vision-map for your explorative journey, which will give you a concrete objective to pursue.

Thus, take a pause, grab your journal, and then pick back up from *Strengths,* as we begin to illuminate your mind regarding the SWOT Analysis tool.

Strengths

Your strength is your inherent capacity to manifest energy or a body of powers in an area—or multiple areas—of your life that gives you a competitive advantage over others. It is the factor that distinguishes you as a person—something that you have as an individual that separates you from the herd. It is the concentration of potent energy in a field of your life that transitions you from the bounds of common manifestation to an uncommon indication. It is your inner Clark Kent (Superman) or Barry Allen (the Flash) in action, the superpower in you manifested.

Identifying your area(s) of strength is a crucial part of unearthing your latent potentials since they form the foundational purpose for the exploration and discovery that you will undertake. Knowledge of your strengths emboldens you in a new way. It gives you confidence in your journey of becoming, as you transition into the best version of yourself. It opens the portals of zest, giving you energy in your effort to explore and discover talents that will make that significant life transforming difference in your life.

From observation, you will notice that a majority of the most confident people are those who operate in their strengths. These individuals have discovered *what is most natural and comfortable for them,* and through the *art of repetition,* they have achieved mastery of their craft(s). They can do this because they understand where their best selves find the most expression. In this zone, they are in cruise control mode. You can recognize this trait in yourself as well. For instance, you probably shy away from tasks that intimidate you, but readily lean toward the ones you are good at. The draw toward the ease is an indication of what your strengths are. It is your zone of least effort.

Your strength is a trait you exhibit at work and at home that holds you back from what you suspect will expose your inadequacies. We always want to show up with our best selves, even more so when we have a competitive streak. Life is all about perspective. No one wants to be perceived as weak. Operating from a place of strength masks your weaknesses. The ideal state is to hinge on your strengths as leverage to eliminate your vulnerabilities. Your powers embolden you, as it should, allowing you to give your very best toward accomplishing your goals and objectives. It is a clear indicator that informs you where your advantage lies.

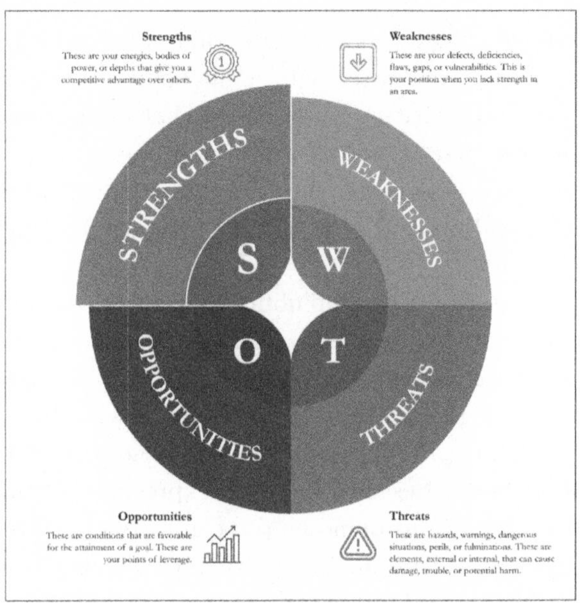

Figure 4.2 SWOT Analysis Matrix Tool: Strength (S)

The SWOT analysis tool (See Figure 4.2), just like in organizations, enables you to understand the *status quo* of your present self in order to help forge you into a better person. It gives you the foundational facts that allow you to plan on how to capitalize on your strengths to eliminate your weaknesses while exploiting your opportunities in order to eradicate all threats that could hinder your efforts to reach your maximum potential. This tool is intended to help you go from good, to better, and to your very best. In the words of St. Jerome, "Good, better, best. Never let it rest. 'Til your good is better, and your better is best."

Are you ready to get down to brass tacks of *Strengths* in the Self SWOT Analysis? Are you unhesitant to dig deep into the substratum of your subconscious self to understand your *strengths*?

Before we delve into the nitty-gritty of this self-discovery effort, I would advise you to put the *art of journaling* to practice now. Grab your journal, and get ready to dig into yourself as you explore your *strengths.* As you read the questions below, take note of *patterns* and *facts* that you unearth in your self-exploration process that you believe are your strengths. The nuggets you note down can transform your life as you begin to process, refine, and polish them to make your future shine. The nuggets you discover will help you frame a new vision toward unleashing newfound hidden potentials in your life for a better future. Do take your time to give an answer to some of the questions listed below:

- **What are my dreams?**

I have made this question the first here as your dreams are a cogent pointer of the strengths you have now, and the ones you should be looking to develop in the nearest future. The journey toward unearthing your innate potentials is a *dream adventure.* You must have dreams on the path to digging up your inherent potential. If not, *what exactly is nudging you on toward wanting to unearth the greatness that you carry in you?*

I am not saying that you must have it all figured out or be completely clear about what the impression or cerebral thought is. It must not be all figured out. It could all be a work in progress. However, when you know the dreams that drive your search, it makes the whole process a lot clearer. Those who dare to dream are the ones who make history. They are the ones who invent and make discoveries. They tap into the depths of their reasoning to unearth wonders that become the world marvels and spectacles of intrigue.

Bill Gates dreamed, and today, we have Microsoft. Mark Zuckerberg dreamed, and today, we have Facebook. Larry Page and Sergey Brin dreamed, and today, we have Google. Elon Musk pictured a world of electric cars and space exploration, and Tesla and Space X were born. Jeff Bezos dreamed of having the *world's most consumer-centric company, where customers can come to find anything they want to buy online,* and Amazon, his brain-child, has morphed itself into a global e-commerce juggernaut. Time and space will fail me as I continue to list all the dreamers who have become world changers. *What is the dream budding within you, right now? What is/are the thought(s) seeking an avenue for expression?*

What are my dreams? Ask yourself that question again. Ruminate on it. Ponder on the words of Debby Boone, the American Pop princess best known for the inspirational 1977 chart-topper "You Light Up My Life," who said, "Dreams are the seeds of change. Nothing ever grows without a seed, and nothing ever changes without a dream." Hence, *what are your hopes and aspirations that you mull over at night?* These *hopes* and *aspirations* could become the seeds of change that could transform your life and generation. Write them down. *What is the succession of images, thoughts, or emotions passing through your mind during your sleep or waking state?* Write down all that springs from the founts of your subliminal-self as you think on these questions. Write them down as bullet points under the **S** quadrant of your Self SWOT Analysis tool in your journal.

- **What is my area of strength?**

Whatever your response is to this question, it should be as detailed as possible. Honestly, the goal of this portion of the book is for you to identify what your strengths are. Your strengths are your hidden assets. It is your point of advantage, your position of leverage, your place of clout, cogency, distinctive equilibrium, and cerebral security. It is that deep-seated factor that gives you a can-do state of mind. All this may sound repetitive, but before proceeding, you must know what you think about your strengths if at all you recognize them fully.

Your area of strength does not have to be limited to just the *tangible* or *hard skills,* which are *perceptible skills* that are teachable and easy to quantify (e.g., an educational degree or certificate, apprenticeship, language proficiency, machine operation, etc.) and acquired through the years. Your area of strength could also be *intangible skills* (also known as *soft, personal,* or *interpersonal skills*) as well. These are subjective in nature, *imperceptible,* and harder to quantify. Some examples are communication, critical thinking, empathy, humor, integrity, leadership, motivation, persuasion, problem-solving, people and systems management, teamwork, time management, work ethic, etc. You would be amazed at what some creative minds have done using the *perceptible* and *imperceptible* skills that they discovered. The opportunities are endless.

So, ask yourself again, *What is my area of strength?*

- **What am I exceptionally good at?**

Have you attained expertise in a field? Do you have a college degree, or some certification, or completed an apprenticeship knowledge in an area? Have you achieved any specialized skill or understanding in some field? It could also be self-learned. Within these fields of expertise could lie the treasures of potentials that could distinguish you. Here, I want you to describe the hard skills you have picked along the way. It could be something you have used in service to others who can attest to it as well as make a recommendation for you as a testament to that acquired aptitude. List it here.

Beyond the realms of these hard skills, you could also be exceptionally good at other things that others may classify as mundane, but, through your creativity, you could tap and hone the ordinary and make it extraordinary. You could harness the common and make it uncommon. Are you good at organizing, drawing, scheduling, acting, singing, or even cooking? You could turn that everyday knack into an exceptional, unique asset for profitability and distinction. For instance, think about *Marie Kondo,* popularly known as *KonMari,* who is a Japanese organizing consultant and best-selling author. She took her love and joy of tidying up to an exceptional level. Today, she has published four books and counting and is the star of Netflix's hit show, *Tidying Up with Marie Kondo,* and founder of *KonMari Media, Inc.*

What you are good at, as we have seen, does not have to be just hard skills gained from college or even soft skills that we saw from the previous question. "*What is my area of strength?*" Don't limit your abilities. Think as broadly as you can about things you have done in the past with a sense of fulfillment at your own excellence, regardless whether it is an unpopular skill, what we want to do is to identify them first. It could be something basic as *tidying,* as we saw with KonMari. Do you have to go to college to learn how to fold your clothes or tidy up your space? I don't think so. However, she made something *great* from it. She created a following for her love for tidying. Discovering her potential has caused a tectonic shift in her life from the good to the better and to the best, as she continues to unearth her potentials.

Another instance worth noting is *Kuro "KuroKy" Takhasomi,* the German *Dota 2* player who, as of 2019, has earned $4,199,926.95 from ninety-six Tournaments and counting. Don't get me started with the eSports macrocosm. This massively growing industry is fast evolving at an astronomical pace. Goldman Sachs has stated through statistical projections that the monthly viewership is going to be 276 million people per month in 2022 and that incomes are surging. For instance, *Tyler "Ninja" Blevins* earns approximately $1 million per month by streaming on Twitch. Today, traditional Pro Sports (e.g., NBA and NFL, and more) are all jumping into eSports to get a piece of the pie of profits.[4] Without belaboring the point on eSports, two to three decades ago, would you have ever thought that playing video games could make you money, especially those kinds of digits?

Think about the question, *What am I exceptionally good at?* X-ray your life as you unearth your innate potentials and look at skills or things that you do that you are particularly good at. *Could you profit from it? Could you take an ability that you have in an area from ordinary to extraordinary? Could you create a market for yourself from that potential?* Think about it and write down your thoughts as you mull over these questions. Hidden in your responses could be the answer to the question about your innate potentials.

---

4 Goldman Sachs & Co. LLC [US] makes an extensive effort in providing us with comprehensive, detailed statistics into the growing world of eSports that I have barely scratched the surface in mentioning. They assert that "With one of the fastest-growing fan bases in pro sports, a youthful global audience that's already larger than Major League Baseball's and top players who are quickly joining the ranks of millionaires—eSports have entered the mainstream." (Reference: Goldman Sachs & Co., LLC. [US]. (2019). Goldman Sachs - eSports joins the big leagues. Retrieved from https://www.goldmansachs.com/insights/pages/infographics/e-sports/). Some high-profile names hopping onboard the eSports hype-wagon by making major investments and acquisitions in eSports teams are the likes of Steph Curry, Shaquille O'Neal, Jerry Jones, Rick Fox, Robert Kraft, Alex Rodriguez, Ashton Kutcher, Mark Cuban, Steve Aoki, Magic Johnson, etc. (Reference: Breakthrough. (2018, August 29). 11 celebrity eSports investors you didn't know about. Retrieved from https://medium.com/@breakthrough_lab/celebrity-esports-investors-you-didnt-know-about-eb9a8c395292).

- **What privilege do I have above other people?**

A privilege is a distinctive right, immunity, or benefit that a person enjoys beyond the advantages of most. Some individuals enjoy some opportunities that give them a competitive advantage over others. For instance, having access to some level of education can be a privilege. Many people across the globe don't have access to basic literacy, much less quality education. Also, the career or skills you have acquired could give you a point of advantage over others. For instance, working at a reputed corporation could be an advantage that you have above others for getting ahead.

Your geographic and environmental heritage could become a point of advantage. Those that hail from socio-technologically advanced and developed societies have greater odds of finding success as compared to those born and raised in developing nations that may be struggling with poverty, poor health, environmental care, inadequate security, and general lack of development. The family people are born into (i.e., their biological-heritage) could give them an immediate position of advantage over others. For instance, being born into the House of Windsor, the reigning royal family of the United Kingdom, you immediately have access to the sovereign benefits of wealth, security, societal distinction, etc.

The economic status of people could grant them a status of privilege over others. Those born into wealth have instant access to capital to execute their business or life ideas, while others who live paycheck to paycheck cannot. People who are less financially privileged may have great ideas but may often lack adequate funds to execute some of those ideas. However, nothing is impossible. Believing is the first step toward redemption and never giving up. Staying creative and continually forging ahead is the birthplace of possibilities.

Your social network status could be your position of privilege over others. A robust social network of people could readily extend valuable opportunities to you. Also, having notable people in your sphere of influence could grant you a distinction above others.

I could go on and on about various privileges that could distinguish you beyond measure. The main thing is being aware of these positions of opportunities and making the very best of them when you have the chance. It will be of no value if you have these competitive advantage privileges and you fail to recognize them to even use them. Once again, the question is, *What privilege do I have above other people?* Your inherent potentials could be buried in these privileges. Think about the weapons in your arsenal that will make your journey considerably smoother and write them down.

- **What achievements am I most proud of?**

The lists of things you have accomplished in your life, especially by superior effort, great courage, etc., could be an indication of where your strengths and your hidden potentials lie. It might sound counter-intuitive at first, but in answering this question, you will better understand the kinds of things you are most likely to excel at and the kinds of achievements that make you most proud of. I do not want you to hold back on your first few thoughts, even if you think it is not a significant achievement. There are no wrong answers in this. The fact remains that your accomplishments could be milestones that could guide you toward your hidden talents or abilities.

When we look at the hall of fame of those who have made remarkable discoveries and achievements, we see people who exerted themselves by exploring the core of their potentials to become, to achieve, and to accomplish extraordinary feats. For instance, it is for this reason that Louis Pasteur, the French chemist, and microbiologist, discovered the principles of vaccination, microbial fermentation, and pasteurization. It is the reason why Thomas Edison, the prolific inventor, and businessman, was credited with several discoveries in the fields of electric generation, mass communication, sound recording, and motion pictures. Your many great achievements are often an indication of the definiteness of your purpose. Your purpose is usually an indication of the expression of your known and latent potentials.

What achievements am I most proud of? Take some time and reminisce about all your accomplishments over the past years. Was it a sporting event you won a medal for? Has your sense of achievement come from organizing things (e.g., a messy desk, room, garage, etc.)? Have you found out that you did an excellent job in raising kind children who treat people with respect and regard? Maybe yours is heading a department in the company where you work or running the company at large? Have you always been applauded and recognized for great empathetic leadership in every organization you have worked? Has yours been a passion for traveling to various parts of the globe in search of an adventure as you experience the sights and sounds of different places you visit?

All these accomplishments are yours, and yours to celebrate. So, relish them and be confident about writing them down. Hidden in these achievements could be life-changing potentials that could distinguish you immensely when unearthed.

- **What are my values?**

Values are the spiritual qualities of mind and character, a moral compass that directs people onto a path of excellence and expression. Believe it or not, your values represent an area of strength in your life, if you are grounded in them. Values produce inherent traits that exude the qualities of your best self. They are the dominant areas of your commitments and are usually aligned with your life purpose, never apart from it. Hence, it becomes potentially advantageous to answer the question, *What are my values?* It could be a leading indicator in helping you identify and unearth your hidden trove of talents from your subconscious *Caves of Wonders*. Let me digress a little by channeling our minds to *Aladdin 2019*, the recently reenacted live-action adaptation of Disney's 1992 classic animated film produced by Walt Disney Pictures, directed by Guy Ritchie, with stars such as Will Smith, Mena Massoud, Naomi Scott, just to mention a few. The *Cave of Wonders* in the epic movie, according to the Disney Fandom website, "is a location in the movie Aladdin. It is a forbidden realm filled with vast riches, magical objects, artifacts, and most notably, the lamp of the all-powerful Genie." Your subconscious can be likened to this place in the movie, full of potential treasures waiting for you to discover them.

Exceptional values in any person are a source of strength. It is upon such values that great civilizations and societies are built. The lack of this intrinsic worth has also contributed to the downfall of empires and nations, past and present. The American Senator, Cory Booker, said, "If you look at great human civilizations, from the Roman Empire to the Soviet Union, you will see that most do not fail simply due to external threats but because of internal weakness, corruption, or a failure to manifest the values and ideals they espouse." Values hold a surpassing sway in one's life. Hence, understanding your values grants you a golden compass that could guide you while exploring the vast mines of your subconscious to unearth your latent potentials.

Do you believe in family and friendships? Do you value loyalty, compassion, fairness, faith, inner harmony, justice, or respect? Do you espouse the values of excellence, respect, success, status, trustworthiness, wealth, wisdom? You could make a list and determine on a scale of priority what you think is most valuable to you. Fun could even be one of the top items on the list of your values, or even fame, happiness or humor. Whatever it is, do yourself a favor and write it down. Remember, hidden in your values could be the priceless gems of potentials that could transform your life. With this exercise, there is no pressure on you to state what you think is acceptable. Do what makes you happy and relish every moment of it!

- **What do people commend me for?**

Operating from a place of competitive advantage to serve and affect change often attracts praise as worthy of confidence, notice, kindness, etc. The things people recognize and praise you for your aptitude, capability, or innate ability are often powerful indicators of where your strength or potential lies. Usually, because these things come easy to you—a clear indication that you are operating effortlessly in your comfort zone—you might overlook them as trivial because of the relative effortlessness with which you do them. However, when people who can't do what you do see you do it with little or no hardship, they admire and applaud that strength and understand its value to you.

Pay attention to the recurrent commendations you get in a specific area of your life as a pointer to the possible potentials that characterize your life. Open your eyes as you explore the possibilities of innate potentials in these accolades. Don't be shy as you explore and unravel yourself in this self-exploration exercise. *What do people say you are good at? What have you received commendation for time and time again? What are you always applauded for in the circles of your associations?* And do not worry if you haven't gotten a lot of admiration for your work. It will come in time. The reason could stem from the fact that you haven't spent enough time around people for them to recognize your strengths. Through the *law of associative interaction,* people encountering you cannot help but notice the best you, sooner or later. There is really no need to worry because there is nothing hidden that won't be revealed, and there is nothing secret that won't become known.

As earlier mentioned, crude oil is formed under pressure from biomass in the earth's subterranean zones. Through extreme pressures, it moves upwards through porous rocks. Meeting an overhead cap rock (i.e., non-porous rock), it gets trapped in this region. Here, it waits to be drilled and released to deliver the products of its potency. In the same way, your potentials want to come to expression. Your abilities have been formed under pressure, through the span of your life in the core of your subconscious. Your experiences, expertise, gifts, intelligence, skills, strengths, or talents funnel upwards and are trapped in the porous zones of your potential possibilities. However, you are still required to dig, to put in work, and to try to break through the cap rocks of limitation(s) to release your potentials for their maximum expression and utilization.

Your point of advantage is welded into the core of your DNA and will always seek a way to express itself. You are fundamentally who you are, just like a leopard cannot change its spots, and your potentials within yourself want to be unearthed for full expression. However, the onus lies on you to discover and unravel the potentials you have hidden within you. Come to bear with your point of advantage and begin to exercise it. Find avenues to operate in your comfort zone and express your potentials. For instance, get involved in volunteering efforts to put those potentials to work. You could also participate in extra-curricular activities as an avenue for self-expression. Not only will you recognize that there is more to you, as you put yourself out there to give your very best, but others will also notice your potential in action and compliment you for it. Therefore, x-ray yourself as you answer this question, *What do people commend me for?* Record your thoughts on this note as they may be a clear indication of what your hidden abilities are.

- **What is the one thing I would like to do more of?**

The final question for the *Strength* (**S**) quadrant of our *SWOT Analysis* as we unearth our latent potentials is, *What is the one thing I would like to do more of?* Certain things pick our fancy, things that are of a positive and negative note that we can't get enough of (NB. Regarding our line of thought in this book in seeking all things positive as we explore our potentials, we will stick to the positive as we avoid the negative). The one thing, or a group of things, that we would like to do more of could be an indicator of what our potential could be.

Some people go the extra mile of having a trail of things that they wish they could accomplish, summed up in their bucket list of things that they want to do in this lifetime. The question that I now propose to you is, *Do you have a bucket list? Do you have a list of things you have not done before but want to do before dying?* Is there a trend or a pattern to the things you wish to achieve? The patterns could be a signal to your latent potentials. Record them and start the process of trying to accomplish them. In so doing, you may unravel your hidden abilities and more.

Your answer(s) to *the one thing I would like to do more of* could be an indication pointing you in the direction of your potential(s) that you are currently not exploiting. Start exploring the things you would like to do more. After dedicating some time to them, you may find out that some or all of these things may not necessarily excite you as much. Nevertheless, there is value in the process of embarking on the journey in the first place. It may assist you in unraveling more potentials currently alien to you. Begin your exploration with an open mind into the things that you want to do more. Write down your thoughts as they come to you.

So far to this point, we have been exploring various questions in the *Strength* (**S**) quadrant of the SWOT Analysis assessment tool. Your strengths are the most significant indication of your hidden potentials. Knowing them grounds you in your purpose. To discover your strengths requires you to dig into the subterranean zones of your subliminal-self. What diamond drill bits could you use to do this? They are the questions that we have explored in the above paragraphs.

The *first* question was, *What are my dreams?* Hidden in the elemental diamond cubic constitution and structure of your dreams could be the priceless gems of your potentials.

The *second* question was, *What is my area of strength?* Your strengths are your points of advantage. They are that deep-seated attributes that give you a can-do state of mind. Don't neglect them. Tap into it.

The *third* question was, *What am I exceptionally good at?* There is something you can do exceptionally well, something you have achieved an expertise of. Check your *hard skills.* However, remember not to forget your *soft skills* as you explore yourself. In these skills that you have listed in your journal could be a strong indication of your inherent abilities, talents, or skills.

The *fourth* question was, *What privilege do I have above other people?* You may have a factor in your life that gives you a competitive advantage over others (e.g., education, career, your geographic, environmental, biological, or economic heritage, social network status, just to mention but a few). Why would you not leverage these factors that give you an advantage over others?

The *fifth* question we considered was, *What achievements am I most proud of?* The chronicles of your achievements and accolades could indicate a trail that typifies your strengths. What feats have you accomplished? Is there a pattern for them? Within these successes could be the foundation of your innate abilities, so do not ignore the track record of your accolades. Review them for consistent patterns, and try to repeat them.

The *sixth* question that we considered was, *What are my values?* As you go deeper into the underground trenches of your innate self, don't neglect your core values. Those spiritual qualities of your mind and character could hold the keys to the portals of your hidden potentials. Use the intuitive minecarts of motivation to haul the potential treasures of your values to the surface of your life and existence.

The *seventh* question we looked at was, *What do people commend me for?* Your gifts are very vital in this process of self-discovery. The things people recognize and praise you for (i.e., your aptitude, capability, or innate ability) are usually a powerful indicator of where your strength or potential lies. Don't ignore or underestimate them. Note them and actively exploit them. Your points of commendation could be your potential position of distinguishing advantage.

Finally, the *eighth question* we considered was, *What is the one thing I would like to do more of?* Everyone has something or a group of things that pick their interest. Some people in collating these interests have established a bucket list of what they wish to accomplish in their lifetime. *Do you have a bucket list?* Ingrained in these interests, as we have seen, could be a pattern that indicates your innate potentials. Note the patterns. Stain and polish them with the varnish of anticipation and pursuit, as you reveal the beautiful models of your inherent skill set.

Reviewing these strength-determining-questions is a crucial step in our journey toward unearthing your latent potentials (NB. These questions are not in themselves exhaustive. You could add or remove to them as needed, tailoring them to your own situation). The answers you have provided to these questions in the *Strength*(**S**) quadrant of your SWOT Analysis assessment will reveal your strengths. As we have seen, your *forces of distinction* play a crucial role in unveiling your hidden potentials. Knowledge of your *competitive advantage concentrations* gives you an arsenal of factors that can help you battle the *internal weaknesses* that truncate the unraveling of your best self ever. Not curbing weaknesses could bring your self-discovery exploration to a definite halt, and could blast your hopes and dreams to oblivion. Also, knowing your strengths can help you combat external opportunities and threats that affect your self-discovery. Thus, don't trivialize this process as it is essential in helping you unearth the factors that give you a competitive advantage in life.

CHAPTER 5

Self-Exploration II: What Are Your Weaknesses?

—∾—

IN CHAPTER 4, WE STARTED our self-exploration journey by delving into the various quadrants of the SWOT analysis tool. We took a thorough look at the *Strengths* (**S**) quadrant of the matrix. In our self-exploration analysis, we have established that your strength is the place where things come to you easy. It is your zone of least effort—your comfort zone. It is your inner superpower manifested, and the *weaknesses* in you suppressed. We highlighted that your strengths can be harnessed as the leverage that helps you mitigate, or preferably eliminate, your weaknesses, both known and unknown. We then asked ourselves several questions to help us unravel our strengths while noting them on our SWOT matrix.

We have heard about the proverb, *A chain is only as strong as its weakest link*. This fact applies to a person as well. I would say that this proverb became very popular since the advent of the famous TV quiz show named *Weakest Link*. As mentioned on its IMDb (Internet Movie Database) page, the show originated in the United Kingdom (UK), which later started airing in the

United States (US). In the game, players were asked general knowledge questions, creating a chain of accurate answers in a row. As each round came to an end, *the weakest link* player was voted out of the game. No one wants to be dubbed *weak,* even in a game. Everyone wants to always put their best foot forward, in any given situation. Everyone wants to be a winner, showcasing the strengths that awarded them their win. People celebrate strengths in others but loathe the expression of weakness.

The fact remains that *a chain can only be as strong as its weakest link.* When pressure is applied to it, it breaks at that point of its weakest link. The weak point makes the whole chain vulnerable to failure. If nothing is done to fix the point of weakness in the chain, it becomes a point that nullifies the strength of the series of links. The inception of this proverb, *A chain is only as strong as its weakest link,* sprung from Thomas Reid's (Scottish philosopher) *Essays on the Intellectual Powers of Man* in 1786. In his words, "In every chain of reasoning, the evidence of the last conclusion can be no greater than that of the weakest link of the chain, whatever may be the strength of the rest."

Everyone has one weakness or the other. However, these gaps, defects, flaws, vulnerabilities, or deficiencies are not to be treasured. Weaknesses open the doors to a plethora of disadvantages that only bring about ineffectiveness, inefficiencies, loss, and waste in organizations, and as we shall see, also in individuals. Weaknesses are attributes that we should always strive to mitigate or eliminate from our lives.

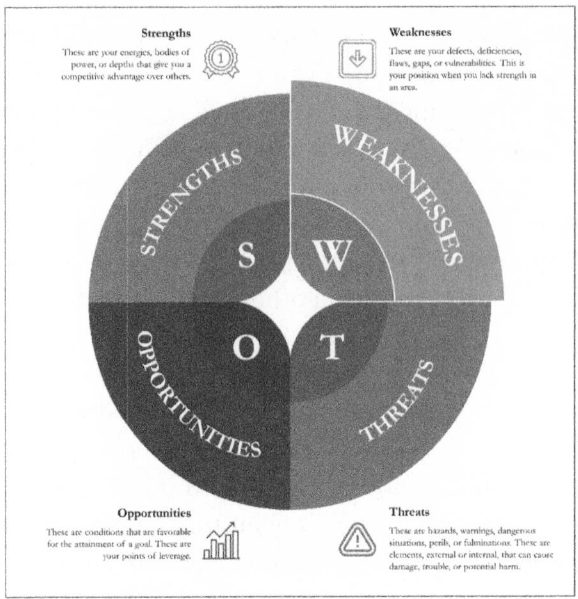

FIGURE 5.1 SWOT Analysis Matrix Tool: Weakness (W)

We will now consider the second quadrant of the SWOT analysis, which is *Weakness* (**W**) (See Figure 5.1). We must approach this quadrant with the same sense of zeal and intentionality as we did to the *Strength* (**S**) quadrant. By revealing our weaknesses, we expose every vulnerability that could bring the mine shafts of our minds crumbling down to our own demise. Let us get to the nitty-gritty of it as we answer the question, *What are your weaknesses?*

WEAKNESSES

Weakness (**W**) (i.e., defects, deficiencies, flaws, gaps, or vulnerabilities) is the lack of strength, firmness, vigor, or the like. It is a state of inadequacy, for instance, in a person's character, in a system, or in an organizational framework. These characteristic places you at a disadvantage relative to others. In the words of Voltaire, "We are all full of weakness and errors; let us mutually pardon each other our follies—it is the first law of nature." Whether it is in systems, establishments, or people, we are all prone to occasionally experience the feeling of weakness. However, the goal is not to bask in its ambiance, but to find ways to overcome these gaps.

There is power in recognition. You stand in a position of strength when you recognize your weaknesses. Our vulnerabilities are problems that we encounter that need surmounting. By identifying them, you now have an opportunity to proffer a solution toward avoiding, mitigating, or preferably eliminating them. Organizations and even people often lean on their strengths to overcome their inherent weaknesses. In the words of Charles Kettering, the American inventor, engineer, businessman, and the holder of 140 patents, "A problem well stated is a problem half solved." As we progress, we will be filling out the second quadrant of our SWOT Analysis, as we determine what our inherent weaknesses are, so be sure to keep your journal handy.

Paying homage to our various mining analogies, allowing weaknesses in your life is akin to courting disaster. This can be compared to the many fatal and catastrophic accidents that spawn from errors in surface and subsurface mining. They are usually caused by human miscalculations, a *weakness* that establishments in these sectors work very hard to avoid. From *methane and consecutive dust explosions* to *blasting related accidents,* many of these happen because of gaps and obstacles at work. Allowing such accidents to occur could lead to irreversible fatalities, like the 1,099 miners who lost their lives during the tragic Courrières disaster, the worst ever mine disaster in Europe, and the second in recorded history, in Northern France on March 10, 1906, caused by methane and dust explosion. Similarly, entertaining weaknesses in your life will bring your vision, purpose, and the unearthing of your possible hidden potentials to a tragic end.

Allowing weaknesses to linger is like recognizing that you have a deep cut on your leg that is infected, but consciously allowing it to fester—out of carelessness—until it becomes infected with gangrene. This disease is caused by the death of soft tissue due to either obstructed circulation, or by a severe bacterial infection, usually followed by decomposition and putrefaction, and commonly affects the extremities (e.g., toes, fingers, limbs, etc.). This decay frequently leads to the extreme medical measure of amputation to prevent the further spread of the gangrene. In the same light, allowing weaknesses to fester would only lead to more decay, and eventually gravitate toward the annihilation of dreams, purposes, and all good intentions.

Having a weakness is mainly approached with disapproval. However, while we all deal with some form of weakness or the other, it is not an easy admission to make by any means. For instance, the interview question *Could you highlight some of your weaknesses?* causes the hearts of many interviewees to always skip a beat. The last thing you want is to be perceived as weak. I mean, when has a weakness ever been an admired quality in any person? However, unless you admit the failings, gaps, or vulnerabilities in your life, you will never have the power to do anything about them. Hence, recognizing your inadequacies is crucial in the journey to unearth your latent potentials. Only then will you be able to stand in a position of strength to tender solutions to them. If you do not see your weaknesses as something to be addressed, you will never be willing to work on them. This is an enormous blunder, as it will only stall your progress.

No one is born perfect by any means. However, while some are more balanced than others, we all have areas we could be better at. There is a plethora of weaknesses that plague the lives of many people. Some instances among many are as follows: giving up prematurely, a limp will power, a lack of self-confidence, a lack of courage, having no sense of urgency, an inclination to always procrastinate, an affinity to a pessimistic thought and lifestyle, being excessively judgmental, self-pity, laziness, irritability, etc. I could go on and on with the various weaknesses that plague people. However, I will leave the analysis of what weaknesses you might face to you in the paragraphs that will soon follow. Don't recoil at the thought of the question, *What weaknesses do you have in your life?* Approach the query and others that follow fearlessly. Be very candid with yourself as I take you on a journey to recognize your gaps or vulnerabilities. Remember, *there is power in recognition.* Write them down in your journal in the *Weakness* (**W**) quadrant of your SWOT analysis.

We all have one form of weakness. However, our approach to the gaps in our lives should be as Michael Jordan—the celebrated American basketball Hall of Famer and businessman—said, "My attitude is that if you push me toward something that you think is a weakness, then I will turn that perceived weakness into a strength." That is what I hope all my readers will do—*Turn your perceived weaknesses into strengths.* Approach your *weaknesses* with the mindset of wanting to turn them into *strengths.* You should never allow your failings or inadequacies to paralyze your onward effort of self-discovery. See your *weaknesses* as potential *opportunities* filled with the potency to become *strengths.* Approach them with a renewed sense of optimism and use the positive muscles of your subconscious to overcome and transform them. That is the mindset I hope you cultivate at this juncture and beyond.

Weaknesses can be contained, and as earlier stated, they cannot be ignored, or the situation could be further aggravated. The recognition of your weaknesses is not only strength, but it is also *a sign of growth* and *grit*. Recognizing your weaknesses allows you to increase and mature to new levels in time. By succeeding to transform your *defects* to *strong points,* your *deficiencies* to *sufficiencies,* your *disadvantages* to *advantages,* your *flaws* to *fine points,* your *gaps* to *gains,* and your *vulnerabilities* to *value-assets,* you can increase the treasuries of talents in the hidden vaults of your subconscious.

In the words of Harsha Bhogle, the Indian Cricket Commentator and Journalist, "Sometimes, your greatest strength can emerge as a weakness if the context changes." I could not agree more with him. The context changes when we recognize our weaknesses, and then we put in the effort to transform them into strengths by leveraging the already existing powers in us.

Finally, we have come to the junction where we can begin to dig deeper into the excavations of our souls. We have come to the place where we bring out the mining drill bits of various questions, as we unearth the weaknesses that lie in the depths of our subliminal-self. *What are your weaknesses?* Don't cower at the inquiry, and don't skip this process either. Write down the answers to the questions below, in bullet points or in detail—whatever you prefer—as you fill out the second quadrant of the SWOT Analysis tool you had begun building.

Some of the questions to ask are:

- **What do I struggle to do?**

What are some of the things that don't come effortlessly to you? Things that come naturally to you, as we have seen in strengths, give you leverage or an advantage over others. You are in your element, in control, and in your comfort zone. Things that you struggle with are things that remove you from your element, and you are not in your comfort zone. *Are there things that you do that require you to exert a lot of effort in order to get them done?* The results do not come readily to you. Others may do the same task with relative ease, but for you, it is a drag. The friction is intense, and often, you just cannot wait to get over it.

To better understand this question, consider a student who struggles with understanding the subject of Mathematics in general. For them, the abstract interplay with various numbers, theorems, and calculations is like dancing *Zanku,* the Nigerian legwork dance, with *Eris,* the Greek Mythological Goddess of Confusion. On the opposite end of the spectrum, the student who loves all things Mathematics positions themselves in a state of confidence. It is pretty much like a graceful and slow waltz with *Concordia,* the Roman Mythological goddess of agreement, understanding, and harmony. What you struggle and contend within your life could be an indication that points you to your weaknesses.

To change the outcome, you must tackle the problem head-on. Shying away from it is defeat, and approaching it with a strategic poise and persistence is your key to succeeding where you struggle. In the words of Robert H. Schuller, the Christian American televangelist, "Tough times never last, but tough people do." If what you struggle to do well at is an essential pillar to your purpose, then engage with the problem, and don't disengage yourself from it. Know that *if you can conceive it in your mind and strive for it. All things are possible for one who believes.* Strive! Strive! Strive! However, I would advise you to only disengage *if and only if* the things you struggle with no longer add value to your essential purpose. If it is posing to be a setback to your whole life's pursuit and design, disengage so that you don't sink your entire ship over something that will add no value to you in the long haul. Sometimes, it is a strength to know when to let go. Engage the struggle but know when to disengage.

As you look within yourself, you could answer this question with some of the things you could say you do not have the *talent* or *patience* for. Instead of it being a source of happiness, it is more like a chore. Again, your honesty is required here. You must be candid as you document your thoughts as you think on this question.

Be real in answering the question, *What do I struggle to do well at?* Document your thoughts as you answer this question.

- **What area of my work do I enjoy least of all?**

One of the most revealing ways to get answers to this question is to look at the job you currently do. *Do you really enjoy the job that you do? How engaged are you at work? What area(s) of the work do you enjoy least of all? What factors make up the reason(s) why you detest what you currently do in your job?* If your answers to all these questions lean on the negative, then you are part of the majority of people who are actively disengaged from work and unhappy with what they do. This is an unpleasant place to be in because you are mostly unfulfilled and not performing at your very best. This is a huge indicator of a weakness in your life as it cripples your will to discover and unearth your hidden potentials.

Several factors show that many people are disinterested in the work that they do. Some of the visible signs are tardiness and absenteeism, poor work quality, low energy at work, a negative attitude, frequent use of social media in the workplace, badmouthing the organization, lack of enthusiasm, etc. These signs and more show that the employee is actively disengaged at work. Not performing at your highest standard is detrimental to both you and the organization. Several factors could contribute to the disengagement, such as unmet job expectations, inadequate resources, underutilization or overutilization of talent, hostile work environment, lack of recognition, and toxic leadership. Knowing the root cause of your disengagement or the areas of work you loathe will give you a vantage point to understand how to tackle it. Confront the root of the source of your displeasure, directly or indirectly.

This is really a revealing question, *What area of my work do I enjoy least of all?* Survey your thoughts as you muse on it and record them. The things you least enjoy at work could be linked to areas of your work life you may not be great at. It could be due to inadequate training, or perhaps you just fail to perform at your very best at it. It could also stem from being lazy, and as a result, you are steadily being held accountable and written up for your poor performance. Most often, the poor performance at work seeps into other areas of your life, making you even more miserable. Confront the foundation of your displeasure. Write down the thoughts coming to you and be very candid.

Remember, being insincere with yourself will cripple your will to unearth your hidden skills and abilities.

- **What values do I struggle with?**

Your values or relative worth, merit, or importance is the signature of your psyche and represents your true nature. The *you* in *you* will always find a way to surface and seek expression through your values. Hidden in your values—or the ones you are exploring and yearning to acquire—could be the potentials that would distinguish you in life. Poor values can paint a bad image of you.

Hence, a weakness that puts you at a disadvantage needs to be changed. Failure to correct the variation in your values could spell ruin for your vision, purpose, and life in general.

Say you want to be better at integrity, but still find it hard to be truthful. It is currently an area of weakness, but you are in no way confined to this diversion. Change is possible. Do you struggle with creating family time? Being respectful to others? Being honest? Being kind and generous? Being compassionate? Being patient and understanding? Being hospitable? Staying committed to a course of action? Doing excellent work? Being punctual? Being effective and efficient? Whatever the intrinsic worth may be, the crux of the matter is that you wish to have them, but you struggle to do so.

Like we have noted, you are not confined to your weaknesses. The fact is that as you ponder this question and more, you are trying to improve your life for the better. It shows that you are not accepting the *status quo*. You are not stagnant but are actively moving toward the mark of change. You are digging deeper within yourself to the core of your reasoning to unearth solutions to your struggle. Still moving in the same spirit of journaling, taking note, and sculpting a vision for yourself, write down these values that you are struggling with. It is imperative that you do.

Next, conscientiously begin to work your way toward turning around the areas of your life where you have previously struggled. Do the direct opposite of what led to the value being a struggle to counter the strain in the first place.

- **What are some of the skills of value that I do not wish to acquire?**

Self-awareness is crucial to living with authenticity, without which your life will be lived unfulfilled. One of the pillars of self-awareness is being brutally honest with yourself. Self-awareness allows you to observe yourself under the microscope of rational logic. It lets you screen yourself. In so doing, you can see the skill you have, those you wish to have, those that you should have, and those that you should avoid. Once you know the things you don't really care to be better at, it frees you up to pursue the things that really matter to you.

Okay, I am not going to delve into every group of skills as I cited in the previous paragraph but will titrate that information to focus on *the skill set that you should have,* but maybe—just maybe—you do not wish to acquire. For example, have you ever been in a situation where you steadily had that unflagging thought that you should really be doing something that you are not? That incessant nudge telling you to acquire a specific skill, but you choose to push the thought away, or you procrastinate? Have you ever wondered about the fact that it could be the Spirit of the Universe trying to nudge you toward your innate potential?

Let us say you do not subscribe to the value of *hard work* and would first pour effort into *smart work.* Sometimes, just putting effort into hard work can be a chore. There is value in pushing yourself and working hard, but it is not every day that you wish to knuckle down. Once you understand that you are the captain of your subliminal-ship, with the sole duty of navigating through the oceans of this life toward the isles of success or failure, you become more at ease with your decision to apply yourself to the tough grind. Hard work is no longer just routine. You now approach it with the value of *smart work* as a mindset, knowing that your effort will no doubt increase your productivity in your life, or on the job.

After all, what I do not want you to do is hold that truth back from yourself because it is unpleasant. In the words of Avigdor Lieberman, the Israeli politician, "People can choose between the sweet lie or the bitter truth. I say the bitter truth, but many people don't want to hear it." You have heard the truth about the skills you may not want to acquire but could infuse some value into your exploration to discover your hidden potentials. Embracing the truth is the only tool that will help you recognize and unearth your latent skills or abilities. Allow this truth to set you free. Remember, this is a process of discovery. The miners who mine for gold cannot sidestep the many strata that lie atop the gold they are digging to find. Likewise, you shouldn't avoid the layers that lie above your potentials in the depths of your subconscious, just because you don't like what you see.

What are some of the skills of value that I do not wish to acquire? Whatever thoughts may be coming to you now, be sure to write them down in the *Weakness* (**W**) quadrant of your *SWOT Analysis.*

- **What are some of my character flaws?**

A person's character is the aggregate of features and traits that form their individual essence. The human character is a cardinal part of every human being that allows them to forge their destinies. A good character opens the portals of many positive potentials in people. For example, when a person has an impeccable reputation, it helps them fit in perfectly in society, opening doors that allow them to explore and discover the best versions of themselves as they relate with others in their communities. It also becomes an advantage to forming meaningful relationships. However, a character flaw in an individual is a weakness and a disadvantage that impacts their ability to fit in properly in society and negatively affects their relationships with others. This could also impact their ability to unearth their innate potentials.

Addressing the entire man is an incomplete exercise without attention to the sum of a person's characteristics. When you understand how you behave, you will better and more seamlessly manage your interactions with the world. For instance, when opportunities come your way, you are better equipped at skillfully working with your personality to make the most of them in any situation life may throw at you. You do not exist in a vacuum. You are a part of a community. Hence, your character plays an essential role in how you will be accepted by others in your immediate vicinity. A flawed character is a quality that, if allowed to persist in your nature, will place you at a disadvantage. That is a position you want to avoid as you explore to unearth your latent potentials. In the game of life, you never want to be playing catch up—you either want to be in lockstep, or preferably ahead. Therefore, it is necessary to dig deep within yourself to expose any flaw of your character so that you can know how to use your strengths to address and eliminate the strain of imperfection.

Therefore, it is crucial that you answer the question *What are some of my character flaws?* as well as you can. You could also invite those closest to you to offer an unbiased perspective of you to give you a candid character-assessment. Should you be presented with an observed character flaw, there is no need to be defensive. Note the points, good or bad, and work to negate the imperfections of your character. In the words of Heraclitus, the Pre-Socratic Greek philosopher, "Good character is not formed in a week or a month. It is created little by little, day by day. Protracted and patient effort is needed to develop good character." The keyword here is *patience.* You must intently work—little-by-little, day-by-day, precept-upon-precept—to re-forge your character. An unknown author once said, "Sow a thought, reap a word; sow a word, reap a deed; sow a deed, reap a habit; sow a habit, reap a character; sow a character, reap a destiny."

Step-by-step, work to rebuild your flawed character. It takes time. There are no shortcuts to the process. Take the first step and keep the momentum moving toward your goal.

—∞—

So far, we have explored various questions in the *Weakness* (**W**) quadrant of the *SWOT Analysis* assessment tool. Your weaknesses are characteristics that place you at a disadvantage. It diminishes the leverage that could help you do better than others in a similar situation, all things being equal. Weaknesses are negative in nature, and we must strive to leverage our strengths to overcome them. To discover your weaknesses also requires you to dig into the subterranean zones of your subconscious self. What diamond drill bits could you use to do this? They are the questions that we have explored in the above paragraphs.

The *first* question was, *What do I struggle to do well at?* Things that you struggle with are things that don't come easily to you. You are out of your elements when doing them. You are not in your comfort zone. What you struggle with may be a sign of an inherent weakness that needs to be mitigated, or preferably eliminated.

The *second* question was, *What area of my work do I enjoy least of all?* Do you enjoy the work you do? Are you excited about Mondays? Or, is going to work more of a drag? Are you engaged or disengaged at work? If your answers are negative, this could be a weakness. This state of negativity will impact your willingness to unearth your hidden potentials. Hence, change is a necessity, not an option. Confront the root cause of your displeasure at work, directly or indirectly. Shying away from confronting it would only feed the source or strengthen its foundations.

The *third* question was, *What values do I struggle with?* What you value paints a clear portrait of your true nature. Hidden in your relative worth, merit, or importance, could be life-changing potentials that will distinguish you in life. Hence, poor values can paint a bad image of you. Imbibe positive values, and strive to make them a reality, because that will help you expunge yourself of negative values.

The *fourth* question was, *What are some of the skills of value I do not wish to acquire?* Here we looked at various groups of skills. However, the words *skills I should have* caught our attention. This group of skills could be a clear indication of where destiny is pulling you toward. However, if you keep procrastinating, you could never fully realize—or even discover—your best innate potentials yet. Hence, keep an open mind to those set of skills that you should possess, but you are reluctant to do so. Break through the barriers of that reluctance, and pursue and acquire those skills, that is your solution there.

The *fifth* and final question was, *What are some of my character flaws?* A good character could give you leverage in life. However, a flawed character (or personality, reputation, or nature) spells doom for your destiny. You need to transform a negative reputation, little-by-little, day-by-day, precept-upon-precept, or face ruin. It may be painstakingly slow, but you need to take the first step and let the momentum of your persistence keep you moving forward toward the mark of your established goals.

In summary, reviewing these weakness-determining-questions is a vital step in our journey toward unearthing our latent potentials (NB. These questions are not in themselves exhaustive, you could add or remove to them as needed; tailoring them to your own situation). The answers you have provided to these questions in the *Weaknesses* (**W**) quadrant of your SWOT Analysis assessment will reveal your weaknesses. Knowledge of your weaknesses could allow you to apply your strengths toward curbing or preferably, eliminating them. Ignoring your weaknesses is not an option. Doing so could bring you self-discovery exploration to a grinding halt. You wouldn't want to do that, now, would you?

Are there elements external or internal to us that we could exploit to our advantage? What could these opportunities be? Let's continue our self-discovery journey as we look at the two remaining quadrants of the *SWOT Analysis* assessment tool as we cover *Opportunities* (**O**) and *Threats* (**T**) in the upcoming chapters ahead.

CHAPTER 6

Self-Exploration III: What Are Your Opportunities?

—∿—

AT THIS POINT, WE ARE making good progress in digging deep into our subliminal-self as we work to unearth our latent potentials. We have looked at *Self-Exploration I* and *II,* in *Chapters 4* and *5,* where we looked at the first two quadrants of the *SWOT analysis* matrix that cover the two attributes, *Strength* (**S**) and *Weaknesses* (**W**) respectively. We discussed that you need to first look inwards at the internal factors *(Strengths* and *Weaknesses)* before we consider looking externally as we contemplate our *Opportunities* (**O**) and *Threats* (**T**). In brief, Chapter 4 allowed us to explore the several possibilities of how we could unearth the innate powers that give us leverage. Technically, our *strengths* manifest the inherent potentials we hope to discover (i.e., if currently, we have not discerned them), buttress, disinter, process, refine, polish, and efficiently apply for ourselves and others. In Chapter 5, we looked at what weaknesses were, and the various questions that could help us expose our innermost vulnerabilities that, if left unchecked, could implode the mine shafts of our mind. By now, I believe we must have built up several points for each of these two attributes on our SWOT analysis matrix.

We are forging ahead successfully. In this chapter, we have come to the point where we delve into the external factors of our SWOT analysis matrix *(i.e., Opportunities* and *Threats).* The journey to unearthing the gems of your hidden talents, abilities, or skills requires you to look at elements in your environment that you could exploit to your advantage *(i.e., Opportunities).* An opportunity is a situation or condition that is favorable to the attainment of a goal. If this situation is managed well, it could be favorably exploited it to create a positive impact on the individual and grant them a competitive advantage. Hence, the possibility exists for the conversion of these possibilities to strengths, if managed well. On the other end of the spectrum, when not managed appropriately, they could become inherent weaknesses, which we certainly want to avoid at all cost.

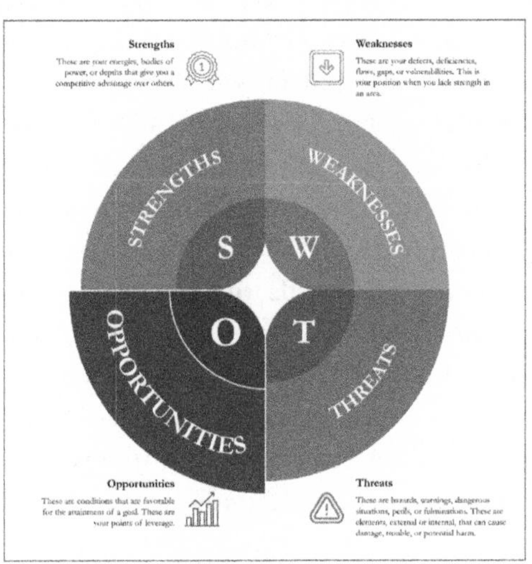

FIGURE 6.1 SWOT Analysis Matrix Tool: Opportunities (O)

We will now look at what *Opportunities* (**O**) (See Figure 6.1) are and establish how we could deploy them in our self-exploration journey. This attribute always comes in a flash, and failure to see it on time means they are gone forever, and we, therefore, need to be attentive to them when time and chance present them to us. We must be perceptive and ready to see, harness, and exploit them to our advantage.

We will explore the various questions that will allow us to unearth the potentials of our openings. In Chapter 7, we will consider the other external factor, *Threats* (**T**), but let it suffice us to say now that if they are not dealt with, there is a possibility that it could damage the pursuit of your purpose, the unraveling of the best *you* in *you*.

At this time, let us now focus on what makes up *Opportunities* (**O**) that we could exploit in our self-exploration process. Also, as we have done in the previous chapters, make sure you are taking notes of the thoughts that come to you as you go through all the questions presented in this chapter. Let us strap up as we delve further into the depths of our subliminal-self to look at our *Opportunities* (**O**).

Opportunities

An opportunity is a situation or condition favorable for the attainment of a goal. It is a good position (i.e., being at the right place at the right time), a chance (i.e., an opening to a favorable probability), or prospect (i.e., a likelihood, or a probable future) that channels you toward a protracted advancement or success. These are elements in your surrounding that you have the chance to exploit to your advantage. Opportunities come like shooting stars. You only have but a moment to catch a glimpse of it and then it is gone. In the words of a Japanese saying, "*Winnow while the wind is blowing.*" The wind blows where it wants to. You hear its sound, but you don't know where it comes from or where it is going. If you miss the chance of an opportune time, that's it. That time cannot be recovered. Catch the wind in your sails when it comes.

If you think about it, right in your hands is a book that has the potential to revolutionize the tapestry of your thoughts and reasonings. It could literally change the frequency of your vibrations to allow you to phase through your limitations. Right in your hands are the golden nuggets of my words, nudging you with every ingot of my verbal effusions, mined from the depths of my gray matter, asking you to *unearth your latent potentials.* The core objective of this treatise is to nudge you toward a journey of self-discovery for you to excavate from the depths and labyrinths of your soul (i.e., your subliminal-self) the real and rare essence of your becoming. You were born to be more than what you are now. Remember, iron can only be hammered into shape at a blacksmith's forge while it is hot. "*The iron stands hot for the striking,*" as similarly stated by Sir. Archibald Clark Kerr, 1st Baron Inverchapel. So, take advantage of this opportunity that has presented itself to you when you have the chance to do so. Do it before you lose your chance to get it done. An anonymous author once said, "A missed opportunity is worse than defeat." Explore the depths of your soul to unravel your point of difference from others (i.e., your innate potentials), and put them to work to distinguish you in life.

Opportunities abound now more than ever before. We are living in an era where possibilities are truly within our hands. The world has become a global village, virtually interconnected with so many chances available to you to leverage and become the best version of yourself. The interconnectedness of the world literally brings information to you at your fingertips in a plethora of ways. Welcome to the era of the Internet of Things (IoT). Living in the IoT age is tantamount to living in an age saturated with knowledge. We are literally sitting on a trinitrotoluene (TNT) keg of information already gone off, with the fireworks of light and enlightenment already raging to the point of delirium. There is so much information at your beck and call for you to leverage as you unearth deeper potentials from your subliminal-self.

Don't tell me you and the enigmatic Loki, the Norse trickster god, are walking in lockstep when it comes to scheming? What excuse can you pull out from your bag of tricks that would absolve you from the very fact that opportunities are at your doorsteps and you cannot deny them? You have none. Increasingly, education is reaching many people virtually through various digital devices. Just by a click of a button, you are presented with a plethora of sources of information, right there from your digital device. What this means is that your odds of improving on your weaknesses have dramatically doubled. The probability of leveraging your strengths as a life-changing assistant is now more feasible and has been greatly multiplied. Not exploiting this increased chance would be a grave mistake. Remember the words of Les Brown, the American politician, and motivational speaker. "In every day, there are 1,440 minutes. That means we have 1,440 daily opportunities to make a positive impact." What this means is that we have a similar playing field with everyone else.

Not only that, there are now opportunities to increase capacity on a global scale. Opportunities abound everywhere around you that you could exploit to your advantage. Many times, like the shooting star we earlier mentioned, opportunities come in a glimpse. If you see it, you see it and tap into it to unearth its hidden essence. If not, it is gone. In the words of William Arthur Ward, the American writer, "Opportunities are like sunrises. If you wait too long, you miss them." Unlocking potentials is a very immersive process that helps you discover your strengths and find opportunities that you can ride on to create the life you envision for yourself. If you are unable to identify the opportunities that surround your life, there is a possibility that you are operating below what you are truly capable of. So, take a clue from Orison Swett Marden, the American writer who founded the Success magazine in 1897, who said, "Don't wait for extraordinary opportunities. Seize common occasions and make them great. Weak men wait for opportunities; strong men make them." Make opportunities, and make them matter as you exploit them to your every advantage. Take the bull of your life by the horns of possibilities when it comes charging. That is your chance to conquer it.

We have come to the crossing where we delve farther into the diggings of our soul. Like we did in the two previous quadrants of *Strengths* (**S**) and *Weaknesses* (**W**), we have come to the place where we will bring out the mining drill bits of various questions, as we uncover the *Opportunities* (**O**) that lie in the depths of our subjective self. This is the penultimate point of our SWOT analysis tool explanation.

What are your opportunities? Get excited as you unravel the factors that you can exploit to your advantage. Note the answers to the questions below, like you have previously done as you fill out the third quadrant of your SWOT analysis tool (See Figure 6.1). Exploiting your opportunities could open the shafts of more strengths or potentials that could contribute positively to your life.

Let us continue discovering the inner *you* in *you*. Some of the questions you need to ask yourself are as follows:

- **Which of my inward strengths/skills do I need to leverage?**

As earlier stated, *Opportunities* (**O**) *on the SWOT analysis tools allows us to look at external elements in the environment that we could exploit to our advantage.* Let us look at some opportunities that we could leverage internally before we look outward to find opportunities in our environment. To do so, we will ask some questions starting with this one, *first, Which of my skills/abilities have I underplayed or overlooked?* Opportunities are sometimes hidden in skills you already acquired but have never used them to their fullest. You must have heard the saying, "*No knowledge is wasted.*" That is very true. Every piece of data that you absorb and invest could become valuable to you if you engage it to gain results. Your skills could be the obvious things you do that you feel don't matter much. Nonetheless, they matter. For instance, it could be a hobby, a sport, a routine, an educational certificate, etc. You only need to shine a light on them to embrace them in their full state.

Still looking inward at some other opportunities, the *second* question is, *What skills can l learn that can be advantageous to me and help me add value?* To be poised to take advantage of opportunities, there are some skills you need to learn and have in your arsenal. It could be a myriad of skills, from technological know-how (e.g., a certification), a language skill, a communicative skill, a behavioral skill, a listening skill, a financial management skill, or a creative skill, etc. The essence of all these skills is to give you an added advantage to compete more favorably. It could be a self-determined skill or one that you were advised to acquire to improve your chances of advancing in your field. From the previous question, you might have recognized an opportunity in an area you do not have any ability, which is where this question comes in. As soon as you identify the skills that you need, commit yourself to develop them. Don't make any excuse. Don't limit yourself. Go all out and earn the opportunities you want so badly. Within these skills and possibilities could be the hidden gem of abilities waiting for you to unearth them to add more value to yourself and others.

The first two questions that we have just considered are introspective in nature, and they allow us to look at the skills we already have and those we could potentially have. These internal skills are opportunities that can be leveraged and exploited for the maximum competitive advantage. The next set of questions for us to use and drill into opportunities are outward looking. Remember, *contingencies are elements in our ambiance that we could exploit to our advantage.* Ralph Waldo Emerson had a perspective of this in his statement, "The world is all gates, all opportunities, strings of tension waiting to be struck." As we dig deeper within ourselves to unearth our potentials—the possible opportunities we could exploit—we see all the gates of possibilities surrounding us. Strike the note of the chord of the opportunities. Take the shot and go through them to excavate the chances that could make you go for gold.

Now, let us look outward by considering the following questions:

- **What immediate opportunities surround me?**

Is the glass half empty or half full? Take a glass and fill it halfway with water. What do you see? A glass *half empty,* or *half full?* The first thing that comes to your mind is your Weltanschauung (i.e., a comprehensive conception or image of the universe and of humanity's relation to it) or your worldview. It is clearly the way you see things. If the first thing that came to your mind is that the glass is *half empty,* then you may have a pessimistic worldview. If the first thing that comes to your mind is that it is that the cup is *half full,* then you may have an *optimistic* worldview on life. I say all this to say this that *life is all about perceptions.* If you encounter a problem, an obstacle, or a roadblock, what is the very first perception that comes to mind? Do you become all out of sorts because of the hindrance you just encountered, or do you see it as an opportunity for you to overcome and reap the rewards of your victory after you surmount it? It's all about Weltanschauung—your perception about your world view.

There are immediate opportunities that surround you. Your surroundings are filled with favorable, or even unfavorable, circumstances that could lead you to discover some abilities that you never knew you had within you. Look at the obstacles around you as an opportunity to overcome. Look at societal needs as opportunities to fill a need. Look at *perceived* impossible situations around you as opportunities that could become possible. Look at trials around you as opportunities that could become triumphs. Look at the chaos around you as opportunities to exploit to your advantage. And yes, *chaos is an opportunity.* That is the reason why astute long-term investors in the stock market capitalize on down market potential by acquiring stocks that take a plunge. As dingy as it may look or even sound—and not a badge I eagerly advocate—that is the reason why arms dealers capitalize on the chaos of war to sell their ware. There are opportunities in everything—even in disorder. Within these opportunities could be the hidden potential to change our lives for the better. Record the thoughts that come to you based on this note. Remember, it is all about your perception and your worldview.

- **What is the competition around me that motivates me to do more?**

Humans, by nature, are competitive. There is a tendency that makes people want to best those around them. No one ever wants to finish in the last place. Everyone wants to finish first, and as a result, they compete aggressively and strive to be at the top of the pack. There is this rush of the happiness hormones (dopamine) when people win, so it is perfectly natural to feel the urge to compete and face it off with others. Many people are averse to coming in the *last place* in any endeavor. One of the factors that make people want to compete with others is that of socially comparing ourselves with others. People want to be seen ahead of others in social settings such as in the workplace or life in general. Competition in humans is a survival trait ingrained in the human genome. In the words of Peter Diamandis, the Greek-American engineer, physician, and entrepreneur, "As humans, we have evolved to compete . . . it is in our genes, and we love to watch a competition." We compete to survive, and we survive to compete—it is a social life-cycle of some sort that everyone can relate with.

We see competition in various spheres of human endeavor. We see people competing in sports. We have seen organized games and tournaments from ancient times (e.g., the Greek Olympic Games) to modern times (e.g., FIFA, NBA, NFL, MLB, etc.). We see competition in economics, in politics, foreign diplomatic relationships, technology races, interpersonal quests (e.g., love), etc. However, the foremost conclusion we can draw from this, as we self-explore, is that the deep interests that launch us into wanting to compete could be a clear indicator of our innate potentials. We struggle to win. We want to exploit the rewards to gain a competitive advantage over others. All this could be a clear indication of where our hidden strengths, abilities, skills, or potentials may lie. The question that we are considering is, *What is the competition around you that motivates you to do more?*

Take a profound introspective look at yourself, and look at those areas or environments that bring out your competitive nature, and carefully note them down. The competition around you that draws you could be a sign of your hidden potentials. Embrace it, process it, refine it, polish it, and use it to your advantage.

- **Is there a principal pain point that I can do something about?**

There is always something in our world that needs to be improved. People always seek change. Whether it be people, principles, processes, systems, or just anything, everything is invariably yearning for some sort of change and improvement or the other. It is a visceral continuous improvement cycle. This fact is essential for your process of unearthing your hidden potentials. Why? Because once you find a pain point that you can add value to, you might just be able to uncover a skill set that has been hidden in you. A pain point is a problem, real or perceived. As an individual, you create opportunities for yourself by manufacturing solutions to those pain points. The answers that you create bring value for everyone involved. With these conjured values often come immense wealth. Therefore, let me ask again, *Is there a principal pain point that I can do something about?* If there is, should you not be asking yourself some crucial questions that could evoke a reaction to the pain points? *How can I proffer a solution to the pain point I am currently experiencing?* instead of asking, *Why am I in this pain point?* Ask yourself, *How can I forge a path to lead me out of this problem?* Asking *Why?* most often evokes a feeling of self-pity and worry, and that of *How?* allows for creative and innovative juices to flow.

The world can be a funny place, sometimes. Some people spend a lifetime looking for ways to avoid or run away from the problems they face, while others spend the same lifetime looking for problems they can solve. The latter do so with a perspective of looking for solutions to those problems. When you provide a solution to a common problem, you instantly add value to a myriad of people, and with value comes a chance for profit. That is what distinguishes the *Haves* from the *Have-Nots.* The *Have-Nots* chicken out of *opportunities* disguised as *problems,* while the *Haves* take a stab at fate by taking the same chicken and transforming them into Chicken Nuggets, and thus the McDonalds and the KFCs of the world are born. The *Have-Nots* cry about the world giving them *lemons,* but *Haves* take the same *lemons* that life dishes to them and they make *lemonade* out of it, and, of course, sell them for a profit. Talk about the irony of life—different strokes for different folks. As earlier mentioned, it is all about perception. Do you see a *glass half empty,* or do you see a *glass half full?* How you see your world is what governs the bulk of your actions, controlling how you react to the opportunities that the universe presents to you. It's all about Weltanschauung—your perception about your world view.

So, the next question you should be asking is, *How do I identify pain points to solve in my life?* It is time to get down to the basics of being practical, as has been the model of this book.

First, start by scrutinizing your surroundings.

Second, you must become attentive. Start listening to all the problems that people encounter daily. Hidden in those problems could be the opportunity of a lifetime and providing the solution would add value to others.

Third, ascertain the various problems that you possess the necessary skills to fix. Maybe you have acquired a college degree that gives you the needed facilities to solve a problem or a self-thought skill on your part. Whatever the case may be, just provide the solution to it.

Fourth, do yourself a favor and proceed to *Go!* Start fixing the problem and don't give in to laziness or succumb to procrastination. Remember, as you do all these things, you could very well be unearthing your latent potentials.

The *fifth* point is that you need to pay close attention to what it took for you to fix the problem and determine if the process is repeatable. The art of journaling and taking note of patterns comes to play with this point. Record your process. In so doing, you could be unearthing some hidden potentials in the depths of your subconscious.

Sixth, how do other people deal with the issue? Are there other solutions that already exist? How does the solution you provided match up to the resolutions others have offered? It is imperative to compare what you are offering to what is already out there. By doing so, you are making sure you are not duplicating solutions.

Seventh, where does your solution stand when compared to the alternative? Is yours above par or below par when compared to the other option(s)? Your solution needs to be qualitative, something that will stand the test of time.

Eighth, eureka! You have found yourself a valuable product or service. You have discovered a pain point that you plainly provided a solution for.

Now, it is time for you to repeat the cycle by PDCA (i.e., **P**lan–**D**o–**C**heck–**A**ct or **P**lan–**D**o–**C**heck–**A**djust). (NB. We will look at PDCA Cycle in more depth in Chapter 8).

Don't bite off more than you can chew by trying to provide solutions to problems out of your reach. Some people overreach by trying to fix a problem that is too broad. In so doing, they always hit a roadblock that stops them right in their tracks and keeps them from achieving their maximum potential. There is wisdom in zeroing in on a specific, niche problem that is within your reach and then providing a solution for it. Search deep within yourself to unearth your latent potentials and leverage the attributes that give you a clear competitive advantage over others. This will form a formidable foundation for discovering solutions to pain points with the purview of your expertise. Solve small problems that are around you and be SMART (i.e., **S**pecific–**M**easurable–**A**chievable–**R**elevant–**T**ime bound) about it. Adopt what I have dubbed as the *V-Principle of Growth* (See Figure 6.2). In this principle, start small from the bottom vertex/ point of the *V*, and fan out to the two arms, and keep growing to infinity. Start small, fan out and keep growing.[5] Simply put, start small and grow big. You can do so by focusing on the immediate problems that surround you. Avoid the trivialities that will hamper the resolutions to your problems. Be persistent in pushing your solutions, despite any frustration or setbacks you may have. Remember to look within and solve your own problem!

---

5 **V-Principle of Growth:** A term of art coined by Ogbonnaya Agom-Eze, that describes a non-stopping growth principle from zero to infinity, from small to great. The foundation of the principle is gotten from the typeface anatomy of the letter *V*. Start small from the bottom vertex/overshoot or bottom point of the *V*, and fan out to the left diagonal serif and the right arms of the *V* and just keep growing to infinity. Start small at a point of your vision, fanout, and grow big in time. The two arms of the letter *V* continue to fan out to infinity, growing wider and wider. When you start something as small as a "point," you have the potential to continue to grow it to infinity. The amazing thing is that the arms fanning out continues to grow, and they will never come to meet at any time. Hence, you can grow anything that you started from a point, as small as it may seem, so great and wide with no limits.

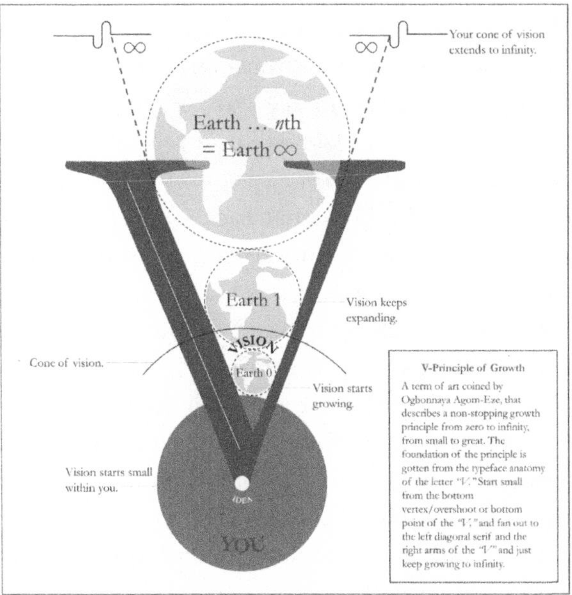

FIGURE 6.2 V-Principle of Growth

The solutions to the problems we experience in life come in different shades and forms. Some solutions are quiet, while others are quite groundbreaking, loud, and very disruptive. Talk about disruptive innovation.[6] They are spawning everywhere

6 According to Clayton Christensen, "Disruptive innovation," is "a term of art that he coined," which "describes a process by which a product or service takes root initially in commonplace applications at the bottom of a market and then relentlessly moves up market, eventually displacing established competitors." Distilling the words of this Harvard Business School Professor, "Disruptive Innovation," takes a complicated innovation—once unaffordable—and simplifies it, making it more affordable for the public. For instance, think the *mainframe computer,* once the awe of all in the early days of its advent. It was inaccessible by all due to its colossal nature and cost. However, through *disruptive innovation,* we have had an evolutional transmogrification of the mainframe computer, evolving to desktops, laptops, handheld mobile computers to the very affordable *smart cellphones,* which in their right are *supercomputers* as

and in every circle. For instance, Microsoft Solutions has disrupted the computing and software marketplace. Amazon has exceedingly buzzed e-commerce bazaar globally. Facebook is screaming *Disruption!* as it sends out a seismic shockwave into the *terra firma* of social media. You revel in awe of the tsunami of the social media buzz that Facebook is conjuring under the helm of Captain Mark Zuckerberg? Exciting, huh? Google is hyper-oozing *disruption* as it has become synonymous to the word *search*. They are also branching out into many more angles, now. In the present and in the future, I see virtual education quickly becoming a disruptor to traditional brick-and-mortar classrooms. I see flying vehicles becoming a disruptor to the several conventional means of locomotion, on land, air, and sea. I see Artificial Intelligence (AI) quickly becoming a disruptor of the traditional workplace and more, where AI will be doing jobs once done by humans. The instances are endless. The unique thing about all this is that people are transforming their pain points to disruptive innovation channels through the solutions they provide. Hidden in many of these solutions are the innate potentials of these individuals.

Some pain points, when solved, become whole new markets. Some pain points, when answered, fill a niche. Examine your life. *What are the current pain points that you are experiencing? Instead of worrying or cowering under the weight of the problem, why not devise a solution for it?* Wallowing in self-pity is a waste of time and energy, a

---

well and even more powerful, when compared to the first mainframe computers. *Disruptive innovation* affords you the opportunity of creating new markets via the conceptualization of a product, or group of products that attract a whole unique set of following in the marketplace, an entirely new customer base. For more information about this principle, check out the reference provided. (Reference: Christensen, D. (2019). Disruptive innovation. Retrieved from claytonchristensen.com/key-concepts/).

weakness that will eventually cause the mine shafts of your mind to implode. Take stock of the things people complain about and think deeply about how you can solve that challenge for them. If you can formulate a solution for the problem, you could open new portals of possibilities for yourself through the value you provide. It could be a thing that you have discerned that could improve the way people live or do things. Be perceptive when you encounter pain points in your self-exploration journey.

What kind of mindset should you have when you encounter pain points or problems? How should you approach it? Remember that your mind is the seat that governs how you see life and how you will eventually experience it. There is power in positive thinking. Reform your mindset by thinking in the frequency of opportunities. Seek how you could exploit them to your benefit. Consider possibility in the face of impossible circumstances. Think advantage when you face disadvantages. Think light when you are plunged into the darkness of hard times. Imagine ability when you face disability. Imagine *How?* under the burden of *Why?* Think about winning in the face of a looming defeat. Think movement in the face of stagnation. In the words of Sam Levenson, an American journalist, *Don't watch the clock; do what it does. Keep going.* Never stop because a *rolling stone gathers no moss.* Just know that hidden in every problem is an opportunity to make an impact. That moment, occasion, event, shot, opening, possibility, or chance could be the hidden wealth of potential that you are seeking. Don't let the opportunity pass you by. Grab it while you may.

Take some time and note down your thoughts.

- **How can I leverage technology in my life and career?**

In line with our mining analogies, we can see that this sector is also leveraging the power of technology to bolster its advancement and efficiency in various mining processes. First, we see more automation in mining. For instance, CAT, Komatsu, and Hitachi are investing big on automated haulage systems. Rio Tinto is spending big on the *intelligent mine,* where the use of robotics could replace miners in the future, with the driving force being more safety and efficiency. Underground excavation is becoming safer with the advent of Underground Mobile Miners, developed by Atlas Copco. We see more surface electric haulage trucks and various kinds of Underground Electric Load Haul Dumpers (LHDs). We see more new innovations in mining software and in sensor-based sorting, where technology is being used to separate the valuable minerals from ores (Steinert and Tomra are big players).[7] As we see, the mining industry is not left behind in the technology race. Hence, it is wise to say that we need to leverage technology as we seek to unearth our latent potentials.

We live in a technological era, one that is moving at a fast pace. In the words of Naveen Jain, business executive, entrepreneur, and founder and former CEO of InfoSpace, "We are now living in a fast-paced technological era where every skill that we teach our children becomes obsolete in the ten to fifteen years due to exponentially growing technological advances." If you are to exploit opportunities around you to your advantage, then you need to leverage the benefits of technology for better

---

7 The mining industry is experiencing its own technological revolution. We see more automation, safer and more efficient underground excavators, the use of more electric vehicles for haulage on the surface and underground, better mining software, more advanced sensor-based sorting, etc. For more information, you can check out the reference. (Reference: Robinson, B., & Morris, C. (2018, January 9). These five technologies will shake up the mining industry in 2018. Retrieved from www.mining.com/web/five-technologies-will-shake-mining-industry-2018/).

efficiency. *What are some things you could do to leverage technology to your advantage?*

First, it can help you reclaim your time. Embrace all technology alternatives that will assist you in eliminating repetitive, time-consuming, and mundane tasks.

Second, technology could aid you in working smart and hard. Today, AI technologies can help you make very complex decisions. It can help you manage your stocks portfolio as it can do all the intricate work for you. AI is also fast encroaching into the accounting and financial world (e.g., Moneytree, AppZen, YayPay, TALK Accounting, Bkper, etc.). In Chapter 3, *Self-Exploration Pre-Activities,* under the sub-heading *Note Your Patterns,* I made this comment that *Every human being is a gestalt—a configuration or pattern—of sequentially learned behaviors that spring from the aquifers of our subconscious.*

Third, there are technology and computer applications out there that can help you track your behavior and habits. Your patterns are born out of your routines. You could use apps to help you map your life patterns.

Fourth, we could leverage technology to help us manage our daily lives via the use of various AI personal assistants like the Google Assistant, Microsoft Cortana, Apple Siri, Amazon Alexa, Amazon Echo, x.ai, etc. These AI technologies and more can help us with things like calendaring, setting reminders, scheduling meetings, natural conversations, recommending, smarter learning, sorting our emails, etc., so does it not make sense to leverage many of these technologies that could make us more productive? By being productive, we could start exploiting these opportunities to our advantage. These tools can keep our lives more organized as we continue to delve deeper within ourselves to unearth our hidden potentials.

Technology—when used correctly—can do many things that help you optimize your chances at unraveling your innate potentials. As we have previously mentioned, we are in the age of knowledge and technology that, in recent times, has become a goldmine of opportunities for the discerning and curious people. We can say that technological advancement is the new gold rush. There is an epic technological revolution in play, today. People are literally building careers out of technology. Now, this is not to say that everyone must develop their careers literally around technology, however, you must study the future prospects of what you do currently and grow your skills in that area. Consider your options about tomorrow and begin to leverage the potentials it generates. Technology is the resounding gong that will be heard in many more years to come. If technology progresses at the rate it is going today, project into the future, where will you be in your life and career 10–20 years from now? How would you have leveraged its several advancements in unearthing your hidden skills and opportunities? Does it not make sense to start dancing to the sway of its tunes now?

Record your thoughts on this note.

So far, we have explored various questions in the *Opportunities* (**O**) quadrant of the SWOT analysis assessment tool. We have seen that *an opportunity is a situation or condition favorable for the attainment of a goal.* Discovering your opportunities also requires you to dig into the subterranean zones of your subconscious self, along with being cognizant of the shots, chances, or possibilities that surround you. We looked at several questions that could help us recognize the opportunities in our vicinity that we could exploit.

Before we started looking outward, we first looked inward. The *first* question was, *Which of my inward strengths/skills do I need to leverage?* We asked two sub-questions to this first question. The *first* one was, *"Which of my skills/abilities have I underplayed or overlooked?"* and the *second* was, *What skills can l learn that can be of advantage to me and help you add value?* These two questions allow us to evaluate any internal skills we could leverage as an opportunity to our advantage. Rummage through your inner depths and see what you can unravel as you do so.

Looking outward, the *second* question was, *What immediate opportunities surround me?* Through this question, we explored the various ways that we see the world around us—our Weltanschauung, our world view. We looked at the *Water Halfway in a Glass* analogy. Some choose to see the glass as *half empty,* adopting a pessimistic view of life. Perceiving the negative side of life always will never help you in the process of unearthing your innate skills. Others prefer to see the glass *half full,* embracing a promising perspective of life. Be rational, and find a balance to allow you to see the complete view. I nudged you to see the opportunities that surround you. There are opportunities in needs, obstacles, trials, and even in chaos. There are opportunities in everything that surrounds us, and it just depends on how you see things—your Weltanschauung, your world view.

The *third* question that we looked at was, *What is the competition around me that motivates me to do more?* Consider looking within yourself or in your environment and note the things that always brings out your competitive nature. The competition around you that draws you could be a sign of your hidden potentials. Don't forget to keep noting the points that come to you.

The *fourth* question was, *Is there a principal pain point that I can do something about?* Pain points are specific problems that you can provide solutions to. We established that in the process of administering solutions to pain points, you could unearth a hidden ability that you have. We saw the benefits of asking *How?* more often. It brings your creative and innovative juices to the surface. Don't brood *too much* over the *Why?* question. Doing so could plunge you into a state of self-pity *if* it is not supported by the appropriate accompanying actions to counter the circumstances that caused the problem. Some people spend a lifetime wallowing in self-pity because they encounter a problem *(the Have-Nots).* Worry, as we saw, incapacitates you. Turn your predicaments to possibilities, and provide a solution to a pain point and join the *Hall of Fame of the Haves.* In so doing, you could unearth the gems of your talents in the process.

The *fifth* and last question we asked was, *How can I leverage technology in my life and career?* You can agree that we are living in exciting times where technology is practically moving at the speed of thought. The questions you should be asking at this juncture are, *What can technology do for me? How can I leverage technology to make me more effective and efficient? How can I leverage technology to unearth the latent potentials that I have?*

In summary, reviewing these opportunity-determining-questions has been a vital step in our journey toward unearthing our latent potentials (NB. These questions are not in themselves exhaustive, you could add or remove to them as needed; tailoring them to your own situation). The answers you have provided to these questions in the *Opportunities* (**O**) quadrant of your *SWOT analysis* assessment will reveal your opportunities. As you are deeply exploring yourself to bring out the factors that will draw out the best version of yourself yet, note the thoughts that come to you because of these questions. Knowledge of your opportunities should give you some ideas on how you could exploit them to your advantage. If you handle them correctly, you could be adding another list of strengths to the innate powers you already have.

As you continue exploring these essential elements in society, you need to be cognizant of the factors that could cause trouble for you and your mission to unearth your latent potentials *(i.e., Threats).* The final question we will be considering as we dissect the SWOT analysis self-exploration tool is, *What are your threats?* Let us continue our self-discovery as we look at the last quadrant of the SWOT analysis assessment tool as we cover *Threats* (**T**) in the next chapter.

CHAPTER 7

Self-Exploration IV: What Are Your Threats?

—∞—

So far, we have looked at *Self-Exploration I* and *II* in *Chapters 4* and *5,* where we discussed the first two quadrants of the SWOT analysis matrix, which cover the two attributes, *Strength* (**S**) and *Weaknesses* (**W**) respectively. We established that you need to first look inwards at the internal factors *(Strengths* and *Weaknesses)* before we consider looking externally as we contemplate the external factors (*Opportunities* and *Threats).* We examined various questions that allowed us to look introspectively as we explored our *Strength* (**S**) and *Weaknesses* (**W**). In Chapter 6, we started looking outward as we commenced considering *Opportunities* (**O**), the third quadrant of the model. Slowly but surely, we have come to the final portion of the SWOT self-analysis tool as we begin considering the *Threats* (**T**)—the fourth quadrant of the matrix—in this chapter. However, before we begin our final push to self-analyze ourselves, it would make perfect sense for us to succinctly summarize *Chapters 4, 5,* and *6.*

In *Chapter 4,* we took a journey to look at several revealing self-analysis questions that would help us dig deep into ourselves to unearth our *Strengths* (**S**). We learned that our innate powers are our inward potentials (i.e., your talent, abilities, skills, etc.) that we need to discover, leverage, and possibly use them to mitigate, or preferably eliminate, our weaknesses. We could also rely on our *Strengths* (**S**) to exploit various opportunities that surround us and also eliminate the threats we face as we work toward unraveling the hidden talents we have buried in our subliminal-self. We established that our inner power is a realm where we manifest our inherent superpowers. It is a place of relative ease, cerebral peace, and tranquility—our comfort zone. It is a place of competitive advantage and leverage. Our strengths are the raw gems of our innate potential in action, all aimed at our every success.

By now, you should have noted your strengths in your journal.

In *Chapter 5,* we dove deeper into the profundities of our minds to unearth the flaws that could make the mine of the subconscious vulnerable to collapse. Here, we considered *Weaknesses* (**W**), the second quadrant of the SWOT analysis matrix. We learned that weaknesses are *defects, deficiencies, faults, flaws, gaps,* or *vulnerabilities* that we should strive to mitigate, or preferably eliminate, from the lexicon of our lives. We saw various examples of what harboring weaknesses could do. Think gangrene! Think about an underground mine collapsing, as instances. When gaps are left unchecked, the result can be catastrophic. In this chapter, we brought to light the cracks in our being that are our flaws and sought to correct them before they cause us to implode. We discussed how recognizing our weaknesses places us in a position of strength. When we spot defects, we can provide remedies. We can only fix what we identify. Failing to see our weaknesses—*intentionally* or *unintentionally*—is a recipe for failure.

By now, I trust you have recorded your weaknesses.

In *Chapter 6,* we dove deeper yet into our subliminal-self as we explored the various depths of *Opportunities* (**O**) that we have, as we considered the third quadrant of the SWOT analysis matrix. Opportunities come in a flash, and we need to be perceptive in order to exploit them. Before we went outward, we went inward by looking at the possibility of us leveraging the probabilities of any inward strengths or skills that we already have, or skills that we needed to acquire. As we started looking externally, we unearthed the various opportunities around us by considering different questions. We established that life is all about perspectives, how we see things, our Weltanschauung—our perception about our world view. We also saw that the competition surrounding us could help us discover our potentials and that pain points are opportunities for us to provide solutions that add value. Finally, we saw that technology can be the principal fulcrum that helps us leverage advantages that we can exploit.

By now, I believe that you must have recorded the points that describe the various opportunities around you.

Threats

We have come to the final and fourth quadrant of our SWOT analysis, the *Threat* (**T**) element of the matrix tool (See Figure 7.1). *Threat* (i.e., hazard, warning, menace, peril, or fulmination) is an element in the environment (i.e., external), or even internal, that can cause us damage, trouble, or some potential harm. Whether external or internal, threats lack any positive qualities; they offer no benefit to you at all. They could be compared to parasites, or should I say leeches. They live off you, offering only harm in return. You want to eliminate parasites, not harbor them. In a similar vein, you also want to get rid of any threats that you face. *Threats* are like *Opportunities* because you cannot change their incidence, or purposely bring them about, but you do have the power to decide how you react to them. When threats arise, the natural tendency is to squelch it before the harm that they carry begins to wreak havoc. Failing to respond to a looming threat could become calamitous, leading to a grave loss. It is tantamount to having a weakness and allowing it to persist until it becomes uncontrollable as it inflicts a sinister and lethal blow. It is comparable to soil erosion that gradually eats away at the topsoil until it wreaks havoc in its wake. Hence, threats must be avoided, or, better still, eliminated as soon as you sniff their presence.

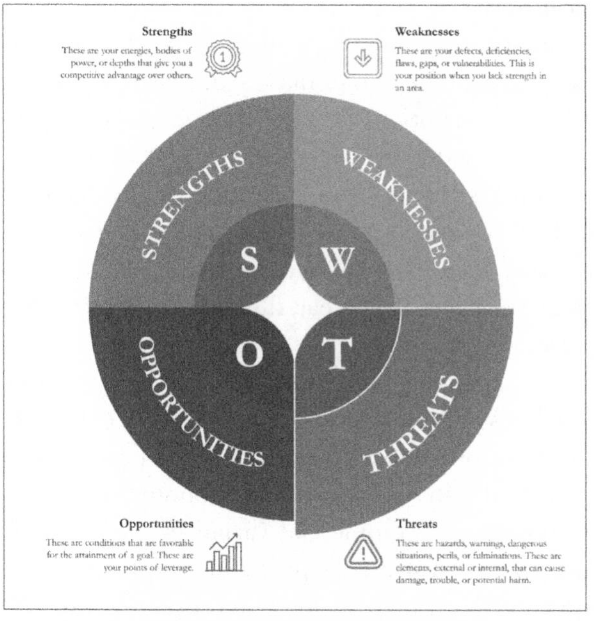

Figure 7.1 SWOT Analysis Matrix Tool: Threats (T)

No one welcomes any form of threat, whatever it is. From a broad perspective, these hazards could be meteorological, social, medical, and geological. Some examples of meteorological perils are drought, flood, flash flood, heat wave, hurricane, tornado, tropical storm, wind storm, firestorm, etc. Some instances of social threats are individual negative behavior (e.g., lone shooter), mass negative behavior (e.g., riots, genocide, etc.), terrorism (e.g., domestic, or international), bombs, hijacking in individual, VIP, or group, biological, nuclear, chemical, and cyber-attacks, etc. Some examples of technological threats are transportation-related events, aviation accidents, rail accidents, vehicular accidents, IT-related events, HAZMAT related events, food, etc. Some medical threats are usually more epidemiological in nature (e.g., pandemic flu, dengue fever, plague, viral outbreaks, etc.). Finally, geological perils could either be *endogenic* (e.g., plate tectonics like earthquakes or igneous activity like volcanic eruption) or, *exogenic* (e.g., slope like landslide, avalanche, mudslide, etc. or weathering like erosion) in nature. Meteorological and geological threats are usually natural, though they can also be triggered or magnified by human activities. Social, technological, and medical threats are primarily man-made. Whatever the threat, they are never occurrences that anyone ever welcomes.

Still paying homage to our mining analogies, we should note that companies in these sectors are not immune to threats either. They face their own shades of obstacles and perils too. Some of the threats that mining companies encounter are energy shortages, economic and commercial variances due to volatility in the marketplace, costly transportation requirements, limited environmental clearance by local authorities, limited permission to operate because of resource nationalism, and natural threats (e.g., flood, earthquake, volcanic eruptions, tsunamis, or hurricane).[8] Some of the menaces they face become so severe that it halts the complete operation of their mines. Hence, in our journey of self-exploration as we unearth our latent potentials, it becomes crucial to be wary of any ensuing threats. All steps must be taken to eliminate them so that they do not halt our efforts toward self-discovery.

The threats you might encounter while unearthing your potential vary from person to person. To be on top of your game, you need to understand what they are and address them accordingly. Some people become a threat to themselves because

---

8 Even the mining industry is not immune to various threats. Kumar and Rathore, in 2015, via an academic article, highlight some of these threats. The *first* biggest threat to mining operations is water and energy shortage. The *second* threat mining companies face is commodity price competition amongst the various mining companies. The commodity markets are highly volatile, and because of this, some companies are not able to plan their mining operations accordingly, leading some of these companies to reshape their businesses, while some of them even go out of business. The *third* threat to mining companies is the colossal capital expenditure (CAPEX) required when it comes to much-needed haulage transportation from pit to port. Profit margins hinge heavily on transportation—the closer these companies are to shipping ports, the higher their profit margins, as they tend to spend less on transportation. The *fourth* threat to mining companies is obtaining the required environmental clearance. The survival of many of these companies hangs on the balance because of the many uncertainties around obtaining environmental permissions to situate their mining operations. The *fifth* threat mining companies face is resource nationalism and license to operate. Countries with abundant mineral deposits are now tightening their hold by instituting very stringent laws to control companies that mine within their borders. Sometimes, their clutch becomes so tight that many companies give up pursuing mining operations in these nations. The *sixth* threat that mining companies face is the threat of natural disasters (e.g., floods, earthquakes, volcanic eruptions, tsunamis, or hurricanes). For a complete review of the SWOT Analysis matrix for mining industry, visit the reference link. (Reference: Kumar, N. P., & Rathore, I. (2015). The need of mining industry—A SWOT analysis. *International Research Journal of Earth Sciences, 3*(8), 32-36. Retrieved from www.isca.in/EARTH_SCI/Archive/v3/i8/4.ISCA-IRJES-2015-046.pdf).

of their negative thinking patterns. Hence, you want to know what paradigm influences your self-perception. Be aware of the changes that could impact your current skill. Be cognizant of those who stand in your way as you push to fulfill your dreams. Knowledge is power. Recognize and address all the threats you face accordingly before they submerge you under a layer of failures that could deal a fatal blow to your dreams.

As we delve into this fourth and final quadrant of our SWOT analysis matrix, I implore you to keep documenting your discoveries as you go through the various questions that will be presented below as we progress in this chapter in our study of *Threats* (**T**). Your guiding lines should be: *Recognize, document, and address whatever threats you discover.* Let's dive into the questions straightway:

- **What are the major concerns in my life right now?**

Life is full of problems. No one can truly say that they are 100% immune to the troubles life dishes daily. We all go through pressure, oppression, and hardship under the press of life. The problems that life imposes can be menacing at times—sometimes inflicting us with punishment, injury, and even the cessation of consciousness to the less fortunate ones. To be in a position where one feels threatened is a place where no one wants to be. It is hard to predict the incidence of threats, but we are vested with the rights as humans to control how we act and react under the shadows of threats, whether active or passive.

So, our first question is, *What are the major concerns in my life right now?* This question could be answered as the depiction of the active threats currently in your life. An active threat is a probable trouble that is in a state of existence, progress, or motion. One which is passive is just the opposite, seeming inert or quiescent.

Some examples of active threats that people face are financial problems, health, debt, unemployment, racial prejudice, physical safety, relationship dilemmas, drug addictions, etc. Passively, a lot of people suffer from the threat of psychological safety in their places of work, in relationships, in their schools (e.g., fear of bullying), in their neighborhoods, etc. Assess yourself and begin to unearth the threats that you are currently facing and note them down.

Threats to our lives can be frightening and very concerning. That is the reason why nations fight to protect their citizenry from various looming threats. You cannot play around with *direct threats.* As Dick Cheney, 46th Vice President of the United States, said, "Direct threats require decisive action." This is the mindset you need to have when you discover any significant concern(s) or threat(s) in your life. You cannot approach any problem or threat you find with any modicum of weakness. You must deal with it decisively in order to neutralize it completely.

Survey your life now for concerns or threats that stand as a hindrance to you becoming the best version of yourself. For your self-exploration to be successful, you must deal with every limiting warning that is present in your life—no exceptions. Note them and act! No procrastination must be allowed when such menacing risks are discovered. The life-defining action you must take is to *"Confront it, head on!"*

- **Could any of my weaknesses be a threat to my life's vision?**

In Chapter 5, we asked an important question, *What are your weaknesses?* We took a while to address this question by understanding what weaknesses were and asked some introspective questions to give us insight into what our own weaknesses were. We saw that *Weaknesses* (**W**) *(i.e., defects, deficiencies, flaws, gaps, or* *vulnerabilities) are the lack of strength, firmness, vigor, or the like, and the state of inadequacy, for instance, in a person's character, a system, or an organizational framework.* Having addressed this previously, there is no need to discuss it here again.

Could any of my weaknesses be a threat to my life's vision? It is a self-defining question. When left unchecked, your weaknesses can, and eventually will, threaten your vision, purpose, and progress, and leave you worse off than you were before. It's like having cracks in the pillars that hold up a major bridge and doing nothing about it. Soon, the cracks will worsen and impact the structural integrity of the entire structure and cause its collapse. Weaknesses, when left unchecked, will worsen and become a looming threat in any circumstance.

Threats are not only external. Sometimes, they are self-imposed and internal when you do not address your weaknesses timely. These gaps or faults have a mind of their own, and they will get worse and become a probable threat to you if you leave them to linger. There is no need to belabor the point on this matter. It is clear as crystal that weaknesses can worsen and become menacing situations. The English Proverb that states *A stitch in time saves nine* is the perfect antidote to resolving the effect of lingering weaknesses.

Once again, note the vulnerabilities that are lagging in your life. Find ways to address them quickly so that they don't worsen and become a threat to your life vision and purpose.

- **Does any area of my life threaten another? If yes, *how?***

Everyone strives to attain a harmonious life. Inner balance brings about the inner peace that allows us as human beings to resonate with the positive energies and forces of the universe. Positive resonance empowers us to function more effectively and efficiently as we attain our life goals. As Marcus Aurelius, Roman emperor and stoic philosopher, said, "He who lives in harmony with himself lives in harmony with the universe." When things are off-balance, a shift occurs to bring the body (i.e., animate or inanimate) back to a state of equilibrium—back to a place of inner peace. A non-equilibrium state can threaten the existence of the whole system as it is inclined to transition into a state of chaos.

I like to always allude to Le Chatelier's principle whenever I think of *equilibrium, harmony,* or *balance.* Although this rule derives its origin from the field of Chemistry, I believe that we can always apply laws to drive home a point in another area other than its field of origin. The principle, from the lens of Chemistry, when put in general terms, simply states that "When a settled system is disturbed (i.e., a change in concentration, temperature, volume, or pressure), it will adjust to diminish the change that has been made to it." In life too, this principle is applicable, because when a body in equilibrium—it could be a system, an organization, or a person—is subjected to a disturbance, the natural inclination is to create an equal and opposite reaction to counter the change to the *status quo.*

It's safe to say that most career-oriented people can readily identify with this question, *Does any area of my life threaten another?* A lot of times, we are pushing to develop one area of our lives and other areas start suffering. We struggle to maintain equilibrium. We shift from a harmonious to a non-harmonious state. For instance, have you seen some people who spend so much energy toward their careers that their family, relationships, and health suffer? It is a frequent occurrence. It could be that you are pursuing a dream, fighting a cause, or bettering the world at the cost of other things that are equally significant. In your journey to unearth your latent potentials, it is highly imperative to strike a balance in the process. You need to have an adaptive mindset that can shift to neutralize the effects and constraints that life throws at you, just like the Le Chatelier's principle. Being in a state of equilibrium is core when discovering your innate talents and abilities.

Personal discovery is an arduous process. It is not just a walk in the park. Digging deep into your subconscious is as tough a business as the job of a miner, if not tougher (NB. On many lists online, the job of a miner is categorized as one of the world's toughest). Maintaining a stable state of mind during the tasking process of exploring your inner depths will help make your search successful. Now, think about every area of your life—your health, career, spirituality, relationships (e.g., family and friends), personal development, recreation, and as many other areas as you can conceive. What areas are suffering? And which ones are thriving at their expense? Once you have clarified this, you will be in a coordinated frame of mind to make a balanced decision about what potentials need unlocking, how you will go through the process, and how you can live a fully utilized existence. Attaining this balance will help you eliminate the threat that may arise due to a shift in the equilibrium.

- **Are my current skills relevant to the future?**

Whatever skills you have right now should be looked at through the spectacles of the future. You need to know if they will be relevant decades from today. Why is that? Because advancement in technology is unraveling at a tremendous pace. I was watching a video from Alux.com on YouTube titled, *15 Jobs That Will Disappear in The Next 20 Years Due To AI,* and there were many startling facts that should make you *pause* and *rethink* your stance regarding your current profession. According to the video, "A study done at Oxford University found out that 45% of all current jobs will disappear in the next ten years, with some of them being completely automated or at least upgraded to a point where the fraction of the workforce will be needed." This is concerning because if you fall into the group whose jobs will possibly be impacted, you will be in a threatened position, should you become a victim of these advancements, trends, and technological transitions.

We are living in exciting times. The professional landscape of today's world is changing very fast. If you are not planning on how to survive these changing times, then you are already in the quagmire of this precarious situation, and you may be struggling and sinking in no time. Failing to plan is planning to fail. You would be stupid to see a tsunami surging your way and do nothing to save yourself. What are some of these industries that will take the biggest hit as stipulated by the people of Alux.com? Some of these professions and trades include drivers, farmers, printers and publishers, cashiers, travel agents, manufacturing workers, dispatchers, waiters and bartenders, bank tellers, military pilots and soldiers, fast-food workers, telemarketer, accountants, tax preparers, stock traders, construction workers, movie stars, etc.[9] I am not saying that this is a self-fulfilling prognostication. However, wisdom would call for caution as you note these points.

9 The advancement of technology is going to make many current jobs extinct. A lot of jobs are at a high risk of automation, as technology and Artificial Intelligence (AI) unravels at breakneck speeds. To gain some perspective on these fields, be sure to check out the accompanying source. (Reference: Alux.com. (2017, October 5). 15 jobs that will disappear in the next 20 years due to AI. Retrieved from https://www.youtube.com/watch?v=r21lu89eUaY).

Is it all doom and gloom for all or most professions? Not at all. Some jobs will thrive with the continued advent of technology. In another video titled, *15 Jobs That Will Thrive in the Future (Despite A.I.),* released by the people of Alux.com, highlights some professions and trades that will thrive, despite the way technology and AI is unraveling. Some of these industries and jobs include robot manufacturers, service management (e.g., Boston Dynamics, Inc.), raw materials management, big data, AI scientists, artificial bodies manufacturers, eSports, psychologists and therapists, gene designers for babies and pets (through CRISPR), and virtual world designers. Some other industries include cybersecurity and private data brokerage, entertainment, real estate developers, biochemistry and tech engineers, private services for the rich, elderly care and end-of-life management, small jobs that are not worth automating-yet, anybody who is in the top 10% of their profession, etc.[10] These are some professions amongst a vast array of other emerging professionals. As you continue to delve deeper within your subliminal-self, does it not make sense to start rethinking your position when it comes to the profession that you are in if you haven't done so already?

So, you need to consider the question, *Is there a future for the tangible and intangible skills that I have acquired? Or, will I need to update them to be more relevant to the changing times?* It is crucial to consider these questions. If your field is one of those that may not stand a chance of survival, you are already in the *eye of the tech-AI storm.* The best time to have reconsidered your stance

10 Advancement in technology and the advent of Artificial Intelligence (AI) is wreaking a lot of havoc currently, and in the future. However, some careers will thrive despite all these advancements. To gain some perspective on these fields, be sure to check out the accompanying reference. (Reference: Alux.com. (2018, November 18). 15 Jobs that will thrive in the future (despite A.I.). Retrieved from https://www.youtube.com/watch?v=6gUrMGnvcfQ).

was *yesterday*, and the second-best time is *today*. The threat is real because lots of people may soon be without a job or in a position where they are not able to add value in applying the skills that they already have, and that is a dicey situation. Note your situation in your journal and start acting without hesitation to change your *status quo* if you really need to do so.

- **What are your competitors doing?**

Life is a competition where we are always vying to come out on top. To be blind to what your competitors are doing is the highest form of ignorance. You must always be on top of your game, and you must be aware of what your competitors are doing. Why? Because your competitors are always looking for ways to outwit and outshine you. They want to be on top of the game and to make sure you never wear the crown of victory in the expression of your highest potentials.

The game of life is a war, and your competitors are out like Spartacus, tagging alongside with the Gauls, Crixus, Gannicus, Castus, and Oenomaus, in blood and sand, eager to see you feel the edge of their thirsty blade. Sounds gruesome, huh? But that is the truth of the matter. Your competitors wish to see you lose the battle. They are there to snuff out your ideas and make sure that your potentials never see the light of day so that theirs could thrive. They want you to be miserable so that you give up and they have the last laugh. Competitors want to steal your market share and leave you high and dry. They want you to cower in fear at their presence. They want to win at all cost. Your failure is their victory dance. To outwit your competitors in all angles of war, you must crave victory more than they do.

In your self-exploration journey, you must be disciplined to your core. You must be as gentle as a dove, but wise as a serpent—ever cautious and strategic to know when to deliver the winning strike to keep you at the summit of the game. You must embrace the eagerness to want to discover the gems of your potentials and come out preeminent doing so. Remember, there are other people in the mines of this life, also seeking the same gold as you. Your competitors also want to find that potential that will distinguish them and give them leverage over you. If you cannot decisively answer the question, *What are my competitors doing?* Then, all I can say is, *Sorry! You are already on the path to embracing mediocrity and every failure as your lot.*

In all you do, study your competition, master your rival(s), and ace your opposition.

—⁓—

So far, we have explored various questions in the *Threats* (**T**) portion of the SWOT analysis matrix, the fourth and final quadrant of the assessment tool (See Figure 7.1). We saw that *a Threat (i.e., hazard, warning, menace, peril, or fulmination) is an element that can cause us damage, trouble, or harm.* To discover your threats, we established that you need to look inward and external. *Threats,* as we have seen in the earlier questions, are not to be toyed with.

The *first* question was, *What are the major concerns in my life right now?* In answering this question, we looked at *active* and *passive* threats that we may encounter as individuals. We also learned that we need to be decisive in dealing with *all* threats. We must approach all menacing situations from a position of strength without any form of weakness. *Confront all threats, head on!*

The *second* question we looked at was, *Could any of my weaknesses be a threat to my life's vision?* We saw that your weaknesses are *defects, deficiencies, flaws, gaps, or vulnerabilities,* and it is dangerous to harbor *weaknesses* without doing anything tangible to curb, or preferably eliminate, them. Weaknesses quickly deteriorate to threatening conditions. Use your strengths to defeat them.

The *third* question was, *Does any area of my life threaten another? If yes, how?* Here, we saw that non-equilibrium in our lives can quickly become a threatening situation. A lot of people face non-harmonious states when they try to focus on one area of their lives while neglecting other areas. We saw the need to be in a state of equilibrium as we seek to unearth our innate talents and abilities. Don't forget to keep noting the points that are coming to you.

The *fourth* question was, *Are my current skills relevant to the future?* We saw that this is a threat worth considering. You will be in a dicey situation if the skills, talents, or abilities you currently have are no longer value-adding in the future. That will render you powerless in your ability to grow to your maximum potential. We saw the need for you to reassess yourself. This will guide you better as you dig deeper into your subliminal-self to ascertain which treasures you need to focus on processing, refining, polishing, and use in your explorative journey to unearth your best self ever.

The *fifth* and last question was, *What are your competitors doing?* You cannot risk being ignorant of what your competitors are doing. Your competition wants all the slices of the pie, and they will do all in their power to get them all. Study your opposition. Do all you can to outwit and outshine them. Always remember that you are not the only one trying to unearth potentials, and your competitors are also at your heels in hot pursuit.

In summary, reviewing these threat-determining-questions is a vital step in our journey toward unearthing our latent potentials (NB. These questions are not in themselves exhaustive, you could add or remove to them as needed; tailoring them to your own situation). The answers you have provided to these questions in the *Threats* (**T**) quadrant of your SWOT analysis assessment (See Figure 7.1) will reveal any warning signals that you need to address immediately and are not to be treated lightly. As you are deeply self-exploring to bring out the factors that will draw out the best version of yourself yet, note the thoughts that come to you because of these questions. Knowledge of your threats should give you some ideas on how you can eliminate them. With this, we have come to the end of analyzing our SWOT analysis matrix self-exploration tool. I believe that this process should have given you a chance to dig deep within yourself. Hopefully, you have learned something new about yourself by now, or even have unearthed some unique abilities that you never knew that you had.

So, what next? We have gathered all these facts from this analysis. What then do we plan to do with all this information? The next question we need to consider is the question of *How?* Now that we have the self-explorative facts that tell us more about our *Strengths, Weaknesses, Opportunities,* and *Threats,* the question to ask yourself is, *In what manner, or by what means, should we unearth our latent potentials?*

That is the question we will be delving into in our next chapter, *How Do You Unearth Your Latent Potentials?* Let us continue our self-discovery journey as we see *How* and *What* we need to do in the next level of our exploration.

Let us stay excited as we keep digging.

CHAPTER 8

How Do You Unearth Your Latent Potentials?

—∾—

AFTER CRUDE OIL IS DISCOVERED and all the necessary tests have been made by geophysicists, geologists, and petrochemical engineers, the drillers drill an oil well into the ground by creating a hole with an oil rig where a steel casing is inserted (NB. The casing contains the conductor pipe, surface, intermediate, and production casings, and the perforated interval). This hole and casing then become the conduit through which the crude oil is extracted. The drilling, depending on the underground reserve along with other factors, can take anywhere between three weeks to a year. The process, as we see, does not take place in a short span. It is a progression of various means over a period, and while it is significantly different from unearthing potentials in yourself, we can assert that the process of unearthing is parallel to the one for crude oil.

In the mining industry, the process of excavating subsurface mines can take quite a while. For instance, according to Mining Technology (i.e., mining-technology.com), the AngloGold Ashanti's Mponeng mine, which is in the Gauteng province of South Africa, is 2.5 miles (4 km) deep—same as ten Empire

State Buildings stacked on top of each other—making it the world's deepest and most affluent gold mine. Mponeng's Shaft No. 1 took five years to complete, from 1981 to 1986. Shaft No. 1's adjoining sub-shaft took another seven years to complete in 1993. Similarly, uncovering anything of value could take time, and it would make much sense for you to invest adequate time to the process of unearthing your latent potentials, if required. The principal factor of note is the need for you to stay persistent with the dig. Remember, *winners never quit, and quitters never have the opportunity to win.* That is a valid fact.

The process of self-discovery or potential discovery requires that you question yourself thoroughly. That is why in the previous chapters that covered self-exploration (Chapter 4–7), we took some time to ask several questions, allowing us to unearth various facts about ourselves that will help us in the subliminal-self-excavation process. At this juncture in our explorative journey through the pages of this book, I will ask you a few more self-discovery questions, so don't give up your journal yet. The answers to these questions will help you to devise a *Plan* (a guided schematic of projected outcomes) that will allow you to *Do* (strategic action-points) the things that will enable you to find your potentials and walk in them. After that, you will *Check* (results vs. projected outcomes), through analysis or appraisals. Finally, you will *Act* or *Adjust* where necessary. Then, you can do it again to keep unraveling your inherent abilities.

Some of my readers may be savvy to deduce the *PDCA Cycle* from the preceding paragraph, a continuous quality improvement tool, made famous by W. Edwards Deming. Yes, we will be using this tool in this chapter to help us answer the question, *How do you unearth your latent potentials?* I don't want you to read this book like a novel or a theoretical college piece. Instead, I want you to acquire some practical tools that will help you utilize the information you gain from its pages. Approach this book as a tool for discovery, as though you are about to find the most valuable part of yourself. Consider all the questions that you are reading in this book as various drill bits that you are using to delve deeper into the depths of your subconscious. Patiently internalize the substance of this book—page after page, chapter after chapter. I am confident that by the time you are done, you would have unearthed potentials that have always been locked in you.

The core of this book, *Unearthing Your Latent Potential,* centers a lot around *self-auditing.* We have previously been discussing the SWOT analysis matrix. By now, you should have been conversant in its use to audit yourself, to bring out your *Strengths* (**S**), *Weaknesses* (**W**), *Opportunities* (**O**), and *Threats* (**T**). By going through the many questions in the matrix, and maybe more, depending on who is reading and your peculiar needs, you should have unearthed some of your hidden potentials by now. The PDCA cycle that we will discuss in this chapter will help you take the next necessary *action steps* toward unearthing your hidden talents. However, before delving into planning, doing, checking, and acting/adjusting, we will look at a few more questions to set the tone for the next level of our self-audit throughout the PDCA cycle.

Throughout the self-exploration self-audit processes, I encourage you to be *honest* in thoroughly answering all questions thrown at you. Some of these questions will require the input of people who know you best. We are not always capable of complete objectivity when we assess ourselves, so if you realize that you cannot provide objective responses when answering these questions, it may be advisable to request input from individuals who know you best—people who can give you their opinion about your real character without bias. Therefore, feel free to ask for their input, since they spend or have spent a fair share of your time with you. The good thing is that you can always verify their answers to see if they are really that well acquainted with you. This would help you have a better understanding of the hidden potentials you may or may not be aware of. Let's get to digging.

Subconscious Search

Let us embark on another subconscious soul search. We have been doing a lot of subliminal-self-auditing by asking a lot of value-pointed questions. The *Art of Questioning* is an efficient, productive, positive, and creative go-to methodology to unravel truths. Asking useful questions goes *in tandem* with good listening. Such inquiries give you the chance to listen to the effusion of the answers that spring from the aquifers of your subliminal-self. Such cogent questions are analogous to the tungsten filament, incandescent, and fluorescent lighting, with excellent color rendition, used in underground mining to ensure clear visibility. They illuminate the paths to the depths of our mind-mine shafts. They allow for better visibility as we dig deeper into the trenches of our subconscious to unearth the gems of our hidden talents, abilities, or skills.

Sound questions help us gather better information, identify obstacles, predict outcomes, and often nudge us to act. Simon Sinek, the British-American author, asserts in his best-selling book title that we should *Start with Why*. However, I would suggest we start with *What,* then *How,* and then *Why*. I think I am pulling off a *Reverse-Sinek* here. Why? Because, starting with *Why* can at times make people defensive. Start with, *What?* Ask, *What can I do?* This question gets your encephalic engines rolling. Then, proceed to *How?* Ask, *How can I?* This gets you up and working to actualize the *How.* While in the process of realizing your *How,* you can ask *Why* to ascertain the root cause that led to the inception of the process in the first place. In this light, innovation is already at work from the onset. Asking the *What* or *How* question pulls people into the realm of logical reasoning, which triggers their innovative juices to proffer solutions to the problems in hand.

Consequently, to unearth your latent potentials, the first thing you must do is question yourself. You need to ask yourself some good, efficient, productive, and positive questions. You need to examine to know *What* your beliefs, biases, and opinions are. By musing on *What,* your mind is already effervescing, issuing forth the bubbles of innovative thought. From here, you need to find out *How* instrumental your beliefs, biases, and opinions could be at unraveling your hidden abilities and bringing them to bare. By pondering on *How,* you are already cudgeling your encephalon to start generating *options* for your next line of action. Finally, you will now ask *Why?* Ask, *Why do I have these beliefs, biases, and opinions? Why are these core factors important, and how can I leverage them to unearth my hidden potentials?* The essence of this is for you to come to your most authentic conviction—to get to a place where you are using the raw materials of facts and figures to develop a *plan* of action, to *do* effectual things, to *check* yourself through self-audit, and to *act* again in order to *adjust* things as required. Answering the questions of *What, How,* and *Why* will help you unearth your latent potentials.

So, *why is imperative to answer all these questions?* The reason is that our individual realities are different. No two persons reading this book can say they have an exact same experience as the next person. As the whorls that constitute our fingerprints are different, so are we all unique in our various ways. For instance, someone born in England might not come to terms with the realities of another born in Rwanda. Similar is with our ideals as human beings. Our Weltanschauung (our world view) of life is quite different. Although we all acknowledge that through increased technology, the world has become a global village, and people can now observe the realities of others beyond their immediate geographic environment, the things that make up their day-to-day are not the same; though neither does the authenticity of one experience neutralize the other. For both parties to engage the world wholesomely, they would each have to *question* and eventually understand that their own reality is not universal. Interred in the answers to compelling questions could lie the hidden gems of potentials we never knew existed.

The *Art of Questioning* allows us to see the world more objectively. In so doing, we can offer our *subjective* opinions in response to the various questions that will empower us to unearth our latent potentials. The more penetrating our queries, the more substantive the potent powers we unravel. It is quite significant that you question what you think about yourself and your place in the world. Everyone exists for an essential reason. What the purpose is could be wrapped in the potentials that we carry within us in our subliminal-self. We all have potentials, known or unknown, that distinguish us from everyone else. That is the very core and foundation of our subconscious search. The questions we have previously asked and the ones we will now or later ask will help you uncover your real capacity. The queries will help you develop an insight into your potentials and enable you to pursue a fulfilling path.

Remember, the questions I have presented in this book for your subconscious search are not in any way exhaustive. You can form questions that relate more to you as a person. As we mentioned in the above paragraphs, we all have different realities that could help sculpt the inquiring assertions that we pose to ourselves more uniquely. Therefore, feel free to inject questions that will help you in the process of unearthing your unique potentials. Whatever the inquiries may be, make sure they embody lucid characteristics. For instance, ensure that they are *identifying, probing, outcome-seeking,* and *action-oriented* questions. Some of the questions I would like you to ask yourself are:

- **Identifying Questions:** These questions will help you recognize or establish *who* you really are, and *what* you can achieve, such as—*What is my purpose? Who am I? What differentiates me from every other person? What are my potentials? Which ones do I recognize having as of now? What value do I add to my family, friends, and society as a whole?*

  As you answer these questions and the ones you generate in this process, you delve deeper into your subliminal-self and continue to identify your hidden potentials.
- **Probing Questions:** These are questions that seek to search into or examine your subconscious self more thoroughly—*What other potentials do I seem to have? What is most valuable about me for my community, state, or, the country as a whole? What else can I offer the world? What else could I do to add more value?*

  Probing questions in this process of self-exploration allow you to dig deeper into the labyrinths of your mind-mine shafts. The deeper you dig, the more you enhance the probability of unearthing valuable talent gems from your subconscious *Cave of Wonders.* Don't shy away from the probing questions.

- **Outcome-Seeking Questions:** These are questions that are end-result-oriented. These are inquiries that seek to elucidate the consequence of our actions—*What do I want to accomplish with my potentials? What benefits do I hope to unearth with my skills? What plans do I have to unravel my best self ever? What else do I need to consider?*

  Such queries envision the end from the beginning—they are revelatory in nature. They reveal the results or outcomes at the end of the tunnel.
- **Action Questions:** These are the questions that transition us to activity or action as we begin to *do* the things that are required for us to go from one state to the other—*How do I unearth my potentials? What will I do to discover my abilities? When will I do it? How long will it take me to do it? How will I know that I am making progress? What are the checks and balances that guide my search? What are my next steps?*

  There is absolutely no benefit in being *all talk and no action.* Hence, these questions are uniquely poised to get you going.

  Like we saw in Chapter 2, *Why Are Potentials Latent?* a lot of people's potentials remain latent because of *inaction.* Why is that? Like we saw, it is because people are given to fear, self-doubt, procrastination, giving up prematurely, and laziness. These attributes cripple them, preventing them from moving forward. Action questions are meant to blast the walls of these obstacles to smithereens. Don't shy away from them. Allow them to do their work. Remember these words as you move forward, *More act, less lag.*

These questions will get the sprocket wheels of your brain spinning into action. As answers start funneling upwards from the depths of your subliminal-self, take some time to write them down in your journal. After you have taken the time to answer these questions, study them for a while and observe if you can identify a thought-pattern that you had not recognized until this moment. Is there a conflict between what you answered and what you admit to people? You would be the best judge of that, at this moment. Consequently, with the emerging patterns that you are recording, you can begin the gradual formalization of a vision for yourself.

Your vision is the golden compass that guides you as you start formulating the plans of your next steps toward the full unraveling of your hidden potentials. With the strategies that you draw up, you should be able to spring yourself into action as you start actively pursuing the goals you have established in your plans. As you go through the process, be sure to evaluate your efforts. Here, you start comparing your current efforts to your expected outcomes. If you notice any variation from the earlier verification of your activities, then you act and adjust yourself for more favorable ends. At this juncture, let us delve into the *PDCA (**Plan–Do–Check–Act** or **Plan–Do–Check–Adjust**) Cycle* tool (See Figure 8.1), as we use it to answer the question, *How Do You Unearth Your Latent Potentials?*

—∞—

PDCA Cycle

How Do You Unearth Your Latent Potentials? Let's look at this question from the PDCA Cycle lens.

In brief, according to the American Society for Quality (ASQ), the *Plan–Do–Check–Act,* or *Plan–Do–Check–Adjust cycle* (*Deming* or *Shewhart cycle*) is a four-step continuous improvement model for carrying out change by *planning, doing, checking,* and *acting,* or *adjusting.* It is beneficial for driving constant improvements to projects, processes, products, or services. *Plan* allows you to develop a framework to change a perceived need. *Do* lets you perform by putting the plan into action. *Check* helps you monitor your efforts to see what you've learned (i.e., what works and what does not work). *Act* or *Adjust* allows you to improve on what you have learned. Hence, successful activities are repeated with a broader scope. If unsuccessful, the plan is adjusted, and the process is repeated.[11]

The PDCA cycle connects perfectly with the self-exploration process of *Unearthing Your Latent Potential.* How? Through the SWOT analysis matrix that we have studied under Self-Explorations I–IV (Chapters 4–7), we *first* recognize the opportunity to unearth our strengths, eliminate our weaknesses, leverage our opportunities, and be carefully cognizant of all the threats. The facts we have gathered allow us to develop a framework to change our perceived need. *Second,* with our structure in

11 The *Plan–Do–Check–Act (PDCA)* cycle is also called *Plan–Do–Check–Adjust cycle, Plan–Do–Study–Act (PDSA) cycle, Deming cycle, and Shewhart cycle.* According to Investopedia (i.e., https://www.investopedia.com/terms/p/pdca-cycle.asp), PDCA was *originally developed by the American physicist, Walter A. Shewhart, during the 1920s; and later popularized by the quality control pioneer Dr. W Edwards Deming, Shewhart's protege, in the 1950s.* It is a four-step continuous improvement model for carrying out change by planning, doing, checking, and acting, or adjusting. (Reference: ASQ. (2019). What is the plan-do-check-act (PDCA) cycle? Retrieved from https://asq.org/quality-resources/pdca-cycle).

place, we will proceed to explore how we can unearth our latent potentials through various actions under the *Do* phase. (NB. We will spend the most time on this phase). *Third,* while *doing,* we'll keep monitoring our efforts to assess what we've learned (what works and what doesn't). *Fourth,* we will then *Act* or *Adjust* our process accordingly.

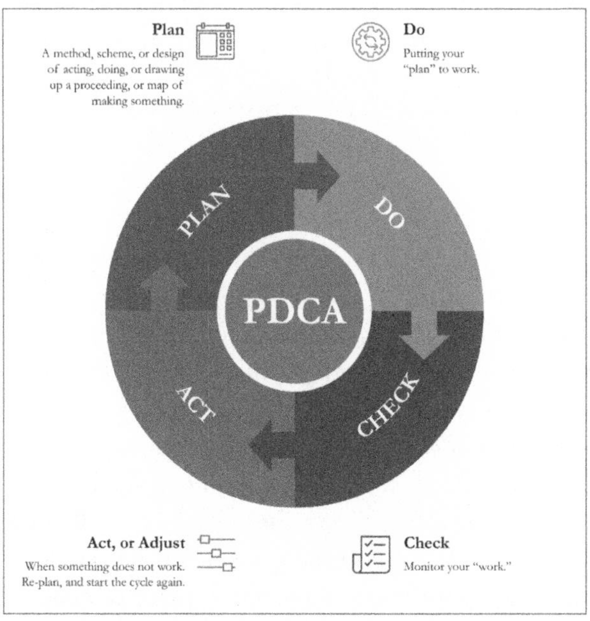

Figure 8.1 PDCA Cycle Tool

This book, *Unearthing Your Latent Potential,* is action-oriented in nature. My goal as you read through its pages is to spur you into action by delving into the acumens of your subliminal-self to unearth the gems of your hidden abilities. You cannot get the best out of this self-explorative process if you are not *doing* the necessary things that will allow you to discover those latent potentials. Remember, *More act, less lag.* Necessity requires that you set in motion your *action-plans.* Your plans will be futile if you don't put it to action by *doing* your stipulated activities. The process of *doing* these *action-plans* is *how you can unearth your hidden abilities.* The rule of *doing* is what answers the question of this chapter, *How Do You Unearth Your Latent Potentials?* That is *why* we need to spend some time on the *Do* phase of PDCA. We will then assess *what works* and *what doesn't* work (*Check*), adjusting our plans accordingly where need be as improve our unearthing process. Without further ado, let's proceed to *Plan* (See Figure 8.2).

Plan

What is a plan? A plan (design, layout, map, method, project, or program, etc.) is *a scheme or method of acting, doing, drawing up a proceeding, or a map for making something. It is a design or scheme of arrangement of a specific project. It provides the framework or pattern from which to operate. It is the establishment of objectives and processes using facts to deliver outcomes or results.* Any endeavor that is worth executing efficiently needs a plan. As mentioned earlier, *failing to plan is planning to fail.* Following a plan carefully guides you in making sure that you execute a specific project accurately. Not following a plan nudges you into a place of chance, where anything goes. Not having a plan can, at times, launch you into confusion. In your self-exploration efforts, a chaotic state is not where you ever want to be. Explore according to a deliberate design.

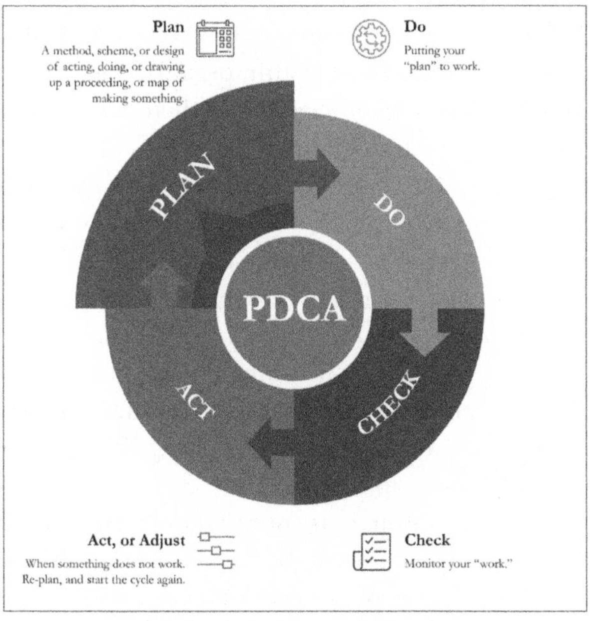

Figure 8.2 PDCA Cycle Tool: Plan (P)

There are various instances of the use of plans. For example, in construction, the first step toward building a house is developing the building plan (i.e., a spatial arrangement according to the intended needs of the users of the space). The architect uses the *brief* or *facts* presented by the client to design the building to their taste. I am an architect. Whenever I commence working on a scheme for a client, I am led by the three-part rule, *Firmitas, Utilitas et Venustas,* that was neologized by the Roman architect and engineer, Vitruvius. The words translate to *Strength, Utility, and Beauty.* Hence, I design my buildings to *last* (i.e., strength), to *properly fit* my client's needs (i.e., utility), and to *appeal* to my clients and the world. All this, in architecture, begins with the *plan.*

Plans are used in many contexts. Before you start a business, you draw up a business plan. Within organizations, teams draw up a blueprint on how to efficiently run their departments. The military draws up a strategic plan for their operations before they engage in warfare. Sports teams draw up a plan of play, as they strategize on how to play a winning game. People sign up for a healthcare plan to have a systematic scheme to take care of their health in the present and in the future. People draw up a strategy for retirement and work toward making all of it happen. There are many instances concerning the use of *guiding designs,* or plans, by organizations and individuals alike. However, ensure that you have a *strategic planning process* that gives you the chance to reach your stipulated goals.

A plan is only as potent as your ability to execute it. I concur with the words of George S. Patton, United States Army General, that "A good plan violently executed now is better than a perfect plan executed next week." In other words, it is time to take the battle to the gates of your opposing set of obstacles with your plans in hand ready to act on them. Remember, *More act, less lag.* You must be resolute in strategically following through on the process of accomplishing the goals highlighted in your purpose maps. Strategically planning your self-exploration journey as you unearth your latent potentials will align you with your vision, mission, and goals. Misalignment brings about waste, so your strategic plan will help you avoid missteps as you progress to discover your hidden abilities. Hence, the question now is, *What are some of the core practical steps of the strategic planning process?*

A strategic plan can be drafted in various ways. We will consider some core aspects of an efficient strategic plan.

First step—Gather Inputs. The SWOT analysis matrix was the tool of choice to gather inputs in this opus.

Second Step—Vision. This drives your strategic planning process. It gives you wings, focus, and direction.

Third Step—Hurdles. These emerge at the creation of vision. Knowing your obstacles spurs you to develop your *How-to-Win* Strategies.

Fourth Step—Resources. You know your *status quo.* You have forged a vision. You know your hurdles. Your resources answer the questions, *What means 'do you have' to deploy to achieve your vision? What resources 'do you need' to unearth your latent potentials?*

Fifth Step—Strategy. In the words of a Robert Stover, an author, and entrepreneur, "*Strategy exists to serve a vision.*" Your strategy looks at the *options* you can utilize with your *resources* to reach your goals.

Sixth Step—Tactics. This pushes you to *make something happen.* It answers the question, *What time-bound and accountable steps do I need to take to unearth my hidden potentials?*

Seventh Step—Check. It is time to monitor and measure your *strategies* and *tactics.* Adjust them where needed as you unravel your best *you* yet.

In summary, *you gather inputs, forge a vision, learn the hurdles to scale, assess your resources, strategize, be tactical, and check your inputs for efficiency.* These are the seven simple steps to crafting an efficient strategic plan to unearth your latent potentials. Planning is a crucial element to realize your set goals and objectives. Hence, to be effective, it must be strategic. I can't agree more with Zig Ziglar, the American motivational speaker, who said, "You were born to win, but to be a winner, you must plan to win, prepare to win, and expect to win." For your self-exploration efforts to be a win, it is imperative that you develop a strategic method for your process.

Now that you know what a plan is and how you can develop one, let us proceed to the *Do* phase of PDCA.

Do

After you have asked all the questions above, you need to act. This brings us to the *Do* phase of PDCA (See Figure 8.3). Here, we are putting the plan into works. According to ASQ, the expected change (i.e., the plan) is tested through small-scale studies or actions. Unapplied knowledge is useless and inconsequential. Iron ore, raw diamond, crude oil and the like are of no value to anyone underground. Their real value is obtained when they have been dug up, processed, and refined into the final products. The same is applicable with your latent potentials. Innate talents are of no benefit to you hidden within your subliminal depths. You must unearth, process, and hone them for their maximum benefit.

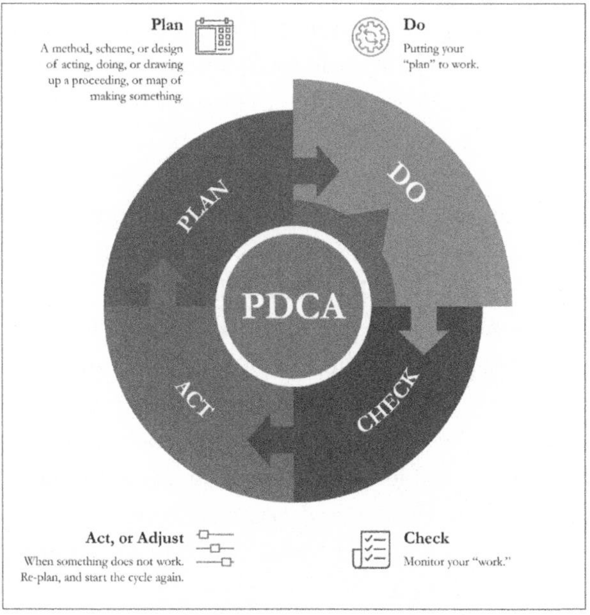

FIGURE 8.3 PDCA Cycle Tool: Do (D)

We explored the functional steps of determining your *status quo* through the SWOT Analysis matrix. Now, we are looking at how you can unearth your hidden abilities using PDCA. However, the value of this exercise is what you choose to do with your findings. At this point, you should have some inkling of what your potentials are. Check your itemized strengths on your SWOT matrix. That should give an idea.

Persistence is key to seeing value being extracted from your potentials. For instance, consider this popular sales concept of follow-up. For every quality sales lead, a salesperson initializes a connection with that lead. The rep introduces their company, products, or services, and subsequently makes a sales pitch to the *potential* customer. After that initial pitch, the follow-up process ensues. Depending on the salesperson, follow-up can start immediately, or a little after the first contact. It strengthens the connection originally established, allowing time for the sale to finally close. Without adequate follow-up, most customers' interests usually wane. Checking-up with *potential* clients is what makes sales tangible. Similarly, if you don't adopt a *follow-up-for-follow-through* mentality with the process of unearthing your innate skills, your efforts will remain a dead loss.

To this point, we have previously discussed a lot of questions to help you delve into the depths of your subliminal-self as you seek to unearth your latent potentials. Now, through the *Do* phase of PDCA (See Figure 8.3), we are proceeding toward the core of more actionable items. The commitment to action is an assured measure of what is further ahead. Nevertheless, here are some useful action-oriented tips that will fast-track the process of unearthing your best self:

- **Identify your strengths and work with them**

Many people struggle and face discomfort in their lives because they fail to operate in their strengths. People in this state are prone to wrongfully assessing themselves. Erroneously working in your weaknesses can instill in you low self-esteem that makes you feel like you are not equipped to achieve much in life. Identifying your strengths is core to unearthing your potentials. It injects a level of self-fulfillment in you, and it serves as leverage to unravel other latent abilities you may have. Like we have seen in previous chapters, you can use the SWOT Analysis matrix to audit yourself and identify your *Strengths* (**S**), *Weaknesses* (**W**), *Opportunities* (**O**), and *Threats* (**T**). Apply yourself to the process of objectively spotting these attributes, particularly the strengths that lurk within the labyrinths of your subliminal-self.

Your strengths need not be in conventional spheres. There is absolutely nothing wrong in wanting to be in your own niche and standing out from the crowd. Walk a unique walk. For instance, your strength could be an aptitude to spot and eliminate weaknesses, or a strong ability to leverage opportunities that come your way. It could be that you are a terminator of threats. Your innate powers can be anything, and you just need to be willing to delve deep within yourself to bring that capacity to the forefront. You are not going through this process of self-assessment to arrive at the same conclusion as everyone else. It defeats the purpose. You are doing this because you want to identify the strengths that are unique to you—in other words, your best self. Focus and amplify your strengths. Don't dwell on any weakness you may have. Curb, or preferably eliminate, them. Leverage your opportunities and make them become your strengths in turn. Be decisive regarding threats, and eliminate them without hesitation.

- **Invest in personal development**

Personal development is an investment in hope. You believe the efforts you are putting into your improvement will pay off. In the words of Brian Tracy, American motivational speaker and writer, "If you wish to achieve worthwhile things in your personal and career life, you must become a worthwhile person in your own self-development." In the pursuit of excellence and higher potential, become worthwhile in your personal development. Such a move will be a highly valuable step toward unearthing your latent abilities as you rise to the demands of new levels of growth.

Before you start working on discovering your full potentials, personal development should be a priority for you. In life, you can only give out what you have. What you internalize is what you eventually externalize. So, do what you need to do regarding personal development. Take courses if you must, read as many helpful books as you can, go back to school if required, engage in mind-stimulating conversations that influence your worldview positively, and do not settle for the norm. Challenge yourself with growth, and you can be sure to get results.

- **Get a mentor**

A mentor is a wise and trusted counselor or teacher who guides their followers called mentees. While the process of finding one is mostly your responsibility, you need mentors on this journey, people who know what it feels like to unearth latent potentials themselves, people who have gone on a similar self-exploration expedition and done so successfully. Finding a worthy mentor who will take you under their wing can take away many years of heartaches and failures that you could encounter. They have gone through similar paths, and they can, therefore, guide you to avoid the pitfalls on your pathway to a new you. If you review the process of searching for gems underground again, you will notice that geologists don't work independently, and neither do the miners. Everyone who is a part of the exploration process brings to the table their expertise to make finding gems or natural resources a more efficient process. The mentor-mentee synergetic relationship and teamwork can be very beneficial. So, your action point is—*Find a worthy mentor and be a worthy mentee.*

Who is your mentor? When you look at every person who has ever become great, quite often, there is a mentor behind them. For Tiger Woods, it was his father. For Mark Zuckerberg, it's Bill Gates, the American business magnate and philanthropist. For Bill Gates, it is Warren Buffett, the American business magnate, investor, speaker, and philanthropist. For Warren Buffett, it was

Benjamin Graham, an American investor, economist, and author. For John Legend, it is Stevie Wonder. For Lee Iacocca, a Charlie Beacham was his first mentor. For Aretha Franklin, it was Clara Ward of the famous Ward gospel singers of Philadelphia. The simple point is—*Mentorship works.* Show me your mentor, and I can tell you who you will become. A mentor will act as a guide for you. Sometimes, mentors, with their keen eye for detail, can recognize potentials in you that you are oblivious to. You mustn't think this requires the physical presence of your chosen mentor. You can be mentored through books, YouTube videos, and other teaching materials. The main point is that *connection* with the message they are delivering. The weight of their message must speak to the core of who you are.

- **Be deliberate about acquiring skills**

There is power in being deliberate. It is a decision made from the mind, from a standpoint that is careful, conscious, cautious, considered, and intentionally weighed. In the words of Clayton M. Christensen, a Harvard Business School Professor, "I believe that we can, in a deliberate way, articulate the kind of people we want to become." Hence, intentional self-development is a path to becoming. Such intentional steps—as an avenue to unraveling your hidden powers—could be the deliberate acquisition of skills, either in a new area or a field in which you already operate. It could also be to get better at something you are not bad at or just gaining a new, higher level of knowledge you yearn to have. The principal factor here is being deliberate.

What skills do you have in your repertoire? Take stock of them. I believe everyone should have one skill or the other. However, if you are absolutely convinced you don't have any skills, then the question is, *What skills do you desire enough to learn?* Remember, skills can be more than just a vocational aptitude, or a college certificate or degree. For instance, it could be the art of persuasion or enhanced communicative abilities and interpersonal interactions that could come handy when making a sales pitch, or it could be management, leadership, financial acumen, etc. Whatever the skill, be deliberate in its acquisition. Remember, you could come upon more gems hidden within you during the skill acquisition process.

- **Practice, practice, practice**

After the commendable step of acquiring a skill or brushing up on it, the next step is *practice.* Put in the deliberate effort into daily practice. Why? Because *consistent practice makes for expertise.* Whatever you spend time doing eventually becomes your experience. Through repetition, you deepen and sharpen your skills, adding value to yourself and getting better at it. No one becomes a professional the first time they try something, neither do they become one the second or third time. Famous athletes like Michael Jordan can attest to this in their recurring failures before eventually becoming a resounding success. Natural talent is a reality that is obvious when observing those who have become celebrated in any activity. However, there is a need to be obsessed with practice to hone the talent buried in your subliminal-self to an expert state. I am inclined to lean on the *10,000-Hour Rule* made famous by Malcolm Gladwell, in his acclaimed best seller, *Outliers.* Practice with a purpose, practice deliberately, and stay committed to it.

Practice will also improve your discipline and confidence when approaching any work. Spend a specific time slot daily toward getting better at your craft. Even if your pace frustrates you the first few times, the key is perseverance and consistency.

Remember that what seems like exertion and failure is often skill development and growth. Will Smith, the American actor, once said, "I've always considered myself to be just average talent and what I have is a ridiculous, insane obsessiveness for practice and preparation." Become insanely obsessed with practice. Duplicate the process, repeatedly—like a Starbucks barista—until you become an expert at your craft. Periander, the second tyrant of Corinth (c. 627–587 BCE), made a comment, "Practice is everything." This is often misquoted as *Practice makes perfect.* In a way, I agree with him. *Practice* is everything.

Keep your goal firmly in front of you, and you will develop the skills necessary to reach the success you aspire to. Practice! Practice! Practice! Practice!

- **Embrace challenging responsibilities**

Challenging responsibilities are opportunities in disguise. As we saw in Chapter 6, if you play your cards well, you can leverage your chances and transform them into strengths. To develop your capacity, you must step up to challenging obligations. Holding back because you have not developed the requisite skills to handle them only keeps you stagnant. For instance, think about how random the challenges of leadership are, often coming so unexpectedly that the leader must provide on-the-spot solutions to them. Because subordinates look up to them for direction, they cannot afford to be without an answer. Just as leaders are met with these urgent challenges that need solving, you must view yourself as the leader of your life affairs in your self-exploration. Instead of ignoring trials when they do come—as they will—address them.

A lot of people have said a lot about challenges, but I am continually drawn to the assertions of a Sai Baba, an Indian religious leader, that "Life is a song—sing it. Life is a game—play it. Life is a challenge—meet it. Life is a dream—realize it. Life is a sacrifice—offer it. Life is love—enjoy it." I will not analyze every part of this statement; it will take another book to do so. However, let us focus on *Life is a challenge—meet it.* There is an opportunity in every challenge. Yet, a lot of people cower at the face of challenges. They are too afraid to meet it. Too many people want the pleasures of life but are unwilling to conquer the pain. When next you are faced with a challenge, take a chance on you and go for it. Meet it with boldness and optimism. It is a chance to perform in a much bigger capacity than you currently operate in, expand your capacity, and unearth more latent potentials in your life.

—∞—

So far, we have considered the *Plan* and *Do* phases of PDCA. A considerable portion of this chapter delves into the *Do* aspect of the model. Why? Because it is futile to have a plan that is not executed. Established objectives and processes are required to be acted upon to deliver the expected results. This is in concord with a statement in the United States Army Field Manual (FM) 100–5 that states, "The final test of a plan is its execution." Consider an army in warfare. If they don't execute their battle plan, they would not stand a fighting chance against the enemy.

Hence, if you have a draft of actions for your self-exploration expedition toward unearthing your latent potentials, but don't perform them, then it is useless to have even drafted a plan. A strategized effort is required to unravel the various gems of abilities within you. This forms the backbone for dwelling considerably on the *Do* phase of PDCA, as we considered various things we could do to put the plans we have into play.

However, the action-steps that we have covered are not exhaustive in any way. Consider the actions as the first steps to gain momentum. Feel free to add more steps to define the moves you take. The main factor here is that you are *doing* something. No matter how small the action, the goal is to keep doing something consistently toward unearthing your hidden abilities. Remember, *More act, less lag.*

Let us now briefly consider the *Check* and the *Act* or *Adjust* phases of PDCA.

Check

You have planned, you have performed, now it is time to *Check* (**C**) (See Figure 8.4) what you have done to see if you are on the right track. You observe your actions to ascertain what you have learned and any gaps that may have arisen during the process. Here, the goal is to scrutinize the results of each of the actions that you have taken in the *Do* (**D**) phase of PDCA to see how they align with the initial design drafted during the *Plan* (**P**) phase. Monitoring allows you to check for successes and failures that materialized in the *Do* phase and documenting any future adjustment that you need to make on the plan that factors in the changes.

The process of unearthing your latent potentials will only be a game of chance without the monitoring phase. In a way, this stage allows you to answer the questions: *How is my digging coming along? What progress am I making in discovering my hidden abilities? What is working and what is not working in my process? What do I need to change in order to make my action plan more efficient?*

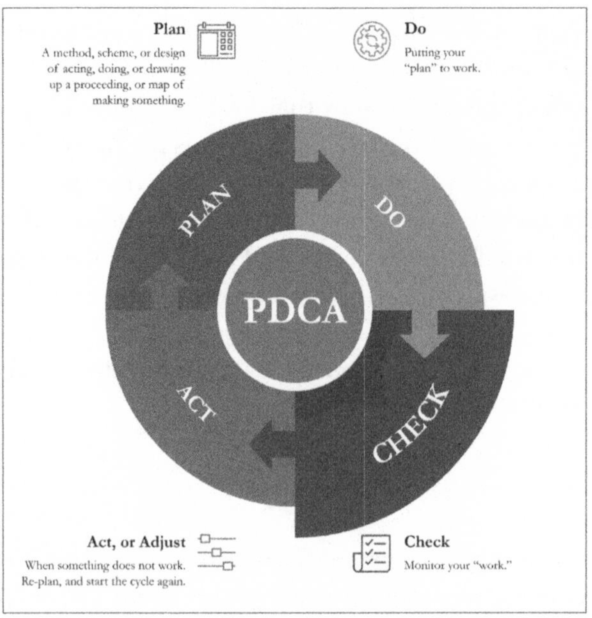

FIGURE 8.4 PDCA Cycle Tool: Check (C)

By answering these questions and more, you will decipher whether your discovery effort is reaching your desired level of performance, or making the desired progress at all, as established in your plan. Sit back and take stock of your progress.

ACT, OR ADJUST

You have planned, you have done, and you have had time to go through your actions. Now, it is time to *Act,* or *Adjust* (**A**) (See Figure 8.5). This is the phase of process improvement where you can act with a focus on what you learned from the *Do* (**D**) and *Check* (**C**) phases. The keyword here is *improvement.* We want to ensure we are getting the desired change in the process. If the actions taken did not pan out as planned, we have a chance during this phase to go through the cycle again with a different set of activities that accounts for the discovered obstacles. If your efforts were successful, you can imbibe your lessons and expand the horizons of your actions (NB. Remember the V-Principle of Growth in Chapter 6 (See Figure 6.2)) for a sweeping impact drive as you delve deeper into the process. Adopting the V-Principle at this stage allows you to expand the horizons of your actions when replicating the successful process as you embrace a broader scope. Utilize what you discovered to devise further improvements, beginning the cycle again.

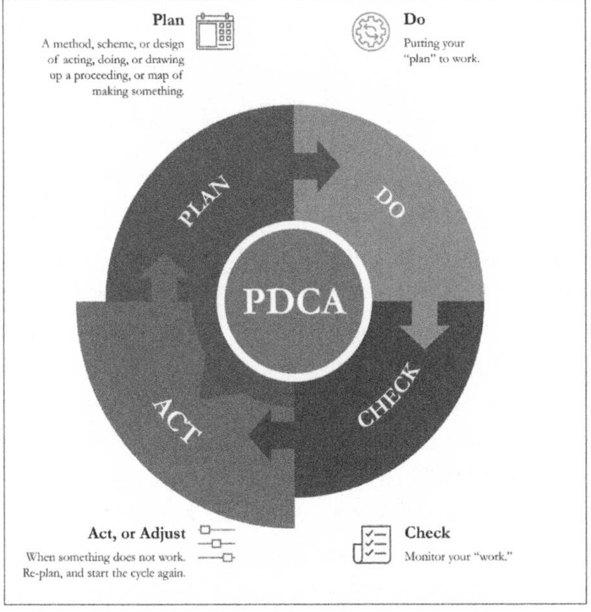

Figure 8.5 PDCA Cycle Tool: Act or Adjust (A)

As you work toward unearthing your latent potentials through the PDCA model, you are bound to detect some obstacles to your *Plan* (**P**) through the *Do* (**D**) and *Check* (**C**) phases. The disparities could be problems from a faulty plan, or from your current actions that need to be adjusted, or even halted. It could also be non-conformities, opportunities for improvement, inefficiencies, and other issues that spawn from your less-than-optimal actions. Whatever these obstacles may be, the *Act* or *Adjust* (**A**) phase of PDCA gives you the wiggle room to delve deeper into the root cause of your discrepancies, re-evaluate risks, and re-adjust your *Plan* with better instructions and standards for your *Do* phase. Act on the changes and keep digging as you explore your subliminal-self for the gems of your inherent talents. Keep the cycle of change going in your self-exploration expedition.

—ꟽ—

The core question in this chapter is *How Do You Unearth Your Latent Potentials?* We took a journey to learn how we can use the PDCA cycle, a four-step model for carrying out change.

Taking a look at the previous chapters in the self-exploration process, the SWOT Analysis matrix we looked at in Chapters 4–7 helps us analyze our current state as we unearth various facts about ourselves. We used it as a self-audit tool to better understand our *status quo*. These facts are raw materials that we transitioned into the PDCA, to spark the momentum that allows us to start the cyclic process of *unearthing* our best selves by *planning, doing, monitoring,* and *adjusting* our process. Hence, you have two tools at your disposal to help you unearth your potentials. One to help you *understand* the *you* in *you,* and the other to help you *bring out* the *you* in *you.* By now, you should already know what those potentials are, believing that you have been acting on all that you have been reading and learning from the first page of this book.

The process of unearthing your latent potentials is a continuous improvement process. The goal is for you to change your *status quo* to a better state through the aid of your innate potentials.

You unravel your hidden abilities by starting with a stipulated design of actions (*Plan* phase). Remember, *Planning is winning.*

You act on the plan through well-thought-out actions (*Do* phase). Remember, *More act, less lag.*

After putting in work through all your targeted activities, the next step is to monitor your actions to ascertain what worked and what didn't (*Check* phase). Remember, *Oversight is chief.*

If it went wrong, you re-adjust your plan and improve the process via renewed actions. If all worked well, then you adopt those actions and expand your horizons with a more extensive scope to keep growing—think V-Principle (See Figure 6.2). This is the process improvement phase (*Act* or *Adjust* phase). Remember, *Change is the only constant.*

After discovering your potentials, what comes next? At this stage of discovery, your talents are unrefined. Hence, the need to bring your newly discovered potential to a *fine* or *pure* state. You don't become a Michelangelo, Mozart, Michael Jordan, or even a Miyamoto Musashi—Japan's Sword Saint—overnight. You do so by continually refining your newfound capacity or capacities through persistent repetition and mastery. Your brand-new potentials need to be deliberately honed and polished to bring their unique qualities to a state of ultimate perfection where you are deriving the maximum utility from all of them.

Hence, having discovered how to unearth your hidden talents, I will be taking you through practical steps to refine those aptitudes, capacities, crafts, faculties, powers, or skills. Remember, every gem that is unearthed must—as a matter of necessity—go through a refining process so that it may become valuable.

CHAPTER 9

Refining Your Newfound Potentials

—⁓—

WHEN THE ORE OF A natural resource is mined, it must be refined. Why? Because in its natural state, it isn't very useful. After solid minerals or other natural resources have been excavated from the ground, they need to be refined into products that are valuable for them to be useful. This goes for most solid minerals and precious metals. They must go through a *process* to bring them to a state where they are valued and beneficial.

For instance, if I give you a piece of raw gold or its rudimentary ore, and you haven't developed a taste or an extensive knowledge about gold, chances are that you will not value it. Why? Because you don't know its value. Depending on its size and constitution, *sometimes* gold ore may look like a piece of rock and the untrained eye may misjudge it to be so—as just a piece of rock. However, the reaction of a goldsmith or someone who has in-depth knowledge about gold and its various states would feel the opposite because they recognize the importance of the gold ore—even those that just look like a piece of rock. But what if I give you a piece of beautifully crafted gold? This gold has gone through the process of refinement and smelted into beautiful pieces of fashionable jewelry that alluringly grants its wearers a tender, graceful, and royal look. Assuredly, your approach to the refined state would be different, because you perceive its finished state, rather than its raw state.

By the way, *how does gold work?* For eons, we have all been enamored by the metal gold. Thought as divine by the Egyptians and Aztecs, the bright yellow and rare metal has always been associated with wealth and power. When it comes to the gold mining process, it is broken down into four steps: *prospecting, mining, extracting,* and *refining. First,* via prospecting, gold deposits are sought out by scientists called *Prospectors. Second,* if enough gold deposits were found in an area, the mining process would begin. A large concentration of gold deposit in solid rock form is known as *lode deposits* (i.e., the gold ore), and could be found either on the surface or underground. In this state, one may not appreciate the gold. *Third,* following the mining phase is the complex extraction process of gold from the lode deposits. In brief, the extraction process includes slurry or powder formation, slurry thickening, leaching, electrowinning, and smelting, where the liquid gold is molded into *doré bars.* The *fourth* and final step is refining, which involves the removal of impurities from the doré bars that remain after the smelting process.

At the refinement of gold, companies that specialize in this process receive the doré bars plus scrap gold, and they re-liquefy the metal in the furnace. In this molten state, borax and soda ash are added to it to separate the pure gold from other valuable and less valuable metals present in the doré bars. Tests for purity are then carried out to measure the gold content. A 99.9% purity usually certifies it as pure gold.[12] At this stage, they are

12 The process of gold refinement comprises four main aspects, which are *prospecting, mining, extracting,* and *refining. First,* gold deposits are found by prospectors. *Second,* it is mined via surface or underground mining activities. The mining process, as we have seen in previous chapters, can be dangerous and negatively impacts the environment. *Third,* after the gold ores are gotten

now re-solidified into the shiny bars (gold bullions, or ingots) that we see, appreciate, and craze to possess. That is the main bulk of the refinement process of gold. Instead of delving more into the alloying of gold, its caratage, or test of its purity, its use in jewelry, health care, and technology, its use in the economy, and its tentative future, let us focus on the core takeaway, here. Gold undergoes a process from when it is mined to when its end results are used.

The same goes for crude oil, which is probably the most popular of naturally occurring resources whose presence has turned relatively unknown countries to become the toast of other nations. When I think of crude oil, the first thing that comes to mind is the image of a thick, black, oozing sludge that spews out of the ground or from a drilling platform. However, when you drive to your local gas station to fill your tank, you probably don't think much about it, though that same crude oil is manifest in the form of the gasoline that keeps you driving on the streets in your automobile. Gas or petrol are among many of the products of crude oil. Some other products include crayons, plastics, heating oil, jet fuel, kerosene, synthetic fibers, and tires. The crude oil, a fossil fuel that ranges from transparent to tar-black in hue, and from water to nearly solid in viscosity, is in its raw state. In this state, the daily-user of its products may see it as useless, but to the keen eye of the petrochemical engineer and other engineers that deal with this natural resource, it is of immense value.

---

from the process of mining, they go through a complex extraction process. The final and *fourth* step is the refinement of the gold, where the impurities are removed. For a detail step-by-step process of how the processing of gold works, see the reference link provided in this footnote. (Reference: Harris, W. (2009, February 23). How gold works. Retrieved from https://science.howstuffworks.com/gold8.htm).

How Does Crude Oil Refining Work? Crude oil is the source of various substances because they are made up of hydrocarbons (molecules that contain hydrogen and carbon and have different lengths and structures). These hydrocarbons contain a lot of energy and can yield gaseous, liquid, and solid products. To obtain these products, crude oil undergoes a process known as *fractional distillation.* The crude oil is passed through the fractional distillation column, where it is heated. At various temperatures (low to high), the numerous by-products it contains begin to separate. In ascending order, with respect to distillation temperatures, the products are: petroleum gas, naphtha or ligroin, gasoline, kerosene, diesel, lubricating oil, dense gas or fuel oil, and residuals like coke, asphalt, tar, waxes, etc. Just like the gold refinement process, the core takeaway here is that crude oil undergoes a process from when it is mined to when its end products are obtained.[13]

The *lode deposits, or gold ore,* in the first illustration is just as golden—if not more—than the gold that is produced after its refinement. However, their value is perceived differently. Inherently, however, they are both gold. Intrinsically, crude oil does contain the potency of its by-products. They are one and the same. However, one is crude in its natural state, while the other is broken into its constituent parts for the maximum benefit of the end users. However, their value is perceived differently. The

13 Crude oil or black gold has affected every facet of life. It is used in making various ranges of products that benefit life. However, in its crude state, many will not appreciate the benefits that it proffers. However, after it undergoes fractional distillation, it's by-products results. For more a more detailed look on the process, you can look at the link that has been provided in this footnote. (Reference: Freudenrich, C. (2019, June 23). How oil refining works. Retrieved from https://science.howstuffworks.com/environmental/energy/oil-refining3.htm).

end-user of crude oil could see it in its natural state as useless to them. Only after it undergoes fractional distillation—when the heat is applied to it—do we begin to see its value.

What changed in the two instances? One product is refined, and the other isn't. The difference in its perception is a product of knowledge. Those who know the potential of gold ore and crude oil are enlightened to the fact that the products of these natural resources have value. Those who don't have this knowledge think the products are the only things of value.

How many times have you had someone in your circle who didn't look presentable at some point in their life? Maybe they were stuck between a rock and a hard place, and circumstances may have just been difficult for them. They may have worn shabby clothes bought from thrift stores. In this situation, they may have had no dressing sense and sometimes may have been under a shroud of shame to be seen in public gatherings. Trust me, people go through such tough times, and they can attest to such a state. However, years later, they walk into a room, and their very presence and entrance make heads turn and leave mouths agape with amazement. Why? Because the individual has undergone an empowering transformation. Fundamentally, it is the same person, usually with the same physical features and mannerisms, but their appearance, carriage, and the way they interact with the world have changed. Over the years, they may have discovered their life-changing potential, refined it, and got better at walking in it, so much that they seem like completely different people.

So, where does this all fit in with your potential and all the unused capacity within you? How will your latent faculties add lasting value to you? In this chapter, I will accompany you through an explorative drill by showing you some of the necessary steps to take if you are to have a viable profit-bearing potential. Your newfound abilities may be crude, but there is a need to hone the talents you have discovered to bring about the best utilization of your abilities. As we progress through this chapter, I will show you the steps needed to translate your potential from its raw state to its refined form, just like that unappreciated piece of gold ore or like that unappreciated, thick, dark, oozing sludge of black crude oil to an almost priceless piece of gold jewelry or the various everyday valuable products of crude oil, respectively. Your potential must have a daily influence beyond you as an individual. The extraordinary value of your newfound intrinsic abilities wasn't built for you alone. They bring significance to you first as the carrier, and in turn, add value to the world at large.

Up to this point, we have already considered how we can discover our hidden and distinctive abilities. In our self-exploration journey, we used the SWOT Analysis matrix, as a self-audit tool, to learn of our various attributes, regarding our *Strengths* (**S**), *Weaknesses* (**W**), *Opportunities* (**O**), and *Threats* (**T**). That gave us the hints to infuse into our plan, serving as a foundation to the first steps for determining *how* we could unearth our innate potentials by the use of *Plan* (**P**), *Do* (**Do**), *Check* (**C**), and *Act, or Adjust* (**A**).

At this stage, you should have some knowledge about what your potentials are. The next phase is to bring your abilities to a robust place of value by refining them such that they could also start influencing others to discover their own hidden talents too. Think about the different people who have inspired your own journey until this moment. When you look at their beginnings carefully, you will see that their own potential was also awakened by someone before them who discovered what was always suppressed within them. Part of the purpose of this chapter is to make you see how you can add beneficial and profitable value to those potentials so that others can find the full expression of their own abilities through and through.

How can we achieve this? By taking the necessary steps to refine the newfound talents that we have unearthed from the depths of our subliminal-self.

—ꟺ—

Refining Your Newfound Potentials

For the beauty in your potential to be revealed, you need to work on improving and upgrading it. Most of us are trained to see value after the process of refinement has already taken place. People are trained by life to see only the successes of our best potentials at work. Many people are oblivious to the hard work that gets people to the finish line of success. People don't see the desire, passion, focus, effort, training, failure, hard work, blood, sweat, tears, doubt, pain, injury, early mornings, late nights, and the like. People fail to see all the sacrifice.

The process of practice and refinement is the birthplace of success. This explains why many people cannot appreciate others who don't look like much. Same reason why we don't acknowledge the value and worth of gold ore or crude oil.

How does refinement directly apply to your latent potentials? To refine is to bring something to superior quality. It means bringing something to a pure state, free from impurities. While refining, you are improving and perfecting the object of attention. You are freeing it from its coarse nature and making it distinct from what it once was. You are advancing the transformation of the object from good, to better, and to the best state possible. As you have unearthed your potentials, I am here to show you how you could perfect the state of your abilities for maximum utilization.

The question we need to ask ourselves at this point is, *How then do you refine your potentials?* I am going to borrow terms from the two refining process analogies that we looked at in the preceding paragraphs (i.e., gold mining refining process and the refining of crude oil). To expand our understanding about how we can refine our potentials, let us look at how the terms *extraction, distillation, and refining* apply to the process of honing our abilities. By working with these refining principles, you should start honing your newfound capabilities to perfection for maximum utilization and profitability.

Let us delve into the refining process pronto.

- **Extraction: The First Step of Refining**

First, you must recognize your potentials. After that, extract them from within your subliminal-self. We have dealt extensively on this process in previous chapters (Chapters 4–8). Referencing our prior analogies, if you don't have any gold deposit in an area, there will be no *lode deposits* or *gold ore* to excavate for further refining. The same goes for crude oil. If you don't have crude oil, how can you refine it through fractional distillation? Hence, without an extraction, there is nothing to be purified. The same goes for your potentials. If they are not extracted from within you, then you will have nothing to refine.

You should have, at this point, discovered and extracted your abilities. If not, pause. Take some time. Review Chapters 4–8 again. Reassess your status with your potentials.

This extraction refers to *the process of taking out.* Sometimes, admittedly, it is done by force. Still, the process separates that which is relevant from that which is not. It is same as the separation of the chaff from the wheat, showing clearly what *is* and *isn't* valuable. The fact is that no progress can be made without this very crucial process. It is like seeing crude oil in its underground reserve without taking any step to extract it out. Cars certainly don't drive themselves on air—at least not yet. Automobiles today, and for now, primarily run on gasoline, though we are seeing the rapid rise of vehicles powered with alternative energies (e.g., electricity, solar, hydrogen fuel cells, compressed natural gas, FlexFuel, ethanol fuel, etc.). However, the fact is *that no crude oil means you have nothing to refine to yield gasoline.* The same goes for your potentials. *They will not be useful lying dormant within you.* Even if the world notices that you indeed have them, they remain useless if not unearthed, refined, and effectively used.

It is like someone who is highly gifted in sprinting. However, this individual only runs occasionally and never does anything of significance with that skill. This may be someone who could potentially outrun Usain Bolt—as of 2019, the Jamaican sprinter still holds the world record for smoking the 100-meter race in a fiery 9.58 seconds in 2009 during the Berlin 2009 World Championships—but if they don't compete beside Usain Bolt or other gifted runners, they will never have the chance to express their potential. The talent remains with them, untapped, unexpressed, underutilized, and uncelebrated. Such a runner will never have the opportunity to be called *G.O.A.T., Greatest of All Time,* when it comes to the 100-meter sprint, and more. They haven't earned it, even though that capacity may exist within them. Their potential if not extracted and expressed, would never be celebrated. It would die with them. Remember Dr. Myles Munroe's statement. "Don't die old, die empty. That's the goal of life. Go to the cemetery and disappoint the graveyard." Why die still *full* of your potential? Extract it, express it, enjoy it!

Extracting your potential is the first step to refining your abilities. Like we said earlier, the *extraction* process could be approached from a vigorous standpoint, meaning that if it comes to it, you must exert yourself, contending earnestly to express the potentials you have within you. To do so, you must *cultivate a mindset* that allows you to break through the barriers of inertia and procrastination. Give yourself the chance to get better at what you have discovered to be an inherent capacity. As we will see below, you would need to commit to daily practice to sharpen the potency of your potentials. You will have to learn under a skilled person in that field if you can or go back to school to acquire the knowledge in an area of your interest. Whatever you choose to do, you cannot sit still, waiting for that ability to somehow bubble up to the surface. Nothing moves until you move!

- **Distillation: Setting a Mindset**

Distillation is the next step, following extraction. Often, *distillation* and *extraction* may occur simultaneously. Distillation means the purification of what you have discovered by the removal of foreign, extraneous, or objectionable elements from a substance. It is the obtaining of the fundamental, real, and invariable nature of a thing after all transient, irrelevant parts have been removed. It could also mean the separation of one substance from another. When I talk about distillation, I am referring to the need to strengthen your abilities by separating the *value-adding* attributes from the *non-value-adding* ones. More importantly, *setting a mindset* (my analogy of distillation) prepares you for the kind of impact your potentials will make.

What do I mean when I say *setting a mindset?* I see the human mind as a palace. The subconscious is the most powerful part of the tripartite human being. It is your *mind abode* with many alcoves. Your mind palace is full of *furniture* and *items* of your choosing, or not—things such as thoughts, intentions, perspicacity, veracities, experiences, motivations, and inclinations. It also includes things that can help you *set* (i.e., arrange, spruce up, or tidy, etc.) the mind space of your subliminal-self. My concept of *setting a mindset* means the removal of the chaotic and the elimination of the foreign, extraneous, or objectionable elements from the mind palace and the rational organization of the fundamental, real, and invariable constituents that are left behind after distillation—the distillates—after all non-value-adding, volatile, or transient parts of the mind are removed.

How do we do that? By deliberately redirecting your focus away from negative, aggrandizing energies, and intentionally move all unnecessary *furniture* and *items* out of your mind palace. Take them to the *landfills of forgetfulness,* and let them be buried there to be dug up no more. Know that *What you focus on, you feed.* Don't feed the volatile elements of your mind. Be ruthless in getting rid of them. After you have done so, you can now focus on what matters, what is left. Now, you need to *set your mindset.* Contain any chaos going on within you by compartmentalizing all that remains through careful and deliberate rational thought into the many alcoves of your mind palace. You cannot refine your newfound potentials with a mind palace that is in a state of entropy (chaos). There must be structure and order. This creates stability when experiencing the impact of your inner abilities. The *furniture* and *items* of your mind that you keep must be in order, aligning to the better-to-best state structure of your subconscious.

For instance, a gem is cut with patience into a beautiful piece of jewelry because the jeweler knows what the *end result* will be. Why? Because the mental image has been formed in his mind. So, notwithstanding how long it takes to transform the unfinished piece of gem into the prized piece, that jeweler will keep at it until the desired result is gotten. Unearthing and refining your potentials starts from the mind—see the end in sight as you continue to sharpen your abilities.

Earlier, I spoke of a person who walked into a room turning heads after their transformation from dressing dismally. The change of appearance garners a different kind of attention. Know that *no real change ever occurs without the change that first occurs in the mind.* Transformation starts from the mind. An uncelebrated position in life is not permanent. Change is always just a thought away. However, the inception of the change you consciously seek begins in the *mindset,* or your *mind palace,* or just your *subconscious.*

As you distill your thoughts, you reduce the chances of submitting to any form of deterrence when it hits you. You will do so because you already have a mental image formed that becomes the vision to drive your potentials. Courage is what gives you the *fortitude* to unearth your potential and the *patience* to refine your newfound abilities. A mind palace that is in chaos bars you from the sustainable energy of self-application. Set the *set* of your mind.

For instance, consider someone who discovers their ability to play the keyboard and has committed to invest time to learn to play the musical instrument. Would such an individual—if after the first week of training, begin to think they are not good enough—ever go far, even if the potential to learn is there? I don't think so. This lack of will to push through is a volatile attribute that needs to be burned away from the subconscious. Hence, at this point, I need you to examine your thought process concerning how you think and what goes on in your mind.

What thoughts are holding you back? Why are you holding on to such thoughts? Let go, be, and thrive.

After you have dug into all limiting thoughts, start working on active distillation by filtering the negatives from the positives. Separate *all* empowering thoughts from the limiting ones and capitalize on the former. *The mindset you carry on your journey to refining your potentials will determine the future of that potential.*

Furthermore, where distilling your strength is concerned, you will have to narrow down your potentials to the things you have the capacity for. While you might have recognized that you can do everything you set your mind on, it does you no good if you spread yourself too thin over many things that you end up being mediocre at. Distilling your thoughts by *setting your mindset* requires you to eliminate everything transient. Focus on the distillates. Hone your potentials by working with a mentor, or practice, or some other method that you can contribute to making it happen. Similar to miners, you are specifying these strengths the same way they determine what section of the crude oil will be used for plastic and which for jet fuel. Hence, deliberately invest your time in the distillation process as described above.

- **Refining: Polishing Through Practice**

Just before we started delving into the sundry ways of refining our potentials, we looked at the word *refine* and considered its meaning. To *refine* is to bring something to a superior place of high quality, without any form of impurities. It is a progressive state of advancement from *good, to better, and to the best state possible.* What better way to refine a thing than *practice?*

In the words of Jocko Willink, an American podcaster, author, and retired United States Navy SEAL, "The more you practice, the better you get, the more freedom you have to create." In this statement, we see the same progressive meaning of the word *refine.* Hence, what you repeat daily becomes a habit. What becomes habitual becomes our experience. We refine our newfound potentials by practice, repetition, or custom, as we progressively get better and better.

I read an interesting article titled *The Making of an Expert* by K. Anders Ericsson, Michael J. Prietula, and Edward T. Cokely, in the Harvard Business Review (NB. From the July–August 2007 Issue). This article highlights some compelling points that show that you can gain *expertise* or *mastery* through practice. Here are some of the illuminative facts I gleaned from this informative piece. *First,* superb performance has a direct correlation with intense practice, devoted mentorship, and social support. *Second,* skill refinement that leads to mastery is not inherent at birth but can be acquired through practice. *Third,* the road to mastery is defined by *struggle, sacrifice, and honest, often painful self-assessment,* as affirmed by the authors. *Fourth,* practice must be deliberate. *Fifth,* it takes time to attain expertise through repetitive deliberate actions. It could take as long as a decade to achieve.

Consider Michael Jordan, the American basketball Hall of Famer and businessman. When Jordan was younger, he was recognized for his athletic abilities as he had begun to play basketball and baseball well. However, after applying these to his high school's (i.e., Emsley A. Laney High School) varsity basketball team as a sophomore, he wasn't chosen. Undeterred, Jordan continued to work on his skills until he got accepted to be a part of the junior varsity team instead where he was noted for his stellar performance on the court. The rejection he got made him commit to getting better at the game such that his performance earned him national recognition. By the age of nineteen, America had started to take note of this exceptional basketball player who had an impressive hang of the game. Still, his best work had not even started. Jordan would go on to score 32,292 points, become a six-time NBA championship winner, bagging five NBA MVP (i.e., Most Valued Player) titles, making fourteen All-Star Game appearances, entering the basketball hall of fame, and setting the bar for upcoming basketball players behind him.

If you are familiar with his story, you must have heard about his dedication to practice. As famous as he was, when he was active in basketball, Jordan would spend at least eight hours daily practicing, perfecting his moves and improving his technique. It was the same skill for which he was initially rejected on that varsity team that took him to the top. After refining his skill on the basketball court, he went on to gain endorsement contracts with global brands like Nike, Coca-Cola, and McDonalds. What am I pointing at? After refining his skills through committed daily practice, it held a more relevant value for Jordan's fans, protégées, and the brands that looked to sign him up as an ambassador. Going down the legacy lane, others have followed his footsteps, such as Kobe Bryant a twenty-year career veteran with the Los Angeles Lakers, who won five NBA championships with many more accolades under his belt. Like Michael Jordan, he honed his craft and perfected his skills by constant practice. They refined their potentials through training. Hence, in order to hone your unearthed potentials, practice is key.

- **Refining: Re-liquefaction through Heat**

In the preceding paragraphs, we saw that the mining of gold falls under four processes: *prospecting, mining, extracting,* and *refining.*

During the refinement stage, we saw that refining companies receive doré bars plus scrap gold that they re-liquefy in the furnace. When the gold is in the molten state, chemicals (i.e., borax and soda ash) are added to it to separate the pure gold from other valuable and less valuable metals that were in the doré bars. At a 99.9% purity levels after tests, the pure gold is re-solidified into shiny gold bullions or ingots. My emphasis on this reiteration is the *re-introduction of heat to cause the re-liquefaction of the gold* to remove any non-value-adding elements that reduce the purity of the gold. How does this connect to the process of refinement of our newfound potentials?

Life, at times, ushers us into some unpleasant circumstances. Sometimes, the fires of these challenges are the metaphorical hammer and point chisel that shapes us into becoming the best we were meant to be. It could be *destiny-ordained* or *self-inflicted* due to our missteps. The challenges that we face are similar to the *heat* used to re-liquefy gold. The intent of this process is not to destroy the gold but to purify it. The fires of challenges we face in our lives are not meant to *destroy* us. Instead, they could be to make us stronger and more perfect, just like gold. On June 5, 2019, at around 8:01 PM, I got the inspiration to define the word *trials* through a Facebook update.

Trials: A fire that reveals the truth about all things. It burns all that is fake. What is left after the fire is the truth.

Some of the processes of refinement happen through the fire, like gold, or pottery, which eventually becomes a ceramic after being passed through the kiln. Sometimes in life, the potentials you discover must go through the fire to become truly refined. In this context, the heat is analogous to the hard times (tests, difficulties, trials, hurdles, etc.) that we experience. If you persist without giving up, the flames you are facing will reveal your true qualities. They will burn away the volatile, transient, and non-value-adding elements from your life. What will be left after the re-liquefaction of your potentials will be the pure, re-solidified *gold bullions or ingots* of your celebrated skills.

Tests become testimonies. Difficulties become deliverances. Trials become triumphs. Hurdles become hopes conquered.

Hence, I will advise you at this juncture to keep at it. Keep showing up to deliver results. Keep putting in those hours of practice. Keep giving it what it takes—your very best and nothing less. Don't succumb to the heat. Don't yield to the pressure. Don't buckle under the weight of any difficulty you may be facing as you work incessantly to refine your unique abilities. Remember that lasting value is extracted from your potentials when they have stable roots. You cannot deliver your best with half commitment. Be all in, no matter how tough or hot the re-liquefaction process is. Though feelings of inadequacy and self-doubt may arise, keep working on perfecting those skills, and in no time, they will bring results beyond your wildest dreams.

- **Refining: The Place of Tests**

During the final step of refining gold, after chemicals (borax and soda ash) are added to the re-liquefied doré bars plus scrap gold to separate the pure gold from other valuable and less valuable metals that were in the doré bars, a test is usually carried out to determine its purity. Let it suffice us to know that 99.9% of gold purity (24 carats or 999 Millesimal Fineness) is considered the purest gold. Without running tests, there is no way of learning the precise quality of the product. Similarly, we go through examinations to ascertain the potency of our refined potentials. This is the final rung in the refining of your potential. The same way you cannot know the quality of gold without testing it, you will not be able to assess how effective your refined powers are without testing them.

Up to now, you have been tenaciously working through the pages of this book to discover your potentials. By now, you should have extracted them, distilled it to a place where they are clear, and started implementing various refining processes. The final refining process, *The Place of Tests,* is putting it out for people to see it. Test it with friends and family, colleagues, and whoever is open to it. In the words of Peter Thiel, the American entrepreneur, venture capitalist, and hedge fund manager, "It's good to test yourself and develop your talents and ambitions as fully as you can and achieve greater success; but I think success is the feeling you get from a job well done, and the key thing is to do the work." Put your refined potentials to the test to ascertain their potency. Putting them to work will develop them and make them more productive. Don't hold back just because in your estimation you think it isn't perfect. Remember, *More act, less lag.* Progress never happens in a day. It is a process.

Another thing to note with the process of testing is that as people begin to give you constructive feedback, it helps you refine those potentials even more in such a way that the result pleases not only you but also the people to whom you have committed to serving with your abilities. A note of caution here, however, is to be clear about the difference between bitter criticism and constructive feedback. There is a need to be cautious of people you let in to test those results with you. People who are green with envy will castigate your efforts and seek for all avenues—through words and deeds—to pull your down, so beware. However, if these people have some skills in your area of interest, you can trust their feedback to have an informed background, based on their previous experience in life, either personally or professionally. No matter what, do put your newfound skills to the test. It will help you develop.

—๛—

In this chapter, we have considered the various ways that you can refine your newfound potentials. Our skills in their crude state can be compared to solid natural minerals deposits (e.g., gold, silver, diamond, iron, etc.), or like other natural resources like crude oil. In these unpolished states, a lot of people are blind to their value. Many people are trained to just perceive potentials only in their finished state. This makes lots of people myopic to deciphering the first-rate advantage of their abilities, therefore missing the goal.

We saw that *Extraction* is *The First Step of Refining*. If there is no product, there cannot be any further process, and everything immediately comes to a halt. However, reading this book is a positive sign that indicates you are not settling. It is an indication that you desire a change to your *status quo*. So far, we have provided you two self-audit tools (SWOT Analysis matrix and PDCA) to unearth your potentials. Put them to work!

In *Distillation,* I encouraged you to *Set Your Mindset.* It is imperative that you distill your thoughts. Simply eliminate all objectionable elements from your mind palace and focus on the value-adding factors. All transient factors must be purged as you get rid of any form of chaos. Finally, with *Refining,* I asked you to refine, through *deliberate practice, leverage the heat of trials, or challenges to purify your potentials,* and finally, *test your potentials.* Put them out for people to see. If you do these things, you are well on your way to refining your potentials.

So, what next? You have extracted your innate powers of your subliminal-self. You have cleared your mind and compartmentalized your distillates. You have refined your potentials, or you are in the process of doing so. Is this where it ends? What can you do with these potentials? What are some possible ways that you can use or express your talents to make a maximum impact to your benefit and to others?

We will look at some examples of *Products and By-Products of Your Newfound Potentials.* Let us stay excited as we continue our self-exploratory expedition.

CHAPTER 10

Products and By-Products of Your Newfound Potentials

—ꟽ—

EVERYONE HAS SOMETHING THAT UNIQUELY defines them, and that includes you. So far, we have laid the groundwork to our knowledge. We looked at what potentials are and considered why they are latent. We started digging deep to explore ourselves via the use of the audit tools (i.e., the SWOT Analysis matrix) to ascertain our *status quo* by learning our *strengths, weaknesses, opportunities,* and *threats.* We then went ahead to see how you can use PDCA to start *planning, doing, checking,* and *acting,* or *adjusting* our plans in a loop. After all this digging, you should have unearthed your potentials. With that assumption in mind, I showed you how you can *refine* your newfound abilities. What then?

In this chapter, we will look at the *Products and By-products of Our Newfound Potentials.* We hear about *products* and *by-products* in various circles, but what are they? Companies manufacture products and services that satisfy different customer needs. As these products are manufactured, by-products are also sometimes produced. A product is simply *a thing that is the result of input labor.* It can also be *a person or thing that results from a process.* A *by-product* is *the result of another action, often unforeseen or unintended.* It is *a secondary or incidental product in the process of manufacture.* Hence, we will look at *incidental products* that appear from our process of delving deeper and finding our unseen talent gems from our subliminal-self.

Keeping in line with our mining analogies, the products of naturally occurring minerals are often not singular. For instance, gold is used to make jewelry, and it can also be used to make sculptures, coins, and as a conductor in electrical products during the manufacturing process. Gold is also used by the National Aeronautics and Space Administration (NASA) in the production of spacesuit visors because of its remarkable quality of protecting the astronaut's face from unfiltered sun rays. The same can be said of crude oil, clay, diamonds, etc. For instance, petroleum is a known product of crude oil. However, this product is used in the production of so many more by-products like fertilizer, perfume, insecticides, soap, vitamin capsules, etc.

You are currently in the process of unearthing your hidden potentials and abilities. Who you become after this process is the product, so to say. The new *you* becomes defined by your discovered talents, whatever they may be. The means of identifying and unraveling your abilities transform your *status quo.* You become the output as your newfound potentials begin to govern your every intention. However, in the process of you discovering your hidden abilities and processing them via the refining process, certain by-products emerge from this action, and it can be either unforeseen or unintended. They are subsidiary products in the process of you becoming the best *you* in *you.* These by-products should not be ignored but leveraged.

Wherever skills exist, there is an inherent capacity for them to be augmented, regardless of whether that multiplicity is a direct result of the potential or a secondary one. For example, your potential to be a leader (i.e., the product) has within it the by-products of problem-solving, people leadership, resource and allocation management, etc. Hence, buried in your potential that is unearthed are other by-products that can also become great positives in helping you refine your newfound abilities and act as a catalyst to discover more skills. It's the *Snowball Principle* or the *Domino Effect of Addition.* Your potentials reveal more potentials.

Whatever you recognize your potential to be, it has this same characteristic, meaning its results are usually not singular. Your newfound potential is a plural platform for more abilities. For instance, a musician might find that in addition to recording great music, they also have an aptitude to inspire others through public speaking. Likewise, a public speaker could discover the potential flair and capacity to be artistic and creative. In both instances, these individuals are expanding the products of their recognized potentials to cover other value-adding skills. This is akin to the words of Christ in the Holy Writ in Matthew 25:29, "For to everyone who has will more be given, and he will have an abundance. But from him who has nothing, even what he has will be taken away." (Modern English Version).

In previous chapters, you already assessed your strengths, showing you some of the latent potentials that you have. What were some of the things that you discovered about yourself? I will list some of the *hard skills* that are possible products of your newfound abilities, but not limited to this list. There could be more unique products that you discover not listed here. Notwithstanding, *hard skills* are *teachable skills that are easy to quantify that you can learn in a classroom, through books, training materials, or on the job.* I am hoping that by looking at this list, you can recognize some of the things that ring true for you, and afterward, you act on them.

- Public speaking
- Songwriting
- Accounting
- Programming
- Arts curation
- Medical aptitude
- Visual arts
- Civic growth
- Singing
- Counseling
- Handcraft
- Engineering
- Language skill
- Sales
- Acting
- Dancing
- Writing
- Research
- IT
- Event hosting
- Journalism

There is more to uncover beyond this limited list. However, it stands as a marker to guide your self-exploration discovery. These *hard skills* are not the only pointers to what your innate potentials could be. Your *soft skills* could also be the expressed talents that potentially distinguish you. *Soft skills,* also known as *people skills* or *interpersonal skills,* are *skills that depict the way you relate to and mix with other people and are more subjective and are much harder to quantify*. Some of them are:

- Communication
- Flexibility
- Leadership
- Motivation
- Patience
- Persuasion
- Problem Solving
- Teamwork
- Respectfulness
- Work Ethic
- Listening
- Storytelling
- Negotiation
- Adaptability
- Critical Thinking
- Innovation
- Deal Making
- Mentoring
- Honesty
- Empathy
- Multitasking

To be honest, I have barely scratched the surface of various examples of *soft skills.* However, I believe that you have gotten the crux of my intentions at this point. These two lists are only *pointers* that would direct you to what your innate potentials could be. Whatever they are, unearth them, harness them, refine them, and use them to your advantage. As you do so, also pay attention to any other *by-products* that emerge in the process of your discovery and leverage them to your benefit.

The by-products of your potential will be closely aligned with your strengths. It may or may not be anything out of the ordinary. Your finding could be abilities you have probably engaged in the past, but for the lack of follow-up, have been left unused. As we explore some of these *by-products,* be sure to leverage them and make them work for you. Just as the by-products of petroleum are beneficial, make the by-products of your potentials useful. Beyond the aforementioned hard and soft skills, your newfound abilities can produce more by-products. These are the intangible elements that are in themselves value-adding. So, what could some of these by-products be?

Skill Expression

The *first* by-product of your newfound potential is *skill expression.* Seeing that *potentials* are unused abilities, it is safe to say that every potential is a skill that seeks to be harnessed and revealed. Skill expression or manifestation is a natural inclination that comes to every human. It is the urge to demonstrate the distinctive qualities that set them apart. When you tap your potential, you will be uncovering skills—tangible or intangible, hard or soft. The process will make you privy to relevant knowledge that will contribute to your effective performance.

If you look at every gold bullion or ingot, you will see that within it is a quality that makes it highly valuable. Having discovered its rarity as a gem, gold is processed and refined to a high standard that makes it treasured for varied purposes, uses, and exchange. Likewise, the skills contained in your potential are the tangibles that you can transact for monetary gain when manifested or revealed. The strategic expression of your newfound skills can make you distinguished, celebrated, marketable, and invaluable to your organization or community.

Discovering and manifesting your potentials not only helps you recognize the skills you have but also helps to see the areas where you can do your best work. Your newfound abilities expressed efficiently gives you a competitive advantage wherever you are putting those powers to use. Whether you are an entrepreneur, if you work with other colleagues in an establishment, or with some employer, your expressed inner powers instill a sense of confidence in you and others. It gives people the chance to trust you and your output.

Confidence

The *second* by-product of your newfound potential is *confidence.* Besides seeking out opportunities to express your abilities, it also gives you a new boost of confidence as a by-product. It is a belief in oneself and one's powers or abilities. A new lease on this trust is a magnet for more opportunities, and it also attracts the credence of others. Let me ask you, *How comfortable would you be giving a crucial job to someone who lacks self-confidence?* You would be very skeptical, wouldn't you? Why? If someone doubts themselves, they have given you every reason not to trust them either.

I am sure you could recall some instances where you have seen such a scenario at play. You see people who possess the abilities to do a job but are oblivious to it, hence falling short by lacking the ounce of confidence required to take the bull by the horns to accomplish the task. When you discover your potential, your confidence soars like an eagle. Take the case of an athlete with low self-esteem who, after performing poorly, gets caught up in that cycle, producing poor results repeatedly. However, if you believe in the ability of your newfound potential, it will give you the confidence to get up and keep fighting for the win. On the other hand, there are also some who are known to give a magnificent performance, even after some repeated cycles of failure. During those discouraging times, these athletes still possess their winning potentials. The difference is that they lean forward confidently, believing that with their abilities, they will eventually fetch a win. Winners never quit, and quitters never win.

Refined talent will always give you a reason to believe in yourself. When working on your potentials, you will record wins and failures alike. Trust me, there will be times when you may not perform at your best. However, that does not give you the impetus to completely cast away your confidence. You must continue to strive in earnest, remembering that as you push forward repeatedly, winning or even loosing, you are only honing your abilities to become sharper and better.

Continue to see yourself win despite all odds. Persistence grants you several reference points to sharpen your strengths. This, in turn, boosts your confidence. Your discovered abilities can produce the by-product of confidence and self-reliance. If you failed in a first, second, third, fourth, or even more trials, lift yourself up and try again, and again. Never lose your confidence, since it holds a great reward for you that is hidden in the refined potentials you put to work. Know that your determination will help you build endurance in your repetition as you push further to accomplish your purpose.

Competence

The *third* by-product of your newfound potential is *competence.* This means having enough facility, talent, knowledge, and experience for accomplishing a specific purpose. It is closely associated with confidence. In fact, confidence cannot be conceived in the absence of competence. This quality is a direct by-product of unearthing and refining your newfound potentials. Your proficiency in an area helps you deliver the needed results.

After discovering your potential, the natural inclination is to express it. The more you make known your potential through repetitive practice, the more self-assured you become. Your increased confidence is directly correlated to your competence levels. The more you practice and polish your brand-new abilities, the more competent you become at using your skills. Your increasing level of expertise through repetitive practice is directly proportional to your growing capability and a direct measure of your competence levels.

The mere perception of what is possible in your becoming the best *you* ever is a spur to grow in your proficiency. The vision of the *possible you* drives you to delve deeper into your subliminal-self to unearth your latent potentials. As you unravel these life-changing abilities, you begin to refine and polish that skill with discipline and determination that improves your relevance in your industry, company, family, and country. In Chapter 9, we covered extensively various ways of refining our potentials. One of the ways we saw was *deliberate practice.* Here, we see that it is a reoccurring theme.

Deliberate practice hones your proficiency or competence. Doing something skillful repeatedly makes you get better at it. For instance, think of a barista at a Starbucks Coffee shop. The first day on the job for a newbie can be a daunting experience. A barista must immerse themselves in all the drink recipes and all the *modus operandi* of the Starbucks Way. Through *deliberate, repetitive practice,* Starbucks baristas make certain their art of making the perfect *Cup of Joe* and other drinks for their customers. They become more competent and confident in their craft, one cup at a time.

It is easy to pinpoint people who are yet to uncover their potential. They lack competence at what they do as they haven't yet identified what their strengths are. Also, they are most likely operating in an area of weaknesses to which they are oblivious. These individuals may also be missing out on leveraging opportunities that come their way. They may also be slipping on every proverbial banana skin that life throws on their way, never apt or nimble enough to learn from the previous catch-22 they may have encountered.

The goal of the whole process is for you to become more competent and confident at wielding the staff of your new powers. You will see that the things you are most self-confident at doing are the things you perform remarkably well. However, if until now you still haven't discovered what your potentials are, pause. Take a step back and review the Chapters 4–9 again. As you repeatedly internalize these chapters, I believe something should click. As you ask yourself the various questions discussed in these chapters, I hope that you will receive guidance to your potentials. Remember, *deliberate practice will make you more proficient and confident as you unravel your potentials.*

Passion and Enthusiasm

The *fourth* by-product of your newfound potential is *passion* and *enthusiasm.* These two go together and are almost synonymous with each other. Passion (i.e., emotion, intensity, or feeling) is *any powerful or compelling emotion or feeling that governs our actions,* while enthusiasm (i.e., interest, passion, craze, or ardent zeal) is *an engrossing or dominating possession of the subconscious by any interest or pursuit.* The compelling emotion here is the desire to unearth our latent potentials. The benefits of our discoveries nudge us to become more engrossed in delving deeper to uncover more gems from our subliminal-self.

Discovering your potentials gives a new lease of life to your passion. This by-product is often an indicator that you have found your inner abilities since we are often passionate about our find. Your innate abilities are often things that thrill you to the point that you lose track of time, or it could just be things that you crave to do. Your new potentials compel you with an intensity to want to express it repeatedly, building your confidence in the process. Uncovered potentials spark a new level of enthusiasm toward further self-exploration. Discovering them gives you a burst of ardent zeal. It creates a distinct learning angle, as you realize you have a knack for it.

Besides giving you an extra boost of confidence and placing you in a position of competence regarding your job, potentials furnish you with something much more to be excited about beyond the workplace. It broadens the scope of your passions. It enlarges the coasts of your vision and purpose. It launches you to higher levels of thought, toward the accomplishment of something more productive and profitable. Those who discover their potentials are often more adventurous and passionate in life than those who have not. These individuals enthusiastically give back to the world from the wealth of their brand-new skills and knowledge.

Our newfound potentials compel us toward wanting to discover more of our hidden abilities. It grows our passions toward this objective. The pursuit fuels our subconscious with a sustaining interest of what we could possibly become. It makes us more enthusiastic toward digging deeper into our subliminal-self. I imagine a gold miner is not as excited about the subsurface earth he is about to excavate as he is about the gold buried underneath that same earth. Discovering your potential gives you purpose to work with and a cause to devote yourself, mastering those strengths and refining them until there is something to trade profitably.

Valuable network

The *fifth* by-product of your newfound potential is a valuable network. The more refined your potential, the more your chances of having a circle of valuable people in your network. Why? Because value attracts value. Unrefined crude oil is not as beneficial when not refined. In its raw state, it cannot produce the things it ought to provide since it is still impure and not as useful in that state. Hence, it is not of much value. Its value amplifies after it undergoes refining.

We already saw in the previous chapter the refining process of crude oil. However, let us note that because it contains short and long-chain hydrocarbons, crude oil is most useful only when separated. The long-chain hydrocarbons have a higher boiling point than the short-chain ones, which contributes to the reason why they cannot be used for fuel. Each different chain length of *unprocessed oil* gives them a unique property that makes them beneficial in a different way. That is the reason why it is processed through fractional distillation where the different hydrocarbon chains are separated based on their vaporization temperatures.

After crude oil has been distilled, various products are obtained. The list of products of this refining process is (i.e., short to long hydrocarbon linkages): petroleum gas, naphtha, gasoline, kerosene, diesel, lubricating oil, and fuel oil, along with residuals like coke, asphalt, tar, waxes, etc. These products attract a network of middlemen and end users. Why? In its refined state, crude oil becomes more valuable as it enters the consumer demand and supply chain network. Just like crude oil, your potentials are more worthwhile—providing more avenues for trade—to you and others when refined. The more you hone your abilities, the more you expand the network and value of those who have access to you.

A successful person would have access to a network of people who can be assets to them, who can provide solutions to personal issues, easing an otherwise arduous public process in their everyday goings. Your refined skills immediately give you an edge at life as you become a high-flier in your arena of operation. That is when your name, time, knowledge, opinion, products, services, and the like become assets that yield value and people want to do business with you or develop an acquaintance with you. The power and value of your network expand astronomically.

Without finding your distinctive powers, it is also possible for you to have a network of valuable people. However, you may still be at a handicap, even with this vast network. Why? Your potential is somewhat of a vector quantity—it gives you direction. In the absence of refined talent or skills, you lack the direction to achieve anything worthwhile. You will lack the scope to leverage your network, which makes it valueless to you. However, the discovery, processing, and refining of your inherent abilities will aid you in attracting the kind of people you desire to be in your network, hence pointing you in your anticipated direction.

However, there is a need for you to be cautious of the *worthless network*. In your journey of self-discovery, there will be people whom you should not have in your network at all. As you unearth and refine your potentials, you will begin to see those who are just detractors. Refine your channels of engagement with others. Cut out those who are non-value adding. Avoid all disparagers. You believe that you can become the best version of yourself yet, but there are chronic cynics who would dissuade you from even trying. You are not the same as those who do not believe the possibility of you unearthing your latent potentials, so do not join yourselves to them.

Service

The *sixth* by-product of your newfound potential is *service,* which refers to an act of helpful activity, or a position where you offer support to others when you place yourself in the state of servanthood. This is possibly the most gratifying by-product of your potential. Every ability, skill, or talent you have is an opportunity to help others. The act of serving will be particularly encouraging for people with a natural inclination to touch lives with their work.

Your ability to serve others with your potentials is a thing of honor. When you uncover your skills, your first instinct is to express it. It builds confidence as you become more competent in deploying your skills with deliberate practice. In the process, your passion, enthusiasm, and your network begin to grow. Out of the product of your potential comes the by-product of service to others. Let this become the catalyst that triggers your passionate desire to help and support humanity with your expressed abilities.

Your ability to serve others is one of the highest forms of humility and leadership. Even Christ taught his disciples in Luke 22:26 that " . . . the greatest among you become as the youngest, and the leader as one who serves."[14] The by-product of your potential, *service,* is the foundation of the timeless concept of *servant leadership,* the phrase coined by Robert K. Greenleaf in *The Servant as Leader,* an essay first published in 1970. In his words, he stated that "The servant-leader is a servant first . . . It begins with the natural feeling that one wants to serve, to serve first."[15]

Serve others with your potentials. Look at the world, those who attain greatness always *serve* others in some capacity. In the words of Kallam Anji Reddy, Indian businessman, "Everyone has a purpose in life and a unique talent to give to others. And when we blend this unique talent with service to others, we experience

---

14 Christ advocated a life of servant leadership via this statement in Luke 22:26—"But not so with you. Rather, let the greatest among you become as the youngest, and the leader as one who serves." (English Standard Version (ESV)).

15 The concept of servant leadership is timeless. However, the phrase, "servant leadership," as we know it today, was first coined by Robert K. Greenleaf in "The Servant as Leader," an essay that he first published in 1970. Three core things are highlighted as the encephalic core of this essay. First, "the natural desire." Servant leadership, " . . . begins with the natural feeling that one wants to serve, to serve first." Second, "the conscious choice." Servant leadership begins with the " . . . conscious choice" that "brings one to aspire to lead . . . " Third, "the best test." What is the best test to ascertain that servant leadership is effective? "The best test, and difficult to administer, is: do those served, grow as persons . . . " (Reference: Robert K. Greenleaf Center for Servant Leadership. (2019). The servant as leader. Retrieved from https://www.greenleaf.org/what-is-servant-leadership/).

the ecstasy and exultation of own spirit, which is the ultimate goal of all goals." Microsoft serves you through your Operating System and other things, Google through *Search* and other applications, and Amazon through *E-Commerce.*

Serve others through your distinctive powers. Let it be your *ultimate goal.* Make it the *core* of your purpose. If you want to be the greatest when it comes to unleashing your potentials, you must have the heart and drive to be the servant of all, so you can serve with your *Strengths* (**S**), leverage your *Opportunities* (**O**), and turn them to your strengths and use them to attend to others. Know that *the more of your potential you discover, the more you can serve people in different capacities. It is like a ripple effect, as your actions of service continue to spread and affect others.*

Embrace service at all cost.

In this chapter, we have seen that something is always produced when labor is inputted in a process. In this case, as you labor to read through the pages of this book, you are unearthing potentials from the labyrinths of your subliminal-self. We saw that your skills could be wrapped in your *hard skills* as well as your *soft skills.* As you are unlocking the gems and core products of your subconscious, certain by-products are also bound to be extracted. Though these by-products may be secondary or incidental; however, as we have seen, they are in themselves potent in the whole process of self-discovery.

The *first* by-product of your newfound potentials that we looked at was *skill expression.* Upon discovering your innate powers, you will find a desire to express your abilities.

The *second* by-product of your newfound potential is *confidence.* Your gifts give you a new boost of confidence. As you reveal them, your confidence grows.

The *third* by-product of your newfound potential is *competence.* As you express your skills, you develop more confidence in wielding the staff of your abilities. In the process, your competence, capability, or proficiency grows.

The *fourth* by-products of your newfound potential are *passion* and *enthusiasm.* Your brand-new abilities imbue a new lease of intensity into you (i.e., passion). In the process, you become enraptured with an ardent zeal to want to dig up more gems of your hidden gifts.

The *fifth* by-product of your newfound potential is a valuable network. Because of your novel skills, your nudge to express them is your natural first move. Combine it with your confidence that elicits a disposition of competence in your newfound enthusiastic passions helps your network to expand. Remember, *value attracts value.*

The *sixth* and last by-product of your newfound potential is *service.* While unearthing your skill-set, make sure *service* is the *core* of your purpose when it comes to self-discovery. As you find yourself, *serve!*

So, what next? What do you do with the *products* and *by-products* you discovered? What do people generally do with the products that they produce? The purpose of manufacturing products or other goods and services is to put them to use, to sell them, and to generate profit. Would the same apply to the *products* and *by-products* of our subliminal discoveries? We will see as we continue our self-exploration expedition in the next chapter titled, *Trading the Products* and *By-Products of Your Newfound Potentials.* Let us keep digging.

CHAPTER 11

Trading the Products and By-Products of Your Newfound Potentials

—⁓—

SO FAR, YOU HAVE DONE an astounding job with identifying your latent potentials, processing them, and refining them. We have also seen the various *products* and *by-products* obtained from our revealed innate abilities. Now, it is time to add value to yourself by trading them for the things you desire, be it an opportunity to serve, money, fame, fulfillment, or all these things combined. The principal question that this chapter is poised to answer is, *How can I trade my potentials and make them valuable to me, or my community at large?* Let's embrace the fun discoveries ahead.

So, what is trade? In the most simplistic form, *trade (i.e., business, commerce, enterprise, barter, deal, profession, etc.) means the exchange (i.e., giving up of something for something else) of goods, services, or both.* When you hear the word *trade* alongside *potential,* what first comes to mind? I bet your inclination immediately gravitates to, *Oh, wow! How do I get to sell my potential for some profit?* Well, whatever you thought, you are probably right on the money. The prevailing fact is that there is an opportunity to *profit* from your potentials. Why shouldn't you? You have worked hard to unearth them, and you should want to make something from the tough grind. I am not talking about any form of selfish personal gain, here, but on the kind of profit that is honorable, positive, and worthy of mention.

Trading has been practiced from time immemorial, from primeval times till date. Even before 2000 BC, the Sumerians of Mesopotamia engaged in trade with the Harappan civilization of the Indus Valley. Also, Hatshepsut, the first female of the Eighteenth Egyptian dynasty occupying the throne, facilitated a thriving ancient Egyptian commerce and industry. Throughout history, we see the caravan trade of Asia and the Arabian Peninsula during the second millennium BC. Trade through the ages led to the invention of money where annals show the use of grain or silver before 2000 BC in ancient Mesopotamia and the use of copper ingots as monetary units throughout the Mediterranean in the later Bronze age. Time will fail me to talk about how the Sogdians ruled the East-West trade routes famously known as the Silk Road (i.e., from the 4th - 8th century BC), or the trade of the Vikings and the Varangians (8th–11th century BC), or the resumption of the European Spice trade in 1498 by Vasco da Gama, etc. What do we draw from this prance through the corridors of trade history? That *trading has been practiced for a long time.*

The concept of trade has evolved amongst nations and individuals for millennia. The advent of cutting-edge technologies, transportation, increased industrialization, and globalization amid the community of nations has led to the expansion of commerce at astronomical and mind-blowing proportions. Countries endowed with specific natural resources leverage this and trade it for a profit while buying other goods and services that they need from other nations. Today, many organizations have spawned because of trade, such as World Trade Organization (WTO), International Organization for Standardization (ISO), United Nations Conference on Trade and Development (UNCTAD), Organization of the Petroleum Exporting Countries (OPEC), World Customs Organization (WCO), North American Free Trade Agreement (NAFTA), International Trade Center, World Fair Trade Organization, and World Fair Trade Organization. The bottom line of all these organizations and more is the liberalization of trade among member countries through voluntary participation. The foundation of it all is *Profit.*

Staying true to our mining analogies, beautiful as gems may be, they are sold with the principal purpose of generating a mutual and profitable value between the people who mine them, the jewelers who fashion them into fascinating pieces, and the end consumers who wear them, or use them for other purposes. The same goes for nations and companies when they mine precious stones, metals, or other natural resources. Their goal is to turn a profit from their endeavors. The same goes for your skills and strengths. They must be traded for profit. Like I mentioned earlier, it could come in the form of financial reward or personal fulfillment through active involvement in the work that lies within the area of your strength. Whether you want them to be a source of wealth for you or a channel to serve people, it is a matter of determining what you want to get out of deploying them. This is why the profit I refer to in this chapter is not exclusively transactional. Whether it is the trade that occurs amongst nations, or the mutual transaction trade of gems and other natural resources, or even your newfound potentials, the foundation of it all is *Profit.*

Gems buried and undiscovered add no value. Only gems that are discovered and put in use create profits. You can sit on land that is chock-full of, say, some of the world's most precious and rare stones, such as the Red Diamond (C), Taaffeite ($BeMgAl_4O_8$), Grandidierite ($(Mg,Fe^{2+})Al_3(BO_3)(SiO_4)O_2$), Serendibite ($(Ca,Na)_2(Mg,Fe^{2+})_3(Al,Fe^{3+})_3[O_2|(Si,Al,B)_6O_{18}]$), Diamond (C), Alexandrite ($BeAl_2O_4$), just to mention a few.[16] Or, you could be sitting on land that gorged tawny gold (Au), or black gold (crude oil). If they are not discovered, processed, and sold, they remain of no value and are useless to you. However, these gems, when discovered and dugout, go through the process of being cut, shaped, and polished, and then are sold in the different forms as needed by end users. It is only then that they become of value. Within this cycle, there has been a considerable amount of value creation, and as a result, profit. The miners will get paid, the people who furnished the machinery (i.e., if loaned) for the mining will get paid. Furthermore, in the value chain, there's the jeweler who also benefits in crafting various pieces. Also, if

16 Gems are intriguing, and therefore, I compare them to the innate potentials buried in us. I stumbled over this article on Forbes magazine that highlighted that "There are over 4,000 minerals on earth," and the author espouses that "we will never see many of them in our lifetime." In this article, the highlighted gems are just a smidge when compared to all the gemstones in the world. However, the author has chosen these due to their value and rarity. "Minerals can be classified as gemstone," Nace asserts. Some of the gems mentioned here, in ascending order, due to their value and rarity, are as follows: Jeremejevite ($Al6B_5O_{15}(F,OH)_3$), \$2,000 per carat; Fire Opal ($SiO_2{\cdot}nH_2O$), \$2,300 per carat; Poudretteite ($KNa_2B_3Si_{12}O_{30}$), \$3,000 per carat; Benitoite ($BaTiSi_3O_9$), \$4,000 per carat; Musgravite ($Be(Mg, Fe, Zn)_2Al_6O_{12}$), \$6,000 per carat; Red Beryl ($Be_3Al_2Si_6O_{18}$), \$10,000 per carat; Alexandrite ($BeAl_2O_4$), \$12,000 per carat; Diamond (C), \$15,000 per carat; Serendibite ($(Ca,Na)_2(Mg,Fe^{2+})_3(Al,Fe^{3+})_3[O_2|(Si,Al,B)_6O_{18}]$), \$18,000 per carat; Grandidierite ($(Mg,Fe^{2+})Al_3(BO_3)(SiO_4)O_2$), \$20,000 per carat; Taaffeite ($BeMgAl_4O_8$), \$35,000 per carat; and Red Diamond (C), \$1,000,000 per carat. In similitude, your talents are even more valuable and priceless than all these gems combined. However, the secret of the value of your potentials lies in their discovery. (Nace, T. (2015, November 2). 12 most expensive gemstones in the world. Retrieved from https://www.forbes.com/sites/trevornace/2015/11/02/12-most-expensive-gemstones-world/#353d79ae1538).

sold to stores, another value chain has been added to this cycle. Remember, this only shows the monetary worth of that chain. Besides, imagine the jobs created throughout that cycle and the number of people who are, one way or another, getting paid by being a part of the process.

Could you just imagine the circle of value creation that your discovered latent potential would create? For instance, look at the many vanguards of great business organizations that I have mentioned across the chapters of this book, the likes of Jeff Bezos, Bill Gates, Warren Buffett, Jack Ma, Mark Zuckerberg, Larry Page, Sergey Brin, Elon Musk, etc. The discovery of their potentials led to the creation of companies through which millions, collectively have benefited, through promising careers and more. What if some of these greats refused to unearth the potentials buried within them? Then there may not be business conglomerates like Amazon, Microsoft, Berkshire Hathaway, Alibaba, Facebook, Google, Tesla, Space X, etc. They have created magnificent value cycles, of which, many are benefiting tremendously. The discovery of your potential can become a triumphant story like these individuals that created disruptive *products, by-products,* companies, and more. Your skills could take you from *ordinary* to *extraordinary,* from *mediocre* to *magnificent* heights. They traded the *products* and *by-products* of their genius intrinsic gems and look at them today. Their transcendence is global, growing, magnetic, and profitable. *Could this also be your story?*

Therefore, we can say without any quiver of apprehension that *trading your potentials is not an option but a necessity.* It's not an *option* if you want to leave an indelible mark on the sands of time. It's not an option if you aspire to disrupt the macrocosmic field of your expertise. It's not an option if you fancy becoming a world-changer, a world-mover, or a world-Quaker. You could be making stunning discoveries and breathtaking changes via your discovered and refined abilities. It's only a thought away. If the *greats* did it, why can't you do it in your *area of specialization,* whatever it is? We have an equalized playing ground—Time. The greats also operate in the same twenty-four-hour day as yourself. They *did* it because they believed they *could* through the *discovery* and *trade* of their potentials. They *did* it because they *invested their time wisely,* shunning any form of procrastination. Remember, like I always hear them say on Alux.com, "Your best day to do anything was yesterday. The next best day is today." You *can* do it in your own right, if you *believe.* You *can* do it if you *invest your time wisely.* You *can* do it by shunning procrastination. Start now. Remember, *More act, less lag.* Follow the process laid out in the pages of this guide and channel yourself to *becoming.* Now that we have figured that out, the ensuing question is, *How do you successfully trade the products and by-products of your potentials? Also, if they will be exchanged for those returns, what are the practical steps you need to take? Do you sell them as a commodity, or exchange them for a commensurate value?*

Without further ado, here are some of the ways you can trade the *products* and *by-products* of your latent potential:

Branding

The *first* way of *Trading the Products and By-Products of Your Newfound Potentials* is through *branding.* In the most simplistic of terms, a *brand* is a *kind, grade, or make, as indicated by a stamp, trademark, or the like.* For instance, *Starbucks* is a brand amid other coffee makes. *Lange & Söhne's* is a watch brand. *Louis Vuitton* is a fashion luxury brand amongst many others. *Nike* is an athletic and lifestyle footwear, apparel, equipment, accessories, and services brand, and a leader in its industry. Apple, Google, Microsoft, Amazon, Facebook, Coca-Cola, Samsung, The Walt Disney Company, Toyota, McDonald's, etc. are all brands.

Anyone will tell you that branded products are esteemed higher than unbranded ones. This isn't just for widely recognized brands, but also true for brands that are not very popular. It's as simple as the preference for a branded bar of soap over an unbranded one, or a branded bag of cereal. In the words of Eva Chen, the Taiwanese businessperson and the co-founder and CEO of Trend Micro, "Build a lifestyle around your brand, and the audience will follow." People like something they can recognize. Hence, as you discover the products and by-products of your potentials, build your lifestyle around it. As you do so, an audience that recognizes and relates to it will celebrate and eventually follow you.

This psychology is backed by the fact that branding projects credibility, trust, recognition, loyalty, consistency, inspires confidence, and legitimizes the authenticity of the product. However, when a product does not have a brand identity, there is always some kind of hesitation to buy or go with it. You continually question yourself, *Can this product be really trusted to deliver the service value that it is offering?* You second-guess yourself at that instance. Likewise, with the product of your potential, when you are known by an identity, it becomes easier to trade the *products* and *by-products* of your abilities and skills. No one really second-guesses your worth and what you have to offer.

You may have heard the statement, *Your reputation precedes you,* a phrase that became popular in the latter half of the 1900s. It means that people have discovered things that define who you are even before they meet you. These things could be *positive* or *negative,* and *true* or *false.* It coincides with the words of Jeff Bezos, Amazon Founder and CEO, that "A brand for a company is like a reputation for a person. You earn reputation by trying to do hard things well." Hence, you do everything in your power to perfect your craft until it begins to speak for you. It becomes what defines you and what people know you for. Your *brand* is your *reputation.* In other words, the *products* and *by-products* of your potentials are the defining elements of your *brand* that precedes you.

For instance, Anthony Robins' *brand* or *product* is *motivation.* His *by-products* are *professional speaking, acting, and writing.* For John Maxwell, it is *leadership,* and his *by-products* are *pastoring, speaking, and writing.* For Oprah Winfrey, it is a colossal *media presence,* as she is daubed *Queen of All Media,* and her *by-products* are *philanthropy, television producer, talk show host, actress, and media executive.* For Wole Soyinka, it is *writing,* and his *by-products* are being an *essayist, a poet, a Nigerian playwright, and the Nobel Prize recipient for Literature in 1986.* These are just a few instances amongst many of how you can correlate brands, reputations, products, by-products, and potentials with each other. The *brands* and *reputations* of the *products* and *by-products* of their revealed intrinsic abilities precede them. *What brand or reputation precedes you?*

Branding is of essence because it is the *quod erat demonstrandum,* the *QED,* the logical or philosophical argument and complete proof that defines your personage before those who will eventually be interacting with you. Your branding precedes you. It will include the things you are majorly known for, that being the qualities that describe your identity. People want to see the consistency behind what you do. It increases trust in your output. This is the reason, like we saw in the preceding paragraph, why you can associate a person with a specific trade. For example, if a person is known for *music* as their *brand,* and that person suddenly announces their involvement in another trade—say, politics—you tend to meet that announcement with hesitation. Why? Because you have known that person in connection with one industry. People would be skeptical to accept them *in toto* for their new brand affiliation until proven worthy of the new area of interest. That is the power inherent in *branding.*

When you are known within a defined industry or industries, depending on how vast your potential is, it gives credibility to the things you produce. People will experience you in those capacities because the reputation you carry in those areas precedes you. It is easier for them to patronize you repeatedly and even recommend you to other people. Your brand will typically include what you do. It will hold the promise you deliver every time people experience your faculties in your area of expertise. It will involve the quality of your delivery and your brand name. This gives you an edge in the industry where you operate in, solidifying the authenticity and trust behind the work that you do.

Some of the things you will need to ponder on in this regard. (NB. These questions are in no way exhaustive, you are always free to add to them as it best fits your situation). They are as follows:

- Having found my potential, what do I want to be identified with?
- What industry does my potential point me toward?
- What do I want to be associated with me and my work?
- What brand currently in existence best mirrors the way I want to be seen?
- What is that one guaranteed value I want people to experience every time they encounter my work?

Product Development

The *second* way of *Trading the Products and By-Products of Your Newfound Potentials* is through *product development.* It is the creation of new products with defined characteristics that are beneficial to consumers. We have seen that refinement will always yield tangible elements that can be traded. In Chapter 9, we saw the various ways that we can refine our potentials. In Chapter 10, we considered that in the process of polishing our abilities, or skills, *products* and *by-products* are obtained, and when traded, yield positive values to us and others. This is the most common way of exchanging value with the results of your potentials. We saw that the various possible products (i.e., hard skills or soft skills) and by-products (e.g., skill expression, confidence, competence, passion and enthusiasm, valuable network, and service) of potentials. How does all this relate to product development?

The product developed could also be in the form of either *palpable* things or other *non-palpable* items. This is particularly common if the potentials you discover *creatively* leads you to marketable ideas that could be developed into viable products for your projected niche of customers. In creating those products, you add something tangible to what you offer to the masses. Product development is a creative process. You move from conceptualizing an idea and *creatively* looking for avenues to transforming that idea into a tangible product that will appeal to consumers. This ingenious process multiplies the impact of using potentials to serve and meet consumer needs, which could give you the means to profit off your discovered newfound abilities.

For instance, Bill Gates' programming knowledge potential yielded the *Microsoft Operating System Product (MOSP)* and many other physical products (e.g., Surface, Surface Hub, Xbox, HoloLens, Mobile devices, etc.) that the company offers today to empower others. For Aliko Dangote, the Nigerian business magnate and investor, his aggressive business acumen potentials bore the product of the entire *Dangote Group, Inc.* The by-products of his ventures are many, including cement, sugar, salt, seasoning, flour, semolina, pasta, technology, among others, all yielding him tangible products of value and profit. For Malcolm Gladwell, the Canadian journalist, author, and public speaker, his potential is *writing,* and at the time of this writing, the products are his six best-selling books and his hit podcast, the Revisionist History. This solidifies the fact that your abilities can lead you to develop products that generate value and profit for you.

After you have discovered your potential, you need to look at it critically to assess how it can be profitable for you. Could it be something that you could sell directly to your audience as some product or service? Does it need to be further refined? You must know the processes involved in making it usable by the end-user. For instance, if you discover your potential in music, you need to determine if you need to learn any skill to augment it. Often, musicians pick up an instrument of choice to learn alongside their ability to sing. You may need to decide how you would want to reach your audience with your music (e.g., releasing an album, or single tracks for upload on iTunes, or on YouTube, or via live performance shows, etc.). Do you have a natural flair for cooking? Could you polish your skills, or broaden the scope of your cooking abilities by learning other dishes not native to you? Or, could you acquire a Culinary Degree in Restaurant Management to buttress your talent? Critically assess your skills to ascertain how you want the product of your craft to reach your final audience.

Whatever creative aptitude you choose to hone, your *personality* alongside your *goals* will go a long way in determining the direction you will eventually take. These two elements will provide guidance on whether you will need to develop a product to bring your potential to maximum fruition or not. However, to attain the best results, you need to immerse yourself in an in-depth search of who you are, what your potentials are, and what is practical for you. Once again, that is the reason you are reading this book.

Here are some follow-up questions to ask in discovering how you can develop valuable products from your newfound potential. (NB. These questions are in no way exhaustive, you are always free to add to them as it best fits your situation):

- How do my goals and personality affect the things I create with my newfound abilities?
- What level of success do I want to achieve with my discovered potential? Do I want to go global or stay local?
- What sacrifices am I willing to make in the process of trading the products of my gifts? Are there any limits to these sacrifices?
- How best do I present the palpable output of my potential?
- What competition does my product face? How accessible and affordable will it be? Is the product sustainable?
- How will this product serve people?

Publicizing, or Advertisement

The *third* way of *Trading the Products and By-Products of Your Newfound Potentials* is through *publicizing or advertisement.* The essence of trading the products of your potential is so that people will know about it and somehow buy into it. After all, advertisement, in its most simplistic term is, *the action of making generally known, or a calling to the attention of the public.* It is your right to choose. However, how can everyone know unless you call their attention to the *products* and *by-products* of your potentials? It is essentially useless having a skill that no one knows about, however great it may be.

Non-excavated minerals are valueless. It is when they are mined that they are needed, valued, and profitable. Dug up ores that have not been processed, refined, and gotten ready for the marketplace offer less value too. In order to have an efficient value cycle, the process needs to be completed from the point of unearthing to where they have been refined and fashioned into the end products for the consumers. Consequently, the output of your refined abilities is not meant to be hidden. You must look for avenues to broadcast or advertise what you can do with your newfound capacities. In the words of Laurence J. Peter, the Canadian educator and *hierarchiologist,* "Early to bed, early to rise, work like hell, and advertise." Let people know what you are about. You must market your abilities for them to yield any kind of profit whatsoever.

In this case, publicizing your potentials has its own benefits. It helps you to strategically introduce the outputs of your abilities to the public so that they can see their advantages. They are also able to interact with them, providing an opportunity to find a mutual connection between your product and their needs. What if your favorite musician never went live with their music abilities? You would never know of their prowess, nor would they ever become your favorite musician. The potential to demonstrate your expertise may be there, but without the effort to present it to the public, the extent to which it can be traded is limited. A lot of people cower in fear, and because of this, they never rise to heights of achieving their highest potentials. They die, still filled with all their innate abilities. Hence, you need to discover, unearth, hone, and publicize your unique skill-set. Shout it on the rooftops. Let the world hear about what you can do. Occupy all corners with your skills in action.

Get out there, and let people know about the potentials you have discovered. Let them know that you can deliver on your promise, so that when opportunities come up, they are aware of your abilities, and they can extend them to you. Do not get sold on the idea that you are inferior in your approach when you get out there and let everyone know what you can do. There is no shame in it at all. People can only interact with potentials that have been discovered, not those buried underground and undiscovered—except, of course, they are in the process of mining for those potentials. Think about the percentage of miners among the number of end users, and you will see that the latter are significantly more. It is a pyramid effect. At the bottom are the many end users or consumers. At the top of the pyramid are the few, the successful, the 1% that have discovered, unearthed, and refined their potentials and are now offering their wares to those at the bottom of the pyramid. So, the blunt question is, *Are you at the top or bottom of that pyramid?* It is for you to decide.

Do not be afraid of getting the word out about your discoveries. Many are the vast array of audiences waiting for the manifestation of those who have seen the light of their potentials. Go public with your strengths! Let people know and don't keep quiet about your discovered potentials. Advertise! Advertise! Advertise! As Leo Burnett, the American advertising executive, said, "Good advertising does not just circulate information. It penetrates the public mind with desires and belief." Make your audiences believe in your unique abilities. Interact with them through as many relevant platforms as you can. Thanks to the advent of technology and the internet, the world has literally become *small* due to increased globalization. Utilize the social and communication platforms of Facebook, YouTube, Instagram, Qzone, Weibo, Twitter, Reddit, Pinterest, Ask.fm, Tumblr, Flickr, LinkedIn, VK, Odnoklassniki, Meetup, WhatsApp, WeChat, LINE, Skype, Hangouts, and others that keep showing up in the market, and get the *products* and *by-products* of your potentials noticed. Leverage all angles of advertisement and take advantage of technology to get the word out about the golden outputs of your self-discovery expeditions. Therefore, you technically have no excuse not to publicize your abilities or talents. You cannot afford to keep them a secret. Make some noise about them. Shout them out on top of roof-tops if you will.

Here are several follow-up questions to ask in discovering how you can publicize or advertise the products and by-products of your newfound potential. (NB. These questions are in no way exhaustive, you are always free to add to them as it best fits your situation):

- What is my fundamental message? Can I compress my pitch about my potential in a single sentence? What tone should I adopt?
- Why am I advertising my newfound skill in the first place? What is my core purpose?
- What problems are my potentials solving?
- What is my audience base going to be? Who will I be speaking to (gender, age, interests, income, education, etc.)?
- How vast am I willing to expand the campaign about my potentials? Am I going global or staying local?

- What are my *products* and *by-products?* What will success look like in the way my audience reacts to them?
- Why should anyone be interested in my potentials? What possible value do I anticipate people to derive from them?
- What is my SMART (i.e., **S**pecific–**M**easurable–**A**chievable–**R**elevant–**T**ime bound) marketing strategy?
- How visible am I? What platforms am I on? How am I leveraging these platforms to broadcast my gifts to the world?
- What amount of time am I willing to dedicate to publicizing myself?
- Will there be any financial obligations for promulgating my potentials? What is my budget going to be for advertising my newfound skills?
- Am I ready for this?

Training

The *fourth* way of *Trading the Products and By-Products of Your Newfound Potentials* is through *training*. In the simplest of forms, *training* (i.e., education, practice, foundation, discipline, or exercise) is *the education, instruction, or discipline of a person or thing that is being trained.* Grooming other people to learn the skills you have acquired in the process of unearthing your potential is another way of trading the *products* and *by-products* of those set of skills. As you train others, you are repetitively instructing yourself. Thus, you are continually sharpening your newfound skills to a level of creative mastery or expertise.

Training is essentially creating a platform for people with potentials like yours to develop theirs, and this is where the result of your potential culminates into something that is positively impactful. In essence, *you train yourself, to then train others, you empower yourself to empower others, and you invest in yourself to invest in others.* That is the value of training in a nutshell. By discovering, refining, and sharing your potentials, by educating and instructing others about the ABCs of your abilities, you enable yourself and others in the process. In the words of John Rampton, the entrepreneur, connector, and online influencer, "Empowerment isn't a buzzword among leadership gurus. It's a proven technique where leaders give their teams the appropriate training, tools, resources, and guidance to succeed." Hence, know that *to instruct others to discover themselves, is one of the greatest and most profound ways to trade the outputs of your own potentials. It solidifies the outputs of your newfound skill through practice.*

The methodology of training can differ and may not necessarily be traditional (through a classroom-style teacher-student setting). There are various ways of offering training to audiences that follow your potentials. You can write books, make videos (on YouTube, through live or recorded sessions), and organize conferences that could be formal or informal, paid or unpaid, depending on your preference. For instance, Tony Robbins deploys several avenues to train his audiences. He does so through his books, website, videos (his Netflix Documentary and his YouTube channel), mentor-mentee sessions, business coaching, and through his conference or seminar events. His *Date with Destiny (DWD)* usually a five-day event, could cost each attendee within the range of $4995–$7995. This is from the testimonials of those who have attended it, and from doing the math via ticketing platforms (e.g., viagogo.com). The closer you get to the date of the event, the more expensive it becomes. For the John Maxwell Team certification program, you could pay as much as $4,997 for the package. They have the value that they are offering by trading their potentials, and they are within their rights to peg a price on it.

Technology has also made it easy for you to produce online courses that people can watch at their leisure, about the value that you are offering in your niche of specialization. Today, we have the platform, *Udemy,* which is the leading online platform and place for anyone who wants to produce an online course and market it. Other alternatives to Udemy are Coggno, Curious, edureka! Learning.ly, OfCourse, OpenSesame, Simlpliv, Skillshare, Skillwise, Teachlr, WizIQ, etc.[17] You must note that educating or coaching others is an avenue to trade the value you have found in yourself. However, it doesn't mean the result of that trade will always be received in monetary value. Often, the utility and satisfaction you receive from it are seen in the aggregate, life-transforming effect of unearthing potentials *en masse* in people who would have had their potential go unnoticed, had it not been for the platform you created.

Whether it is a live coaching concourse or a physical class, the goal is to pass on some of your skill sets to your audience. The core of it all is to take others on the journey of self-exploration and refinement even as they discover unused creativities

17 I have highlighted that *creating an online course* and marketing it for profit is one of the avenues that you could use to train others as a way of trading the outputs of your discovered new abilities. Udemy is by far the most popular, but there are other alternatives, as highlighted in this article by Learning Revolution. The options to Udemy highlighted are Coggno, Curious, edureka! Learning.ly, OfCourse, OpenSesame, Simlpliv, Skillshare, Skillwise, Teachlr, WizIQ, etc. The list is in no way exhaustive as more platforms are being developed from time to time. I have provided the link to this source for you to dig deeper and gain a more precise understanding of each in brief. The fact is that there are platforms out there that can assist you in sharing various training about your newfound potentials (Cobb, J. (2019, April 10). 10+ true alternatives to Udemy for selling online courses in 2019. Retrieved from https://www.learningrevolution.net/alternative-to-udemy/).

within themselves. Training benefits the trainer as well as the trainee. It is not going to be a prance in the park, but trust me, if you don't throw in your towel, training others is trading your potentials practically toward setting up yourself as a champion. That is why the military of every nation trains. In the words of Publius Flavius Vegetius Renatus, a writer of the later Roman Empire (late 4th century), "We find that the Romans owed the conquest of the world to no other cause than continual military training, exact observance of discipline in their camps, and unwearied cultivation of the other arts of war." Anyone who strives for mastery and great success in any endeavor must train. To attain great conquest in trading your potentials, coaching yourself and others is a must and not an option. Whatever you do, just *Train! Train! Train!*

Here are a few follow-up questions to ask to help guide how you go about using *training* as a tool for trading the products and by-products of your new potential. (NB. These questions are in no way exhaustive, you are always free to add to them as it best fits your situation):

- Is training a valuable and profitable part of deploying my potential?
- What kind of people will best benefit from the various training options I will offer?
- How can I best design a training program out of my potential to make it practical and attractive?
- Do I want to create an online training platform, or do I want to train through an in-person or face-to-face platform?
- What materials or methods will I need for adequate training? How would I go about sourcing them?

- What steps do I have to take to keep unearthing my potentials and keeping my skills relevant?
- How can I keep the training sustainable and continuously relevant?

Entrepreneurship

The *fifth* way of *Trading the Products and By-Products of Your Newfound Potentials* is through *entrepreneurship.* The *entrepreneur* is *the individual who organizes and manages any enterprise, especially a business, usually with considerable initiative and risk.* Knowing your potentials gives you leverage when starting an enterprise. It gives you the direction to eventually drive your business and a vision of where you want to go with your newfound talents. If your potentials lead to the production of *tangible* products or services, what better way to trade them than venturing into a business of your own? *Entrepreneurship* as a tool for bartering your unique discovered skill sets is without a doubt highly efficacious.

The spirit of entrepreneurship is the heartbeat of the American Dream and a part of the human spirit. It is a culture, a responsibility, a cauldron of creative ideation put in action that is filled with value. Entrepreneurship is an innovative device that allows you to put your potentials to work through a business that creates wealth by putting your brand-new abilities to work. In the words of a Caroline Ghosn, an American businesswoman and daughter of former Nissan and Renault CEO, Carlos Ghosn, "Entrepreneurship is a muscle, and winning is an endurance game." It is like running in a marathon. The spirit of entrepreneurship is the life-force of endurance that gives you the boost to continue running the race of doing great things with the innate potentials that you have discovered.

Entrepreneurship is an avenue that you can use to deploy the products and by-products of the newfound potentials that you have discovered. Many great companies that we see today started under the influence of the spirit of entrepreneurship. The founders of these great establishments saw their discovered abilities as an avenue to crank the machinery of entrepreneurship to life, creating the great companies that we see today. The potentials you find can inspire you to start a company that meets the specific needs of a group of people. As your company takes off and becomes successful, it causes a chain reaction of events in the time continuum as it provides a new channel and platform for people to unearth their own potentials. It produces a ripple effect of innovation, birthing more discoveries of some sort.

For instance, Microsoft today has become a grand behemoth of an organization with the vision of *empowering every person and organization on the planet to achieve more,* and they are doing just that impacting lives positively. This entrepreneurship venture started with the concept of primarily two men, Bill Gates and the late Paul Allen on April 4, 1975, as a software company that has mushroomed into a major multinational technology corporation. Today, the *potential* of the duo has led to the creation of more than 131,000 *abilities* of people working for the corporation, as of the fiscal year of 2018.[18] For Amazon, the *potential* of

18 The Microsoft Corporation is a product of entrepreneurship via the budding genius of the duo, Bill Gates, and Paul Allen (Late). It is a testament that the *potentials* of a few can lead to the birthing of the *abilities* of many. From statistical data, the number of employees that now work for Microsoft has steadily been on the increase—61,000 employees in 2005, and 131,000 in 2018, approximately a 115% increase. (Liu, S. (2018, August 30). Microsoft Corporation: employee count from 2005 to 2018 (in 1,000s). Retrieved from https://www.statista.com/statistics/273475/number-of-employees-at-the-microsoft-corporation-since-2005/).

one, Jeff Bezos, has led to the discovery of 647,500 plus *skill sets* of people working for the corporation on a full-time and part-time basis as of 2018.[19]

Entrepreneurship allows you to monetize your strengths and innovative ideas. It can avail you the opportunity of reaching a considerable number of people with the powers you have uncovered about yourself. The late Steve Jobs could have had the technical know-how of computing, but it wasn't until after he made it a business (i.e., Apple, Inc.) that the products he created started to reach people across the globe. Now, imagine a world where Apple products, such as Macs, iPhones, iTunes, are nonexistent. Strange, right? That is the power of entrepreneurship. It might interest you to know that at the time of this writing, Apple, Inc. trends to be the first United States (U.S.) based corporation to hit the $1 trillion valuation mark, four decades after it was founded. Also in second place for the U.S. public company $1 trillion valuation threshold race is Amazon.

If we are talking about trading the products and by-products of your potential, entrepreneurship isn't something you should ignore. To do so will be the height of disregard at its best. Entrepreneurship is like creating something out of nothing, adding the *extra-* to the *ordinary,* and removing the *im-* from *impossible.* It is innovation. It is creation. In the words of Robert

19 The Amazon Corporation is also a product of entrepreneurship, like Microsoft, Facebook, Google, just to mention but a few, via the budding genius of Jeff Bezos, the founder, chairman, CEO, and president of Amazon.com, Inc. It is a proud testament that the *potential* of one can lead to the accouchement of the *skills* of many. From statistical data, the number of employees that now work for Amazon has steadily been on the increase—17,000 employees in 2007, and 647,500 in 2018, approximately a 3,709% increase. (Clement, J. (2019, February 5). Number of Amazon.com employees from 2007 to 2018. Retrieved from https://www.statista.com/statistics/234488/number-of-amazon-employees/).

Herjavec, the Croatian-Canadian businessman and Shark Tank Television personality, "What is great about entrepreneurship is that entrepreneurs create the tangible from the intangible." The *intangible* is what you are doing now, *unearthing your latent potentials from your subliminal-self,* as you read this book. You then take what you discover and make it tangible, marketable, and profitable. Think in terms of *sustainability* through continuous self-development and a constant process of unearthing. Just like the search for naturally occurring gems is not limited to one geographic area, as an entrepreneur, you will also have to figure out how to manage the different parts of your potentials.

Here are a few follow-up questions to ask yourself to help gain a better understanding of what *entrepreneurship* means as a tool for trading the products and by-products of your new potential. (NB. These questions are in no way exhaustive, you are always free to add to them as it best fits your situation):

- How can I trade the *products* and *by-products* of my potentials?
- What is the best way to do business with the *products* and *by-products* of my newfound abilities? How do I stay true to my potentials in the process?
- What kind of people need the *products* and *by-products* of what my new skill sets offer?
- At what price do I think the *products* and *by-products* of my potential should sell for?

VOLUNTEERING

The *sixth* way of *Trading the Products and By-Products of Your Newfound Potentials* is through *volunteering.* As previously

about the utility you can derive by helping at your local soup kitchen, shelter, or even a battered women's shelter, or the service you could offer by volunteering in a local place of religious worship. There are many other places where you could enlist your pro bono services for the greater good, like an animal rescue shelter, national parks, Habitat for Humanity, the American Red Cross, local libraries, during political campaigns, etc. Look around your community, and you will find several avenues to serve. Would it not be satisfying to know you are part of something more inclusive as you extend your newfound skills to the service of humanity in your community or nation? Notice that it does not leave you without some sort of compensation, so to say.

Volunteering opens you up to new service opportunities, a network of value-adding people, and it increases the value of your potential. The experiences you gain from using your abilities are the ones that you can bring to the table when you volunteer. It's a win-win scenario—a *quid pro quo.* The organization benefits from your skill sets, and you from them as it helps you further hone your skills. Volunteering is an opportunity to show yourself at your very best. It is an opportunity to put the *products* and *by-products* of your potentials to work. It is a selfless but strategic way to trade the outputs of your gifts. It offers you a free opportunity to publicize or advertise your potentials. It is a free way of garnering recognition and building an audience. Volunteering in some capacity or the other is a key to opening doors of profit that you can be fortunate enough to walk through and benefit from. Given how trade is so well tied to money and monetary value, take a moment to think and ask, *Could volunteering be the*

Retrieved from https://www.nationalservice.gov/pdf/katrina_volunteers_respond.pdf).

key to opening the potential portals of profit for me? Also, could I leverage it to eventually trade the products and by-products of my potentials?

Here are a few follow-up questions to ask yourself to help you better understand how *volunteering* could help you eventually trade the products and by-products of your new potential. (NB. These questions are in no way exhaustive, you are always free to add to them as it best fits your situation):

- How can I volunteer with the gifts that I have discovered?
- Who will benefit from my willingness to volunteer?
- What potentials can I refine through this volunteer process?
- What other skills could I unearth on this journey as a volunteer?
- What are opportunities can I leverage as I volunteer in an area of service?
- What do I anticipate gaining through my volunteer experience in the short-term and on a protracted long-term basis?
- Is there anyone I am currently serving that I can tell the profit I seek to earn from my offer to volunteer? Can they help me achieve my goals?

Add Value as An Employee

The *seventh* and *final* way of *Trading the Products and By-Products of Your Newfound Potentials* that we will be considering in this chapter is *adding value as an employee.* The fact is that there is nothing that bars you from trading the outputs of your potentials as an employee of a business outfit or corporation. As a matter of fact, working under someone else's leadership or better still, in a company, already implies you are trading your skills and expertise on the job for the monetary remunerations of a wage and other financial and non-financial benefits and the chance of gaining a progressive growth advancement in your career.

It is valuable to note that being a value-adding employee in an establishment gives you something to confidently trade with (i.e., your skill set) in a space where the amount of risk you carry is significantly less than if you branched out alone. Working in an organization means any ensuing uncertainty of risks is spread out more equitably among other associates in the corporation at all levels. However, the weight of the claim becomes more cumbersome as you climb higher up the corporate ladders of the organization. However, high, low, or mid-level on the totem pole of the corporate ladder—whether employees know this or not—everyone is trading their time, skill sets, and abilities.

On the job, the *products* and *by-products* of your newfound abilities, in conjunction with those of other associates in the organization, are being used for a common goal, which works toward the advancement of the company vision, goals, and objectives. In turn, this helps in unearthing the *known* and *unknown* potentials of the organization. Having gone through several chapters of this book already, you would agree with me if I say quite emphatically that *technically,* everything has *potential,* as a stipulation of fact. Provided you play your part with keenness and dexterity, your work at that business establishment contributes to the company's ability to realize its own *potential* as an organization. That is the reason why organizations started by just one individual, maybe a couple or even a few people can quickly balloon to an organization the employs hundreds of thousands or even millions of associates—think Walmart, think Amazon, etc. Hence, I can say that *potentials have a creative and multiplicative effect—potential births potentials.*

The business trades its trust on you for its ability to realize its own potential while you do the same for yourself. You become an integral part of the organization's vision, or goals and objectives, as you deploy your own potentials in helping to attain that collective focus. Hence, you might be doing yourself tremendous discredit if you go despising the role you play in any system. Among other things you are there to trade the *products* and *by-products* of the potentials that you uncovered, be it your ability to strategize, implement, organize, or analyze, just to mention but a few. Whatever it is, you are not only trading the outputs of your newfound strengths for the salary, benefits, and other compensations that you will get as agreed on from the time of your hiring, but you are also exchanging your time and skill sets for access to a business platform, access to a network of value-adding people, fulfillment in doing work that matters to you, and a chance to sharpen your inherent capacities.

Here are a few follow-up questions to ask yourself to help you better understand how *working as an employee* could be of potential benefit to you for ultimately trading the products and by-products of your new potential. (NB. These questions are in no way exhaustive, you are always free to add to them as it best fits your situation). If you currently work as an employee, do take some time to give an answer to these questions:

- How can I introduce the *products* and *by-products* of my potential into the work that I do in my place of employment?
- Have I been trading the *products* and *by-products* of my potential at my job? In other words, am I operating in my area of *Strength* (**S**)?

- Which of my *Weaknesses* (**W**) hamper my efficiency at trading the *products* and *by-products* of my potential on the job? How can I curb them?
- What *Opportunities* (**O**) can I jump on in my place of work that will allow me to trade profitably with the *products* and *by-products* of my potential on the job? How can I leverage them?
- What *Threats* (**T**) do I need to avoid or eliminate in the place of my employment? Are any of my work habits toxic, thus being a threat? How can I eliminate them?

—~—

The process of trading the *products and by-products* of your potentials can include either all or some of the ways mentioned above.

First, we saw that we can trade the outputs of our expressed powers by *branding.* We are defined by certain qualities that sculpt the reputation that precedes us.

Second, through *developing a product* that could be *palpable* or *non-palpable* that we can exchange for monetary gains.

Third, through *publicizing or advertising* the outputs of our newfound potentials. People won't know what you can do until you tell them.

Fourth, through *training.* The more we educate others, the more we sharpen the new skills we have discovered.

Fifth, through *entrepreneurship.* It is simple. *Start a business with your newfound capacities.*

Sixth, through *volunteering.* Sometimes, we can choose to share the outputs of our gifts without hitching it to monetary gains. We enlist our efforts for a sense of fulfillment, access to others, or an avenue to learn a new capacity, etc.

Seventh, by being an *employee.* We can trade our unique skill sets by working for others.

In all, it should be noted that all these strategies are directed toward profit, monetary or otherwise.

After going through this chapter, we can agree that it would be of utmost benefit to be more *deliberate* about how you trade the outputs of your potentials so that you can get the best results from your efforts. In the words of Robert Fulghum, the American author and Unitarian Universalist minister, "Patterns of repetition govern each day, week, year, and lifetime. Personal habits is one term we use to describe the most common of these repeated patterns. But I say these habits are sacred because they give deliberate structure to our lives. Structure gives us a sense of security. And that sense of security is the ground of meaning."

Let us form personal habits that help us build a structure of trading or exchanging the products and by-products of our newly discovered potentials for profit. In so doing, we will establish a rhythm or pattern to the specific strategy we chose, thereby honing our ability to trade to perfection. This will usher you through the portals of every success, giving you a sense of security and meaning. As we do so, we guide ourselves to a place where we will be *enjoying the rewards of our newfound potentials.*

CHAPTER 12

Enjoying the Rewards of Your Newfound Potentials

"ALL WORK AND NO play," they say, "makes Jack a dull boy." However, on the polar end of the spectrum, "All play and no work makes Jack a mere toy," as said by Maria Edgeworth, the once prolific Anglo-Irish writer of adults' and children's literature. Hence, a need to embrace *equilibrium* in life.

Rewards are amazing! Everyone who has worked hard wants to receive something in recompense for their expended time, effort, service, hardship, etc. In this chapter, we will focus on *Enjoying the Rewards of Your Newfound Potentials.* This is the part of unearthing your latent inner powers where it seems like your hard work of self-discovery is finally paying off. So far, you have found, excavated, refined, and traded the various *products* and *by-products* of your potentials. You have come to the juncture where it is the time to enjoy the benefits of those trade.

Everyone desires to benefit from the work they put into a process. It is only fair, to say the very least. Hence, when we have done right by our potentials by going through the arduous process of self-excavation, it is perfectly okay to desire the results. There is absolutely nothing wrong with occasionally splurging on yourself as a reward for the hard work you have put in to create a living hinging on your discovered inner abilities put to work. There is no trade without profit. Likewise, there is no unearthing of potentials without value. And here, the chain of events regarding delving into the depths of your subliminal-self to seek out the gems of your innate abilities will eventually lead to profitable results.

This part of the process is highly gratifying, as you begin to see tangible results to celebrate the work you put in from the beginning. Paying further homage to our mining analogies, the gems start to bring in profits when sold to the eager end users who are ever willing to fork over any amount as they splurge on themselves. The crude oil, its products and by-products, begins to be desired by international communities that yearn to satisfy their energy needs. The same goes for your discovered abilities, your potential begins to put you in the spotlight, in the face of people who eagerly desire the *products* and *by-products* of your unique skill sets. The gems of your subliminal-self possess the combination codes to the safe-portals of every success. It will grant you access to relevant people who will positively impact your life and you theirs. Now, there is something to show for all your effort that gives you a voice as an expert in the areas of your newfound strengths or abilities.

It is at this juncture that the seemingly *ordinary* add the prefix *extra-* to their becoming *extra-ordinary,* and the best versions of themselves yet. It at this position that the *common* become *uncommon.* It is at this station of life that the *commoners* become *celebrities.* Everything changes. The public who have not put in the same effort to become uniquely distinguished like these immediately and erroneously label them *overnight successes,* but there is nothing *overnight* about the process of unearthing one's potentials. You have paid the price through hard work, so *why shouldn't you reap the benefits of your efforts? Why shouldn't you bask in the euphoria of your long-awaited successes?* You have undergone a process that must have taken you weeks, months, and even years of what will often look like a thankless task to accomplish your goals of unearthing the gems of their subliminal-self. At the time you are going through this process, not very many people may know or have heard about you. However, as your light begins to shine, as the cameras start to roll, as the Ethereal Director yells "Action!" And the movie of your success begins, many, bamboozled by your greatness, will think that it just happened. Nothing just happens.

The presumable *overnight success* is a product of a methodical process. *First* was the *discovery* phase. You came to the realization that you could be more than your then *status quo*. This is a process which might have been met with some elements of self-doubt. However, you broke through the mold of those limiting thoughts, and you embarked on the arduous journey of unearthing your latent potentials. *Second,* after discovering the native treasures of your subconscious, you put them through a process of refinement, which is just as time-consuming as the process of unearthing. During the process of polishing the gems of your subliminal-self, various *products* and *by-products* of your potentials ensue. *Third,* you took the outputs of your discovery to market to make a profit, monetary or otherwise. Now, you are reaping the benefits of the seed-efforts that you have sown. So, as you can see, the alleged *overnight success* is a product of grit and unflinching resolve.

You have become a beacon of hope that guides the weary sailors of fortune to the Isles of Success. At this point in the cycle of unearthing your potential, people see your work, the *products* and *by-products* of your abilities, and decide they want to be like you. The clout that comes with being the owner of treasuries of your newfound talent gems begins to make room for you, as opportunities commence cantering about the meadows of your now-distinguished life like equines of great worth and renown. Your work begins to hold value beyond what you thought was possible. People, brands, and even nations start to see your real value. They begin to perceive that with your potential, you can inspire their target audiences to take part in what they offer, as they dub you an ambassador. People want to befriend you, and they start sharing your story, using it as a case study for those who are going through their own process of discovery. You literally are becoming the brand that people all over can relate to. Your reputation begins to precede you everywhere you go. You are technically becoming a legend in your own right.

Interestingly, you start to see what people see as you begin to appreciate the value you bring to the table. You recognize that you are no longer a *by-word* at the mention of your name. You gradually become the *main-word* on everyone's lips, but now, not as a standing joke. Talk about a progressive transformation happening all before your eyes. All because you took the *deliberate* decision to *unearth your latent potentials,* poised, as you tap into the *gems of your subliminal-self.* However, the fact remains that the journey of your continuous improvement is just in days or even years of its infancy. Roll up your sleeves. You are just getting started, and your journey is just beginning. You recognize that there is still a lot of work to be done on yourself in unleashing the other potentials you still have within you. However, since you have made self-discovery a habit, pushing deeper into the underpasses of your subliminal-self becomes more of a *lighter-load.* At this point, putting in the work does not make you uncomfortable or frazzled. You are ever ready to delve into whatever is necessary to excavate the rest of your potentials buried in the depths of your subconscious.

Although you might not be able to express it, everyone desires this station: a place where we have embraced our strengths and now trade them with relative ease because we no longer work ridiculously hard to get people to notice the value in them. They just see it. It is crystal clear. Try picturing a well-known, successful, and accomplished person whom you admire. Have you ever wondered how it could have been for them when they started out, the struggles they faced, the losses—unknown to you and all—they suffered, the ridicules they endured, the many sleepless nights they spent laboriously honing their craft, or the many protracted hours spent steadily chipping away at the marble stone of their destiny, sculpting the *magnum opus* of their potentials that now drips with recognition.

This stage of enjoying benefits is what I like to call the sweet spot of unearthing potentials. The gains are numerous. Those who pay the price to unearth their latent skills enjoy several benefits. *First* is *inner peace.* You are literally at peace because you are in sync with the statements of the Roman Emperor Julius Caesar, who said, "Veni, vidi, vici," which roughly translates to "I came, I saw, I conquered." You came to the realization that you needed to discover yourself. You saw the opportunity to do so (e.g., reading this book). You conquered the quest of unearthing the gems of your subconscious and traded the outputs for your dream life. *Second,* you will enjoy the fulfillment of self-discovery. *Third,* you will relish the benefits of personality refinement. *Fourth,* you will discover the deep-seated courage to do the impossible. *Fifth,* your inner peace and courage will steady you in the face of challenges. *Sixth,* you will become an epitomic role model worthy of emulation. *Seventh,* you will attract value-adding relationships that yield mutual benefits. *Eighth,* you will develop a more profound sense of appreciation for things. *Ninth,* you will become a person of power and influence. *Ten,* you will transition to the Hall of Fame, where the world will hear your name.

Your potentials will make you a people magnet. In these times of great success after unearthing your inner powers, people will want to access what you have to offer, and your work takes on a new significance in the hearts of people. Myriads of people will flock to you. You will be pumped to impact their lives positively as you *train* or *educate* them on how they can also unleash their potentials. This will be an exciting time of networking on a large scale. However, these are the times to also be cautious. You must embrace the perception of discernment. You must be perceptive of those who are genuine, and of those who want to just take advantage of you and your new elevated status. Sieve your relationships and determine those who are there for *real reasons* and those who are just *faking a quest for friendship.* Whatever the case, it is fabulous to know your potentials can give you wings in many aspects of your life, hence, if for any reason you haven't found your potential, I implore you to take the time to do so because you are truly missing out. For those that haven't found their inner talent gems, you should make concerted efforts to discover them pronto, now that you see what you would be missing out on if you don't. In the words of Robert Herrick, the 17th-century English poet, and cleric, "Gather ye rose-buds while ye may, Old Time is still a-flying: And this same flower that smiles today, Tomorrow will be dying." Simply put, *time's ticking and it ain't waiting for ya,* speaking in present-day lingo.

If nothing else convinces you, let the fact that your potential holds value challenge you. The fascinating thing about this is that no one who sets out on a self-discovery expedition with the mission of unearthing or discovering the hidden potentials buried in their subconscious really knows the extent of what they will discover. The possibilities are endless. For all the research done on the numerous amounts of naturally occurring minerals and gems available in the earth, the best investigations can only attest to an estimated amount. Likewise, you can only expect a tentative appraisal of the variety of potentials that you have. They could be a lot. However, you will never know the extent of your potentials until you embark on a self-discovery adventure. Until you start unraveling, you will remain blinded to the possibilities. Also, you will only leave yourself hollow and unfulfilled with nothing to benefit from.

To live a full life, to know what fulfillment feels like, to feel like you are truly living your best days ever, it is imperative you unearth your potentials. You will start to look forward to every day instead of dreading them. Also, instead of lazing around in bed, or drowning yourself in Davy Jones' Locker of the tears of self-pity as you binge-watch every episode of your favorite sitcom because nothing excites you, your focus changes as you jump up every morning, pumped about the work you must get done in maximizing your potentials. It no longer feels like a chore anymore. Why? Because every second of grinding is now extremely satisfying for you. Your goals now revolve around the core of uncovering your intrinsic abilities so that you can outperform, outwork, out-hustle, and outshine your way to the very best life ever. Your life will become an investment in hope.

Ask the people who always complain about life and their work if they have found their potential. More importantly, ask them if they have taken the first step to unearth them. I bet you their answer will be a resounding, *Mba nụ!* Meaning an emphatic, *No!* Umm! But, *maka, why? Kedụ ihe mere o jirọ ya kpọrọ ihe?* Translating, the rhetoric sage asks, *'Why? Why is unearthing their latent potentials not a focus for them?* Channeling my native African lingo, Igbo. Because many people are unsure of themselves and what they really want from life, they cower in fear and procrastinate their lives away. However, when you discover what you are capable of, things take a turn for better in your life. Could this be your season of enjoying the rewards of your new-found potentials? You tell me. The ball is in your court to play as you deem fit.

—~—

Life is chock-full of people, who, having found their potentials, discover, refine them into various *products* and *by-products,* and trade them profitably for their utmost joy and benefit. I believe you have known people like that or have admired from afar. You may unquestionably be aware of successful people who are living the life you aspire. I am not excluded. I too have people I admire, and I strive to attain their status and even surpass them in the long run. There is no harm in dreaming or aspiring to accomplish the best destiny allows you to be. Dreams guide your inner beliefs—a vector quantity that gives you direction.

One such people whose life's story is widely known is Colonel Harland David Sanders, the American entrepreneur, and businessman, and Founder of Kentucky Fried Chicken (better known as KFC). Before starting his business, Colonel Sanders had worked different jobs in different industries, occupying many different positions—some of which were the result of him getting fired repeatedly for various reasons at the various occupations. It could really be discouraging when failure becomes a pattern. However, Colonel. Sanders was relentless in his pursuit of a breakthrough past the jinx of his employment woes. Finally, he found his niche after many failures. In his 40s, he was running a food service station where travelers could feed. That is the genesis of his breakthroughs, yet not without several tough times ensuing.

As a small boy, his father had died, and because he was the eldest of his siblings, the duty to care for them rested on him while their mum went about her work. The young Harland Sanders would often fix meals for his younger siblings, and this was the earliest display of the potential the young Harland had in him for cooking. For different reasons throughout his lifetime, however, he wouldn't explore cooking professionally until he hit his 40s. On a side note, your potentials could be that fun hobby that you are neglecting. Can I re-echo the Psalmist (i.e., Psalms 118:22) that, "The stone the masons discarded as flawed is now the capstone!" (The Message Bible). Time and again, the knack you always neglect ends up being the thing that distinguishes you, ushering you into the halls of your maximum potentials.

By the time he was in his 60s, he had perfected his fried chicken recipe and successfully sold it in the service station he had opened. After the numerous challenges he encountered, he was able to franchise KFC across America. Some of us quit after we fail a couple of times. By some accounts, his recipe was rejected 1009 times before anyone accepted it when he tried to franchise his restaurant. When he died in 1980, Harland Sanders was worth an estimated $3.5 million (i.e., approximately $10.6 million inflation adjusted in 2019). Also, he became the brand ambassador and symbol for KFC, and his logo still embellishes every box and bucket of chicken that is sold that shows his face and his signature goatee, white suit, and western string tie. Talk about enjoying the benefits of your potential!

Today, when the names of culinary greats are mentioned, it is hard to skip Colonel Harland Sanders. The potential to turn chicken into a meal people would queue for was there, but needed to be developed, and soon enough, it had a loyal following far beyond the passing of its founder. The same can be said about the potentials that lie latent in you. There is a chance that thousands, even millions of people, will be positively affected by your action if you did something about those potentials. So, *why wouldn't you hitch your wagon on the potent dream of unleashing your innate abilities?* Your aspirations are tied to your skill sets. It is only after successfully trading the outputs of you newfound gifts that you get to enjoy the benefits and fulfill your deepest aspirations. Do you want to be widely known for what you do? Be fulfilled? Become wealthy? Have a platform to serve from? Travel the world? Unearthing your latent potentials gives you access to those opportunities.

Regardless of what your goal from unearthing your potential is, I guarantee you the process will enhance your life exceedingly. After all, they are potentials for a reason—they could become more. They are pregnant with possibilities that seek to manifest after their gestation periods. Each potential in you is potent with its own replicative power. What happens after those possibilities are released is that they begin to bear in multiples just the way a seed will always produce more than what it initially was. It is self-sustaining when in motion, just like a chemical chain reaction. According to Encyclopedia Britannica, "a chain reaction, in chemistry and physics, is the process yielding products that initiate further processes of the same kind, a self-sustaining sequence."[21] So, how does this reasonably relate to your potentials, skill sets, or abilities?

---

21 Chain reaction is a self-sustaining sequence that ensues, in chemistry and physics, when products interact and initiate further processes of the same

First, you *initiate* your potentials via an agent. For example, through the light of enlightenment, the heat of being uncomfortable with your *status quo,* or through the catalyst of feeding your mind with information that motivates you to action (e.g., reading this book).

Second, your potentials go into *propagation,* where the outputs of your newfound abilities go into a repetitive cycle. With your newfound gifts acting as intermediates, you continue to develop more potentials repeatedly, as we mentioned in Chapter 8 when we talked about the PDCA (i.e., **P**lanning-**D**oing-**C**hecking-**A**cting, or **A**djusting) cycle.

Third, you deliberately *cancel* your search for more potentials when you see that you may be spreading yourself too thin, or when you realize you have not perfected the crafts of your already unearthed skill sets. The goal is to expand sustainably. Grow reasonably and don't overwhelm yourself to the point of incapacitation. Be strategic in excavating potentials. Perfect the *outputs* and *trade* of a block of abilities before beginning a new cycle of discovery. Don't become a *jack of all trades and a master of none.*

Thus, it is clear that your *potentials in action* are analogous to a chemical chain reaction.

Let us look at the life of Jeff Bezos, Founder of Amazon.com, Inc. In 1994, at the age of thirty, Jeff quit his job on Wall Street to start what is today Amazon.com, Inc., the second company

---

kind. Some examples in Chemistry are the "combustion of fuel gas, the development of rancidity in fats, knock in internal-combustion engines, and the polymerization of ethylene to polyethylene," per Encyclopedia Britannica. An example in physics is the process of nuclear fissions. The three stages of a chemical chain reaction are "initiation, propagation, and termination." (Reference: The Editors of Encyclopedia Britannica. (2019). Chain reaction. Retrieved from https://www.britannica.com/science/chain-reaction).

in U.S. history—behind Apple, Inc.—to hit the $1 trillion valuation mark. To start the company, he solicited funds from his family members, friends, and prospective investors and was able to raise $1 million. His parents were among the twenty that said, "Yes." According to the Securities and Exchange Commission (SEC) filing, his parents invested $245,573 in Amazon in 1995. With the funds that he raised, he started Amazon.com, Inc.[22] He funded his dream and fueled his potentials, never being risk-averse, and his bet has paid over a billion-fold. That money—unknown to him and the people who made initial investments to start Amazon—carried with it a potent economic seismic force that has rocked the global business landscape from the time of its inception until date. When he started though, Jeff Bezos just perceived an opportunity in the technology space—specifically leveraging the power of the internet via e-commerce—and he sure did not want to miss out on it.

Currently, the collective net worth Jeff Bezos and family, at the time of this writing, is in the range of $165 billion, give or take. He currently ranks as the richest man alive. Unleashing his potentials in the tech space has given him mind-blowing wealth and unparalleled success. The extreme financial stability

---

22 The inception of Amazon.com, Inc. is a remarkable story of guts to glory. Here is a man, Jeff Bezos, who quits the perceived security net of his 9–5 job on Wall Street to pursue his *dreams* of building an internet-based business of selling on the World Wide Web. He bet on his potentials that he could achieve his novel idea, and he sure did. He was not risk averse and took the gamble, and today, he sits as the richest man alive. His parents, family, friends, and other initial investors believed in his dream and supported him. Today, Amazon is a resounding success of enormous magnitude. (Reference: Mejia, Z. (2018, August 2). Jeff Bezos got his parents to invest nearly $250,000 in Amazon in 1995—they might be worth $30 billion today. Retrieved from https://www.cnbc.com/2018/08/02/how-jeff-bezos-got-his-parents-to-invest-in-amazon--turning-them-into.html).

gives him the chance to pursue more of his dreams and interests, hence unleashing more potentials under his belt. Today, he explores an interest in the aerospace industry and space travel, seeking ways to commercialize it through Blue Origin, a company he founded in 2000. He is also the proud owner of The Washington Post, a major American daily newspaper that is published in Washington, D.C., with a distinct emphasis on national politics and the federal government, which he acquired in 2013 for $250 million. His wealth also allows him to afford the luxuries he desires for himself—lavish properties, Gulfstream G650ER private jet, private security, etc., provide jobs for well over 745,000 people across all his organizations (i.e., Amazon, Blue Origin, The Washington Post, and Whole Foods Market), and to contribute to philanthropic endeavors. That is the awesome power of potentials in action.

In case you worried that unearthing your inherent abilities would make you conceited, I hope these illustrations have convinced you otherwise. I have reiterated through this book that potentials do not serve themselves alone. They cannot, when they meet needs beyond your own. A musician could be so focused on his craft that he ignores the beauty it creates for someone else. However, that doesn't rule out the effect the music has on the people who hear it. All the strengths within you are screaming out and begging for expression, and it is not without benefit to you. The books, inventions, programs, support, management, leadership, etc. that you have are some of the potentials waiting on your action to become a reality so that you and the people who will be direct beneficiaries can have a better life experience.

—w—

Potentials are not selfish things that steal your time and make you miserable while you toil away in obscurity. They are much more rewarding and fulfilling than you know. There is nothing wrong in enjoying the profits of trading the outputs of the potentials you discover. No one enjoys being an acclaimed failure. Everyone wants to become a resounding success. That is why you struggle to create a living. You want to enjoy some level of comfort in your life. So, *Why not take a chance of embarking on the self-explorative journey of unearthing your latent potentials?* While you discover your potentials, don't be shy about trading its outputs. Do so with every ounce of courage and master the craft of your trade. Don't let fear or procrastination rob you of the possibilities you could discover and unleash in becoming your best self ever. The opportunities that await you could literally be limitless. However, you will never taste the victory of success if you fail to venture out and discover the gems hidden in the labyrinths of your subliminal-self.

Stay persistent like Colonel Sanders of KFC. You may repeatedly fail in your effort to discover your potentials. However, you must never give up. I coined a phrase over twenty-five years ago: "Determination today will always lead to success tomorrow." No matter what happens, stay determined. Stay the course of the journey as you delve deeper into your subliminal-self. An unknown author once said that "Only optimists make history. No monument was ever built to a pessimist." Do you think Jeff Bezos would be the richest man on the planet if he clouded his dream of starting Amazon with the thick-dense fog of pessimism? I think not. Another unknown author said that "Pessimism is an investment in nothing; optimism is an investment in hope." Be hopeful as you push to discover and trade your abilities.

Do yourself and others a favor and unearth your latent inner powers. You stand to benefit immensely, and others will do so too. So, the next time you think about enjoying the profits your potentials will bring to you, think about the people who will also benefit from it and the fulfillment they will get from interacting with the brilliance of your discovered strengths and abilities. Commence your self-exploration expedition. Also, be sure to make it *long-lasting* and *sustainable.* Don't invest in *nothing* by being a perpetual skeptic. Do yourself and others a favor and invest in hope by unearthing your latent potentials and make them work for you and others. The world is waiting for your manifestation.

CHAPTER 13

Sustaining Your Newfound Potentials

—∾—

WE HAVE COME A LONG way from the beginning of our journey. We have discovered, refined, and traded the outputs of our potentials, and we see the benefits. Honestly, no one wants any good thing to end after it starts, *right?* We all want to see the positive benefits of any endeavor we are involved in to continue and not stall. We want to keep discovering more potentials. We want to continue refining the new abilities we find in order to extract more *products* and *by-products* of those potentials. We want to diversify our efforts and not put all our eggs in one basket. To do so, we must think sustainably. Our aim in this chapter is to look at ways we can sustain our newfound potentials.

Nations that explore, mine, drill, and refine their natural resources look for avenues to *sustain* those resources for continued earnings. They seek out regenerative ways to expand the reins of their economic earning potentials in order to stay relevant in the community of nations. An example amongst the few is Dubai, one of the seven emirates of the United Arab Emirates (UAE), a noted oil-producing city in the world, and now a thriving global economic nerve center. Dubai, despite its oil trade boon, has keyed into the truth-laden notion that *oil reserves are finite natural resources that won't last forever.* There are estimates that these reserves will eventually run out before the end of the century. Such news would make the hearts of oil-producing nations to skip a beat. *After its depletion, what next? What will Dubai and other oil-producing nations do to survive in the dawn of an oil apocalypse?*

Surely, they wouldn't keep their hands folded and allow such event of epic proportion blindside them economically. Despite being built on the metaphorical camelback of the oil industry, Dubai has taken steps to ensure the fast depletion of crude oil does not take a drastic toll on them. They have re-invented their economy by making themselves a commercial capital of the Middle East and the world, now known as the *shopping capital of the Middle East,* thanks to their many souks and countless shopping centers. They have taken substantial steps to guarantee a sustainable economy through sectors like construction, financial services, IT, real estate (now highly acclaimed for it), aviation, gold (fondly referred to as the *City of gold,* thanks to its nearly 250 gold shops), and tourism (a 20% stake of the city's GDP).

When you mention Dubai now, chances are high that even before thinking of its oil wealth, the initial thought that comes to mind is the notion of the city as a favorite tourist destination. Dubai is an architectonic wonderland that would make any architect or architectural connoisseur giddy with excitement. Different tourist lures like the Burj Khalifa, Dubai Mall, Dubai Aquarium, Bastakia (Old Dubai), Sheikh Saeed al-Maktoum House, Burj al-Arab, Jumeirah Island, the Atlantis, among others, attract tourists yearly from around the world. With this and more, Dubai has been able to take its many naturally occurring and man-made *potentials* to a transformative new level where they are transforming themselves into something people want to engage with, globally. Dubai is taking no hostages in the race toward unearthing and polishing its potentials. Instead of focusing on just a couple of sources of potential—which remain very profitable—that is, their gold trade and oil production, the city is continually delving into various other powerful potentials to trade.

Today, Dubai is one of the most prosperous cities in the world, which can be attributed to the resolute commitment to maximizing the potentials available to it, with other cities now aspiring to the same level of achievement. In the words of HH. Sheikh Mohammed bin Rashid al-Maktoum, Emir of Dubai Emirate, Vice President, and Prime Minister of the UAE, "I want Dubai to be number one. Not in the region, but in the world. Number one in everything: high education, health, and housing. I want to give my people the highest way of living." He is bent on making Dubai No. 1 in everything, avidly tapping into the metaphoric mines of various potentials that are transforming Dubai in leaps and bounds. In his words, again, "Most people talk; we do things. They plan; we achieve. They hesitate; we move ahead. We are living proof that when human beings have the courage and commitment to transform a dream into reality, there is nothing that can stop them." Their resolve is a no-holds-barred determination toward becoming the first among equals.

Before tourism and oil even became a thing in Dubai, the city, from time immemorial, had always been the principal trading hub for foreign tradesmen. This was before the discovery of oil in the early 1950s. However, Dubai leveraged the availability of pearls and gold influx from trade, as well as its strategic location to attract foreign trade. Without that resourcefulness, Dubai wouldn't know the kind of riches it knows today, now receiving up to 15 million visitors annually, making it the *fourth most visited city destination worldwide after Bangkok, London, and Paris, according to the MasterCard Global Destination Cities Index* (according to *www.statista.com*). This growing influx of tourists further expands its sources of revenue, creating more dynamic potential opportunities to unearth under the auspices of tourism. In consonance with the example set forward by Dubai, the same should be the goal of the individual who recognizes, unravels, refines, and multiplies the products of their latent potentials.

There is a need to find an avenue to *sustain* the profitability of your hidden potential, just like Dubai has done. The city could have chosen to rely on its rather lucrative business in the oil industry. However, they have chosen not to put all their eggs in one basket, should their oil reserves deplete in the coming years. Profitability is the result of trade. Multiplying the avenues of your resourcefulness increases your earning potentials by expanding your reach through various streams of income. *Diversification* is the name of the game in sustaining any growth trajectory. Hence, if you want to create wealth and maintain it, you can't continue to center your wealth on just one thing alone. It is far too risky to do so. At the core of diversification is sustenance. You see, if people, cities, states, and nations don't look for ways to sustain their wealth, they will not survive an economic downturn when it comes.

—~—

Sustainability Bits and Your Newfound Potentials

I read a great book several years ago that paints an appealing intellectual portrait of sustainability. The book titled, *The Necessary Revolution: How Individuals and Organizations Are Working Together to Create a Sustainable World,* was written by

Peter Senge (the American systems scientist, MIT professor, and author), Bryan Smith, Nina Kruschwitz, Joe Laur, and Sara Schley. Senge et al. excellently expound on many concepts that buttress our understanding of the notion of *sustainability*. However, I am not about to do a full-scale review of the book. My goal is to discuss some ideas that will better help in the comprehension of how you can sustain your newfound potentials.

By the way, *what is Sustainability?* In the most simplistic of terms, it is *the ability to be sustained, supported, upheld, or confirmed.* In technical terms from the purview of environmental science, it is *the quality of not being harmful to the environment or depleting natural resources and thereby supporting long-term ecological balance.* Senge et al. define it as "the need to live in the present in ways that do not jeopardize the future." The word spawns from the root word, *sustain* (i.e., continue, preserve, prolong, supply, support, shore up, keep going, etc.), and *ability* (i.e., experience, energy, knowledge, or expertise—the power that results from capacity). We seek to *sustain* an *ability* of worth. The earth is of value. That is why, we endeavor to preserve our environment today so that those who live tomorrow can have a future that is not endangered. We want to sustain our lives, business, economy, culture, society, relationships, etc. In a similar vein, we also need to shore up the potentials we have discovered. We don't want them short-lived.

Part I of The *Necessary Revolution,* named *Endings, New Beginnings,* cites the need to rethink and curb our environmental impact through new choices for the sake of posterity. The industrial age led to gains technologically, though at the cost of increased pollution and the depletion of renewable and nonrenewable resources. Despite these side-effects, myriads still live in denial or in a bubble.

Here are some of my contemplative views on how Part I of Senge's book can help us in the bid to preserve our newfound potentials. The process will not be a pie-in-the-sky-rhetoric. It really is a possible feat. The future you desire that is viable, profitable, and sustainable is attainable. It resides in the choices you make today. You need to embrace a new way of thinking, and this book you are reading now will help you to do just that. A sustained, reinvigorated potential necessitates a seismic shift of the tectonic plates of your reasoning faculties. To sustain your newfound abilities, think systemically. You need to see the whole picture of your *status quo* and who you want to become. This will guide your actions. Don't live your life in a bubble where you are seated in the comfort zone of your *status quo.* Don't deny the need to develop a regenerative potential that allows you to flourish repetitively through practice.

Furthermore, to sustain your newfound potentials, you must be capable of *seeing systems, collaborate across boundaries, and create your desired futures,* as espoused by Senge et al. in the book. These capabilities must develop side by side. *First,* systemic thinking reasons beyond the norm of the *status quo* to see all ensuing *patterns,* both positive and negative. While surveying your current conditions (e.g., via the use of the SWOT Matrix and PDCA), do well to expunge the negative, but leverage and enhance the positives. Seeing the panoramic view of the meadows of your life encourages you to make strategic choices to eliminate threats. *Second,* you may need to collaborate with others (e.g., by seeking mentorship, or expert advice, reading, research, etc.). *Third,* you need to shift from being *reactive* to your *status quo* (e.g., via spasmodic problem solving, or quick fixes), to being *creative* (e.g., strategic or outside the box thinking). Create and sustain your new future through the possibilities of your newfound potentials. (We will return to these capabilities later in this chapter).

Part II of The *Necessary Revolution,* named *The Future is Now,* is a summary of individuals and groups who have taken a critical look at the sustainability *status quo* and acted to make a positive impact. Solo, Per Heribert Carstedt introduced Flexi-Fuel cars into Sweden. As a group, The Coca-Cola Company and WWF's joined forces in 2007 to conserve the world's freshwater resources.

Shaping life beyond *the bubble* of your *status quo* requires that you believe that the *momentum* you have started can be sustained, or constant. This casts my mind back to high school physics. In Newtonian mechanics, momentum (**p**) was simply the product of an *object's mass* (***m***) and the *velocity* (**v**) (i.e., $\mathbf{p} = \boldsymbol{m}\mathbf{v}$). In the context of sustaining your newfound potentials, momentum here is the product of *your ability to see the mass of larger patterns, or gestalts* (***m***) and *taking small steps toward your goals by using your newfound inner powers* (**v**). (NB. I call this *The Momentum of a Sustained Potential (TMSP),* or just momentum (**p**), in this case, relating to your innate abilities). Hence, you must never doubt your capacities toward maintaining this translational drive toward your best self. Think of Per Carstedt and his little steps in Sweden that ballooned.

Part III of The *Necessary Revolution,* titled *Getting Started,* is a strategic guide on where to start. It calls us to break away from the typical limited one-dimensional view and embrace multidimensional viewing strategies. Through engagement via dialogue, a compelling case can be made for sustainable causes and adopted through small steps and meaningful questions.

You cannot sustain a potential that has not already taken flight. So, first things first, *start!* Unearth your latent abilities and build yourself into a sustainable or green brand and reap the benefits. Sustaining your potentials benefits you by eliminating dormancy, creating a continuous profit cycle, gaining leverage, creating a point of differentiation from others, shaping your marketplace, making you become the preferred brand, and re-branding when needed. Keeping your brand green means you are continually creating value by addressing current issues, leverage all learning opportunities, continuing to transform your *status quo* through innovation by unearthing and deploying more new potentials. This will hold your growth trajectory on the upward rise.

Sustaining your potentials means you are keeping people engaged with your brand. Because you have unearthed some new abilities, don't become sated with that level of growth. Stay inspired as you continue to aspire toward more celebrated accomplishments through more novel potential discoveries. To keep your brand green, become an *animateur (someone who leads and encourages participation in a particular activity and especially in a cultural or artistic activity).* In other words, become someone who *brings to life* a new way of thinking and seeing to create a focus or energy toward unearthing and doing something worthwhile with your newfound skill sets.

Part IV of The *Necessary Revolution,* titled *Seeing Systems,* is an encouragement toward cultivating the art of seeing larger systems or patterns in life. This art allows us to look deeper and farther beyond the limits or boundaries we face in life. By developing this art, we can project ourselves forward into our possible futures, editing and re-editing life as we go.

We cannot sustain the outputs of our newfound potentials if we are prone to blaming others for failing to achieve the best we were made to become. The system of your life—your *status quo*—spawns from the way you think. This governs your lifestyles and creates the natural order you experience. Your life is a sum of your thought life. To sustain the outputs of your newfound abilities, you must move from being reactive to becoming proactive in addressing issues as they come.

Buckminster Fuller, American architect, systems theorist, author, designer, inventor, and futurist, once asked, "How big can we think?" Sustaining the outputs of your newfound abilities hinges on your capacity to think big. Thinking big is stretching the boundaries of your subconscious, as you attempt to fulfill your aspirations within the limits of your established extensions. It means going out of your comfort zones to embrace more and thinking more significantly means going beyond your limitations. Learn to itemize the limits to your growth and break them repeatedly. What do I mean? You should set goals for yourself. Establish boundaries for that goal. Accomplish those goals and then broaden the horizon and set new goals again. Keep the cycle going. The more you extend your depths by unleashing more potentials, the more sustainable they become. Therefore, it is factual to say that you can never sustain your newfound skills with limited thinking.

Throughout our journey, I have presented a lot of inquiries or questions in various chapters for a reason. They help you stretch the borders of your thinking faculties. It is crucial to sustain your potentials. Through inquiry, you begin to extend the limits of your subconscious possibilities. To support the lifespan of your newfound abilities means that you are expanding your time horizons—that is, you are proactively forecasting into the future. Doing so reveals any limited boundaries that are limiting your vision as you observe your future from a bird's-eye perspective. Spatial boundaries shift as you determine the *who, what,* and *how* questions on preserving your new success flows. However, while expanding horizons and conquering limiting boundaries, be logical and reasonable. Do not try to do too much at once.

If you wish to sustain your newfound potentials, you must actively see the effects of your choices. Don't choose the easy way out by being symptomatic (i.e., offering quick fixes), when it comes to your potentials. Aim for long-term, innovative solutions. The process may take time, but your solutions will stand the test of time. Being resolute is necessary for sustainability. Stay regenerative—think in PDCA cycles. Key into a self-reinforcing, replicative structural mindset. This is a mindset that wants to grow in duplicates—in geometric progressions or sequences (i.e., 1, 2, 4, 8, 16, . . . *nth,* and so on). This is an accruing form of snowball thinking. With every turn, the snowball on the wet and sticky ground grows. The same applies to your potentials.

Part V of The *Necessary Revolution,* titled *Collaborating Across Boundaries,* paints a portrait of the human face of system thinking (i.e., a perspective of seeing patterns in a meshed, linked, or interchangeable parts that form a complex and consolidated whole serving a definite purpose). To collaborate involves having good aims, communication skills, empathy, and genuinely shared aspirations.

Sustaining your newfound potentials will at times require you to collaborate with others. In the words of Simon Mainwaring, American businessman, on collaboration, "Effectively, change is almost impossible without industry-wide collaboration, cooperation, and consensus." Some of the avenues of cooperation could be in the form of seeking mentorship, counsel, or expert advice. Effective partnership rests on your ability to bring people together, listen, and nurture a collective commitment. It is all about building relationships that stand on the underpinnings of genuine care and empathy supported by the sense of psychological safety.

It is useless to collaborate with mentors, counselors, or experts with a closed mindset to their opinions. Be humble enough to see through their eyes to learn from the strategies they offer that will help preserve your newfound potentials. To get the best from these sources, you must, *first,* keep your views to yourself and listen to their opinions (i.e., suspend your assumptions). To best achieve this, Senge et al. advise that we use *The Ladder of Inference* (i.e., a tool allows you to make sure that your decisions are made based on facts). *Second,* stay passionate and curious. *Third,* be open to change where needed. Remember, *change spawns change.* It catalyzes sustainability.

Therefore, to sustain your newfound potentials, I will advise that you continue to create and innovate. Tap into the core of your generative DNA that creates that spark that fuels your commitment to the cause of unearthing more potentials and innovations. However, it is imperative to note that fostering the engagement you need to sustain your newfound possibilities could be challenging at times. Nevertheless, to keep you inspired, I nudge you to think global. What should drive you to preserve the successes of your outputs is more extensive than you. Let this be your motivation to continue despite the difficulties that you face.

Part VI of The *Necessary Revolution,* titled *From Problem Solving to Creating,* establishes that the global sustainability requires a level of creativity that embodies *inspiration, aspiration, imagination, patience, perseverance,* and *humility.* Creativity hinges on the future of possibilities. Creative organizations don't just solve problems but convert sustainability challenges into strategic opportunities.

To sustain your new potentials, you can never halt the dynamics of creativity. Keep creating. To do so, as Peter Senge et al. posited in my short review of Part V, you must embrace the mindset characterized by *inspiration, aspiration, imagination, patience, perseverance,* and *humility*. You need to operate with an expansive mindset, not a limiting one. Your capacity is far-reaching, beyond what you could possibly fathom. Put the *V-Principle of Growth* (See Figure 6.2) I introduced in Chapter 6 to work as you unleash your creativity.

Cynicism will hamper your ability to sustain the positive and impactful potentials you could keep unearthing, so you must instead immerse yourself in the positive vision of your possibilities. Operate from the foundation of faith, not fear. You can preserve your potentials and their products by focusing on the doughnut and not the hole. Stay optimistic and positive and pay attention to what you truly want to achieve. Continue to forge ahead by preserving the outputs of your possibilities via aspiration and not desperation.

To sustain your newfound potentials, don't limit your vision by succumbing to the pull of *emotional tensions* (e.g., fear, anxiety, stress, anger, sadness, resignation, or even despair). Instead, embrace *creative tension (*i.e., the image of the gap between your future possibilities and your *status quo*). Let your resolve be to see your *status quo* drawn upwards to your vision and not vice versa. This is the pathway to sustaining your new abilities. Stay creative. Stay innovative. Stay perceptive to more opportunities that you can leverage. Don't settle for less, don't settle for mediocrity. Shun negative influences, embrace positive ones and stay resolute to the cause.

Sustaining your newfound potentials is both a creative and a learning process. Once you stop learning, you immediately begin the downward spiral toward stagnation, and your progress starts to atrophy. In sustaining your discovered skills, you don't have to know all the answers right off the bat. Ask for help when you need it. Senge et al. posit two benefits associated with asking for help. *First,* it produces *remarkable diversity and depth of ideas. Second,* it engages *people in changes that really matter to them.*

To sustain your newfound potentials, I encourage you to go beyond reaching for just the low-hanging fruit. Don't settle for the easy work or the quick fixes just to get by. Don't just be sated for the most accessible and most obvious potentials you can quickly see in the depths of your subconscious. Yes, they are beneficial, but you can be much more. Go the extra mile in unearthing more cutting-edge skills to sustain the cycle of your achievements. Going the extra mile is why Microsoft invests substantial resources into neo-tech through novel designs in the future of productivity (e.g., Fluid Framework, Surface Hub Wall, Windows Lite, etc.). That is why Amazon is solidifying its grip on retail, betting big on cloud computing, and evening branching into health care (e.g., acquisition of PillPack, data mining patient records, opening its own clinics, etc.).

No matter what happens, always be on the lookout for more strategic possibilities you can hone and tap into. Broaden the horizons of your vision by having growth contingency plans that give you the chance to expand and explore the future opportunities of your potentials. Have Plans A, B, C . . . etc. for unearthing your potentials, if need be. No matter what, expand the limits of your vision and possibilities. Don't put too much emphasis on what your idea is. Instead, put more emphasis on what it does. Your mind palace ideation crucible needs to bud both from your heart and head. The drivers of your vision need not be solely monetary benefits.

Part VII of The *Necessary Revolution,* titled *The Future,* from the time of this writing, foretells what the future might hold as it relates to corporations, enterprise variety, leadership, our relations, and just us in general. Here are my thoughts as I review the last part of this thought-provoking book:

Essentially, no one is excluded from whatever happens on our planet. From the time of its writing, which was in 2008, Peter Senge et al. espoused that *"80% reduction in global emissions* from established facts in the book, needed to happen two decades from then. It's been a decade and a year so far, and nine more years to go. I won't get into the nitty-gritty of what has transpired since then to tell the world that climate change is real. A lot has happened, some of it being quite catastrophic.

Whatever happens from the time of this writing, we are its architects, its authors, and its builders. We are all in this together, through thick and thin we go. A song I was taught as a child growing up in Nigeria resonates a need for urgency because time is no longer a friend to the planet. It goes, *'Tick,' says the clock, 'Tick! Tick!' What you have to do, do quick! Today,* which is the next best day to *yesterday,* is already abysmally late. Whatever we do, we must act now. Remember, *More act, less lag.*

Lastly, *how do my thoughts from Part VII of this book spillover on sustaining the outputs of your newfound potentials?* Let me start by saying that to have a robust future regarding your possibilities and its products, don't misallocate your assets (e.g., the productive resources of time, energy, funds, etc.). Don't plan only for the short-term. Look to the future, and think long-term. Know that your actions to unearth your hidden abilities today is a long-term investment on your tomorrow, so do not see it as a waste of your time. It will all pay off, in time.

In your efforts to sustain the outputs of your new abilities, understand that *variety is the name of the game.* A monoculture-mindset will hamper your ability to preserve the ends of your skills. Nature is enamored by diversity, and you should be, too. Keep discovering diversified possibilities. At some point, you will hit critical mass, and come to *The Tipping Point,* as established by Malcolm Gladwell in his book, *The Tipping Point: How Little Things Can Make a Big Difference.* That is a point when ideas start snowballing or replicating as viruses do. Your potentials are not excluded from this effect. Your goal should be to come to a point where your possibilities hit critical mass, tip, and begin to replicate in different proportions. Start your *diversified* journey where you are and morph and replicate into what you aspire to become.

To wrap up this journey in unearthing sundry sustainability nuggets from Peter Senge's *The Necessary Revolution,* I urge you to lead your own self-awareness and self-exploration expedition. Have a low commitment to the *status quo.* If sustaining your new-found potentials will be a reality, you must let your mind be open to the new. You can't have a mind diseased by the Black Plague of pessimism and expect to thrive in your abilities.

The most significant disincentive toward unearthing and sustaining your latent potentials is *fatalism.* It is the philosophy where you believe that you can do nothing to shape your future. Fatalism motions people to accept all things and events as inevitable—a lethal resignation to fate that kills your dreams and most noble intentions. Courting this philosophy will defeat any will you have toward unearthing your hidden abilities from your subliminal-self. If you have ingested the idea of fatalism, allow the 105,000 plus words of this book to become the mental molecular hydrogen cyanide (HCN) that you need to put an end to that misery. Kill it a million times over. Whatever you do, you cannot allow it to survive

You can become more. You have potential. Don't believe otherwise. Develop the capacity to help yourself by unearthing your latent possibilities. Have that deep-seated conviction that *you can* and *you will,* if and only if *you try*. You can never become more until you make the deliberate choice to be so. The power of unearthing your potentials is grafted in your decision. You shape or reshape your future by discovering your innate abilities.

The essence of sustainability, as seen above through the various sustainability nuggets, is to have something for the future. Human life is finite, and we need to think about the generation following us. By preserving our sustenance, we can ensure those coming after us will also benefit from those conserved resources. Take fossil oil, for instance. Imagine every drop of it is extracted and tapped by one generation. *Where does that leave those coming behind? What legacy do we leave behind? What are we doing to create sustainable avenues for the future energy needs of our progeny?* The future is now. We must remember that the choices we make today are already shaping our tomorrow, and we must be conscientious about it.

Sustainability is crucial to living. Life demands it. That is why there is a continual succession of births, growth, death, births, and the cycle continues. Nature avails the female gender of all animate beings to give birth to babies to ensure the continuity of animate life. Seeds germinate into plants that further bear fruits that yields more seeds. Ideas procreate more ideas. Innovations inspire more, greater innovations. It is for this reason that substantial research is going into finding other renewable sources of energy apart from crude oil. When the last oil reserve is empty, the world will still need the *products* or *by-products* of crude oil or at least the alternatives to these.

The sustainability movement is remolding our mindfulness when it comes to the conservation of resources. Although small, you are preserving energy by turning the lights off when you leave the room or house. The same goes for when you turn the water faucet off after use. Whether it is to wash your hands, doing the dishes, or even the laundry, you have the awareness to conserve finite resources. These ways may seem insignificant, but the goal is to sustain and avoid waste as much as possible. In the words of Shari Arison, the American-Israeli businesswoman, philanthropist, and billionaire heiress, "Sustainability is the key to our survival on this planet and will also determine success on all levels." Baby steps by many become the quick march that produces a lasting change toward our continued survival.

All we have talked about sustainability is analogous to how we can preserve our newfound potentials. Our goal is to continue trading the outputs of our abilities, as we saw in Chapter 11. However, no trading of the outputs of your skills will continue if there are no discovered potentials in the first place. One way to ensure there is always something to trade is to put your newfound abilities to work. Remember Jesus' *Parable of Talents* in Matthew 25:14-30. Three servants received a total sum of eight talents from their master who was traveling. According to their abilities, each of the servants received a specific amount. From the first to the third, they each got five, two, and one talents respectively. Upon their master's return, he requested each of them to account for the talents entrusted to them. The first two doubled theirs. However, the third buried his and yielded no profit. Well, he got what was coming to him—"a recompense commensurate to his laziness and inaction." In other words, *Be wise. Don't fleece your destiny and punish yourself by not unearthing your talents to the fullest. Don't leave your abilities buried and dormant.*

Sustainability, in this context, is not the same as squirreling away the potentials you have. Keeping away your abilities is a counterproductive way of working to sustain them. Reserving your skills just to yourself will lead to them festering from lack of use. Not allowing your abilities to work for you will only lead to missed opportunities. Missed chances are equivalent to bungled profits. Exercising your skills makes them better, not hiding them. Remember, *Practice makes perfect.* To sustain your new capacities means you continue to hold them up so that they continue to remain relevant.

You would need to continually update your skills. Aspire to get better at the use of your new abilities. Don't get comfortable with your current discoveries. Ask yourself, *What more could I become? What other talents do I have that I can hone? What other gems can I excavate from the depths of my subliminal-self?*

Take yourself through the many self-analysis exercises and questions detailed in the previous chapters. They will help you keep discovering the strengths within you, repeatedly. It is hard to know the limit to the range of potentials you can carry. You can only learn this by discovery and re-discovery.

Diamonds possess the quality of being the hardest scratch-resistant natural substance known to man. Because of its durable nature, they have the potential of cutting through other solids, including other diamonds themselves. They are used as abrasives, engraving bits, in x-ray machines, etc. Crude oil is replete with several products and by-products, as we saw in previous chapters. All these and more are the diverse ways of using these materials. It is similar with your potentials and their resulting *products* and *by-products.* Because of their diverse nature, sustaining them becomes more of a necessity than an option.

Now aware of your potentials and having found purpose within them, the onus lies on you for their continued sustenance. In *your purpose, through your novel abilities, begin to reveal more purpose by unraveling more potentials.* The world wouldn't help you with that. It is too busy sorting out its own problems. Therefore, it is on you to do it. So, the question is, *Will you be comfortable with the immediate result of your newfound potentials alone, especially knowing that what you have in you and can be much more? Will you really be okay with the barest minimum? Or would you rather stretch yourself and try to discover more unique gems in the depths of your subliminal-self?* Remember, it is not for your sake alone. There are several generations behind you that will benefit immensely from them.

—∾—

The pursuit of sustainability of potential is one you will have to keep paying attention to throughout your lifetime, especially if you want to remain relevant through the time of your ephemeral walk upon this planet. New innovations are coming up as the world steeps deeper into craters of technology, and you cannot keep the rudiments of your thoughts and actions shallow at the surface. You must be consistent in maintaining relevance, ensuring your depth matches the change in innovation spawning all around us at breakneck speeds. To be at the top of your game, you must do more than what the average Joe brings to the table.

Knowing these things, *how then do you sustain your potential? How do you perpetuate your potential beyond a small area of influence? How do you build something lasting, a legacy even, out of your potential?*

Before diving into a couple more analogies to answer the *how* questions presented above, I encourage you to start with the *sustainability bits* proffered above. These sustainability nuggets spawned from my review of the book, *The Necessary Revolution: How Individuals and Organizations Are Working Together to Create a Sustainable World,* by Peter Senge et al., to better understand the concept of sustainability and how it could be applied to sustaining our newfound potentials. Start with these wisdom bits and progress to the other bites in the following paragraphs.

When miners dig for gold in a selected area, they are always looking for specific geologic markers that point to the presence of gold.[23] The copious presence of these geologic indicators often elicits the commencing of deeper prospecting and further mining for more gold. If substantial amounts of gold are discovered, more surface or subterranean mining goes on to unearth the prized resources. The same goes for crude oil. There are geological markers to the presence of crude oil too.[24] As

---

23 What do you look for when prospecting for gold? At the time of this writing, I stumbled over an article titled "Eight natural geologic signs pointing toward gold" by Chris Ralph a few years ago. Some of the geologic signs that he points to that indicate the presence of gold in an area are as follows: color changes, iron staining, and gossans, quartz vein matter accumulations, productive rock types, correct topography, extensions of known mineral or placer areas, and similar geologic zones nearby. (Ralph, C. (2011, September 2). Eight natural geologic signs pointing toward gold. Retrieved from https://www.minelab.com/community/treasure-talk/eight-natural-geologic-signs-pointing-toward-gold).

24 I came across this Geology blog that stipulated some of the geologic signs that indicate the possible location of oil reserves that crude oil prospectors look for. These geologic signs that indicate the possible location of oil reserves

far as prospectors continue to see these signs, they will stay the course on prospecting and eventually begin digging and mining operations to find more and more of these natural resources.

To successfully sustain the presence of your potential and turn them to a constant source of the specific kinds of profit you seek, you need to keep digging, just like the gold and oil prospectors. Keep looking inwards, prospecting for more potential indicators by using the self-reflective tools provided in this book (i.e., SWOT Analysis Matrix and PDCA) and *more.*[25] You must continue to delve deeper into your subliminal-self to identify the strengths within you, analyzing the opportunities available to you, and sharpening your existing strengths through continuous self-development.

---

are gravitational changes, magnetic changes, or via the presence of hydrocarbons in the area. (Geology. (2013, April 17). Signs of oil deposits. Retrieved from https://geolnew.blogspot.com/2013/04/signs-of-oil-deposits.html).

25 The SWOT Analysis Matrix is a powerful strategic tool that organizations use to ascertain performance. To understand how individuals' function and further establish their *status quo,* I adopted it as a reflective self-analysis tool in this book. However, the SWOT Analysis Matrix tool is *not* the only strategic tool that organizations or even individuals could use to determine performance. At the time of this writing, I stumbled on an article on GeekExpos.com that highlighted *The 9 Best Alternatives to SWOT Analysis.* The alternatives to the SWOT Analysis Matrix are as follows: PESTLE Analysis (i.e., **P**olitical, **E**conomic, **S**ocial, **T**echnological, **L**egal, and **E**nvironment); Scenario Planning; Critical Success Factor Analysis; SCORE Analysis (i.e., **S**trengths, **C**hallenges, **O**ptions, **R**esponses, and **E**ffectiveness); SOAR Analysis (i.e., **S**trengths, **O**pportunities, **A**spirations, and **R**esults); NOISE Analysis (i.e., **N**eeds, **O**pportunities, **I**mprovements, **S**trengths, and **E**xceptions); SCOPE Situational Analysis (i.e., **S**ituations, **C**ore Competencies, **O**bstacles, **P**rospects, and **E**xpectations); Porter's Five Forces (NB. The five forces are: competition, suppliers, buyers, substitution, threats, and new entry levels); and MOST Analysis (i.e., **M**ission, **O**bjectives, **S**trategy, and **T**actics). (Archer, S. (2019, April 12). The 9 best alternatives to SWOT Analysis. Retrieved from www.geekexpos.com/the-9-best-alternatives-to-swot-analysis/).

Despite the diminishing levels of crude oil, it may seem like we currently have enough because of more drilling and prospecting still continuing. However, at the rate we are going, there is every likelihood that we will soon face shortages. Though the peculiarities of the detrimental environmental negatives of the unremitting drilling of fossil oil exist, it is something beyond our scope in this book. Instead, our focus revolves only around the *process of unearthing* these natural resources.

Taking a cue from the above brief analogies, the need to continually search for new potentials bubbles up to the surface. The abilities you discovered yesterday must be updated to remain relevant to the ever-changing technological innovations that surround us. For instance, *what is the relevance of a mechanical typewriter when compared alongside a laptop keyboard or even the QWERTY phone keypad?* While all can do the work of typing, one or two are more favorable than the other. However, a *typewriter* was once the first choice to get typing jobs done. With the quick evolution of technology, methods that were once *favorites* fast became obsolete. The same goes for the potentials you discover. To preserve their relevance, you need to not fall behind with the times. You need to uniformly evolve along with the fast-paced, innovative macrocosm. When innovation moves, you move. That is it.

Throughout the volume of this book, we have continuously compared the process of mining to the means of *unearthing potentials.* Why? Because of the strong correlation between the two, as the mining process—which includes prospecting, mining, unearthing the natural resources, processing, refining them and getting the products and by-products ready for market—clearly mirrors the self-analysis and personal development process, which are at the core of the cycle sustenance or sustainability. In the mining process, we are continually asking ourselves the question, *How long will these natural resources last?* That question is at the nucleus of the issue of global sustainability. Because of this, we try to conserve resources or at least look for alternative means to the fast depleting resources. Comparing this to our self-discovery initiative to unearth potentials, beyond the need for preservation, we must make efficient use of the abilities we have discovered today. We must endeavor to replenish those strengths, skills, and abilities.

Considerations on how to sustain your potentials must reflect on how they contribute to your growth trajectory. No matter what happens, you must continue to move in the path of positive evolution through the continuous use of your abilities. This means updating your skills often. Even if it implies going back to school, working with a professional coach or mentor to unearth more strengths, or offering to take on responsibilities that you would usually shy away from—keep your forward momentum, never relenting, no matter the challenges that you face. Planning toward sustainability is no less important than any of the processes we have considered in this book, be it the process of unearthing, refining, or trading.

All the processes we considered in the previous chapters rely on in-depth self-analysis. Hence, it would be beneficial for us to reflect on more of such issues about sustaining our newfound potentials. (NB. These questions are not in themselves exhaustive, you could add or remove to them as needed; tailoring them to your own situation):

- What are some of the ways through which I can sustain my potentials?
- How can I ensure my skills stay relevant despite changes and innovations?

- How can I update myself as an individual to live up to the increasing expectation of excellence?
- What strategies do I have to put in place to solidify what my potentials offer?

—∾—

A lot has been covered in this chapter. This tour on sustainability is gradually bringing us to the end of this book. To capture everything in one word, without having to rehash all the facts abstracted here, the word *continuity* captures the very essence of the whole chapter. Sustainability is the soul of continuity. If you wish to preserve the successes you attain from your newfound potentials, you must embrace a mindset of sustainability. You don't want the achievements of the outputs of your possibilities to be short-lived.

In summary, you should leverage the opportunities that come your way in order to sustain your potentials. Multiply all avenues of resourcefulness you encounter. Remember, *diversification is key.* Embrace all prevailing patterns in your life that ensure continuity. Never shun help if you need it in the journey to unearth your potentials. Become creative and not reactive. Let nothing ever dampen your forward momentum. Beware of the daunting of skeptics. Stop shuffling your feet due to fear or procrastination and make a move toward attaining your future mark.

Think big, always. You can never go wrong with that proposition. Thinking small will only limit your options. Thinking big is a direct investment into *variety,* which is the key in the sustainability game. As a matter of fact, try to think global. Go the extra mile in delivering the outputs of your newfound potentials to the world. To gain a significant foothold in your upward trajectory, do well to advertise your skills. Publicize them without shame.

Sustainability is the long rope you need to keep your potentials churning.

So, *what next?* The next chapter is my call to you to begin your expedition. There are no excuses left for you, at this point. Stay with me, as we gradually bring this book to a close.

CHAPTER 14

Begin Your Unearthing Expedition

WE HAVE COME A LONG way through this book. From stating what potentials are, to delving deep into unearthing our abilities using various strategic tools (e.g., the SWOT Analysis Matrix and PDCA), abstracting the outputs, refining them, trading the *products* and *by-products,* moving on to enjoying the benefits, and making sure that our successes are sustainable. At this juncture, we can say that we have gained a firm grasp on what *potentials* are. We can say affirmatively that we have an inkling of what to practically do toward unraveling the gems of our subliminal selves. No excuse will stand to absolve you, should you choose inaction as your *modus operandi.* The ball is now in your court. Whether you decide to make the hoop before that final buzzer goes off is totally up to you. No carelessness this time. Take aim, be precise, be careful, be laser-focused, and shoot! Make that basket and win the game!

We are winding down on our explorative journey, and all I can say is that it has been a fruitful expedition so far. We have come to the penultimate chapter of *Unearthing Your Latent Potentials. It is important to act on all the information you have garnered up until this point. No buts. No excuses.* Why? It is simple. Because, without acting, none of the things we have talked about will be of any use. It would have been a share waste of time on your part and mine, to say the very least. Chapter 14, *Begin Your Unearthing Expedition,* is nothing but a clarion call to you, the reader, to begin your journey toward unearthing their latent potentials. Consider this book to be my memorable monologue to you—my war speech to spur you to action as you fight to annihilate mediocrity and launch yourself into the waiting arms of every success and victory.

J. R. R. Tolkien's *Lord of the Rings: The Return of the King,* the famous 2003 epic fantasy adventure film—co-produced, co-written, and directed by Peter Jackson—was a masterpiece with some exciting battle scenes. Aragorn's impassioned speech as he rode back from the Black Gate always catches my attention and resonates a flaming passion of someone who wanted glory and victory at all cost. In his remarks, he said:

> "Sons of Gondor, of Rohan. My brothers. I see in your eyes the same fear that would take the heart of me! A day may come, when the courage of men fails, when we forsake our friends and break all bonds of fellowship, but it is not this day! An hour of wolves and shattered shields when the age of men comes crashing down! But it is not this day! This day we fight! By all that you hold dear on this good earth, I bid you, stand, men of the West!"

Reader, the task to *unearth your latent potentials,* quite honestly, may seem cumbersome and daunting, as did Aragorn and the Sons of Gondor, of Rohan, about to go into a battle that will claim their lives as they fight against the enemy. Your courage may seem to fail you by just thinking about everything you have to do. Quitting may seem like a preferable option at this point.

However, like he said, "But it is not this day! This day we fight!" Move forward, take charge, and conquer your fears. Use all the tools provided in this book to unearth your hidden abilities.

Don't let this time you have spent surveying this book be in vain. Remember my value proposition to you from the *Introduction* of this book, that *my commitment to you is that the time you will spend interacting with this book will be nothing more but an investment in a productive, meaningful unearthing of your purpose as you discover your hidden potentials.* I firmly believe I have delivered this value proposition in giving you a lot of substantive information that you can apply to your growth and advantage. However, you must take up all the tools you have garnered from this book and put them into use. The biggest regret you will ever face in life is not the times you failed while trying, but the times you failed by not making an attempt at all in unraveling your best self ever. That, my friends, in the fellowship of this discourse, will be your biggest regret—not trying at all.

Architects, with the plan of their designs, would usually give builders the blueprint to turn it into a building that people can inhabit. If that didn't happen, the architectural drawings (i.e., floor plans, facades, perspectives, construction documents, etc.) would only be a work of art to be desired, but not functionally useful. The architectural drawings and other construction documents would continue to be a desirable image of a *potential* house on paper. Yes, the architectonic designs have the full capacity to become a house, but its potentials remain dormant to the medium where they are drawn. Until the plan is *set to site* and constructed into what the design stipulates, their full potentials can never be achieved. In a similar vein, having all the information in this book and not taking the steps required of you to unravel the treasuries of gems locked up in the labyrinths of your subliminal-self is tantamount to that *potential* house on paper or on the hard drive of the architect's computer. Brilliant as the architecture might be, it only becomes fully appreciated after it has been translated to brick-and-mortar. Also, as vivid and potent as your personal gifts may be, you cannot understand nor appreciate their value unless they are discovered and unraveled.

Take the story of Harry Louis Bernstein, the British-born American writer who wrote freelance pieces and worked for a movie production company before retiring at the age of sixty-two. A name probably unknown to many, but his story remains the most authentic story yet about *potential* that I can tell you through the pages of this book. Harry Bernstein (May 30, 1910–June 3, 2011) did not have a pleasing nor mostly comfortable life in his days. Jay Z, American rapper's, famous, *Hard Knock Life* debut rap music chorus that flows, "It's a hard knock life for us, it's a hard knock life for us, instead of treated, we get tricked, instead of kisses, we get kicked, it's a hard knock life," paints a picture-perfect-portrait of the youthful days of Harry Bernstein growing up. It was a life riddled by poverty, anti-Semitic persecution, abuse as a child, discouragement by his teachers to pursue his dreams of becoming an architect, all of which led him to start writing, and then the struggles to become a writer. While he did eventually gather some form of public attention in his nineties. Mr. Bernstein was not a typical American celebrity. From a young age, Harry started writing pieces that he would get people to read. Harry published short stories in magazines but never gained any fame through them. Harry once tried to publish a novel he titled *Hard Times and White Collars* with Simon & Schuster, but that proposition fell flat to its face. However, the fact remained that he could write, and this was a potential he continued to refine for more than four decades.

A sliver of light pierced through the darkness of the gloom he experienced when he gained employment to become a script reader for Columbia Pictures with the aid of Clifton Fadiman, the chief editor of Simon & Schuster, who rejected his book. His potential for writing was gradually making room for him by just a smidge. Finally, at the age of ninety-three, he started to write a book that seemed to reward the years of staunch commitment he had put into writing. It took him from the dimness of obscurity to the limelight of success. That book would go on to gain public acclaim unlike any of his previous works. The title of the book was *The Invisible Wall: A Love Story That Broke Barriers* that didn't get published until Harry was ninety-six years old. After The *Invisible Wall,* Bernstein would go on to write three more books titled *The Dream* (2008), *The Golden Willow* (2009), and *What Happened to Rose,* which was published posthumously in 2012. Some people would have shackled the pegs of their wills to the iron-balls-and-chains of self-pity and perpetual discouragement, but not Harry Louis Bernstein. He refused to cower at all the lemons life threw at him. He just kept making lemonade with the citrus press of his writing potential. Instead of sitting with despair at how little his writing potential had fetched him in those four decades, he continued to write, taking advantage of the platforms he had. Even with little success, he did not stop honing his writing potential.

In an interview he granted while still living, he was asked why he had written that book, the first of his memoirs. He responded that there was an emptiness in his life caused by the loss of his wife of seven decades, Ruby, an immigrant from Poland. After this loss, *writing* became his therapy to fill that void. He cast his mind back to his life's journey, reminiscing on his sad past, challenges, and failures, scripting all his experiences down in his memoir, walking down memory lane. On July 1, 2019, at 6:00 pm PST, I posted on my Facebook page: "Pain: The battery that powers the lamp of your motivation; that lights the pathways of every success." For Harry, his loss became the batteries that powered light of his writing potentials and lit the paths of every success he experienced in his old age. Harry dove into the depths of his subliminal-self through his past experiences. In his words, he said, "I realized then why I had failed in writing novels because I turned away from personal experience and depended on imagination." The latent potentials that distinguished him were his *experiences.* You probably have your ideas about whether he could have succeeded as a fiction writer. However, we can see through this story that *your potential is not something that exists outside of you, but it is in you.* The onus is on you to find the catalyst for discovering your potentials—which I hope this book does for you. For Harry, that catalyst was the death of his wife.

Work with the things I have shared with you in this book. Put them to good use. Don't let the copy of this book that you have in hands gather dust on your bookshelf. It would really be a waste. The rudiments of knowledge and wisdom it contains are meant to be used in the discovery of the golden nuggets of *potentials* that will transform your life. Peruse through the book the *first* time, read through it thoughtfully the *second* time, marinate your thoughts in the brine of its profound wisdom the *third* time. Whatever you do, *Be the Few! Be the Proud! Be the ready Reading-and-Doing Literary Marines! That will put the products of this book to the test.* Allow its wisdom to transform your life. Like the United States, Marine Corps motto says, "Semper Fidelis," meaning "Always Faithful!" *Stay faithful to the course of unearthing your latent potentials.* Don't let your talents go to the grave with you. The cemetery is already rich with too many unused skills. Don't add yours to it. Get up! Get excited about the riches of your abilities. Get pumped about the opportunities inherent in them. Also, if you feel like you're still waddling through the whole process, stay the course. Don't throw in your towel even before you have started. Trust me, *it is better than doing nothing.*

Don't accept defeat. Don't beat yourself up because you are not where you thought you would be, by now. Don't let the failures that you have faced in life drag you into the quagmires of despondency. Don't let fear cripple your zeal to become the best you yet. Don't procrastinate the thoughts that come to you, profusely beckoning on you to embark on a life-changing self-exploratory journey. Don't put it off till tomorrow. Remember, *you have today, and tomorrow is not guaranteed, so take the leap of faith while you can.* Don't throw away your confidence. Hold it tight with all the strength you can muster. Remember, *your confidence has great recompense of reward.* Stay the course of the marathon. Remember, *only those that cross the finish line will win a prize.*

Don't be timid or shy about unearthing your latent potentials. Be fearless! Be ruthless as you charge forward to conquer the depths of your subliminal-self. Stay determined always. Remember, *determination today will always lead to success tomorrow. Remember the life of Harry Louis Bernstein.* Don't stop by the wayside as you journey to unearth the gems of your abilities. Don't quit! Stay the course! Give your very best as you charge ferociously to the end zones of discovering your very best potentials yet! Remember that *life is a journey, as is the process of refining your potential.* It is a journey that will continue throughout your lifetime, so don't give up on yourself. You have far too much in you for the world than you know. Pursue it! Overtake it! Recover all in the process of digging deeper into the depths of your subconscious!

Unearth your golden potentials! Let the world see the resplendency of your best self yet! Stay motivated! Stay on course

—∞—

"Ignorance," they say, "is bliss." Concerning unearthing your potentials, ignorance is not bliss, but rather a misery in waiting. Ignorance is not an option after having gained all this knowledge from this book. There are certain dangers to procrastinating after learning extensively concerning how to go about unraveling your innate abilities. There is a certain sense of urgency behind the process of unearthing your talents or gifts. After all the information you have garnered, you should have embraced it by now. The reason is simple—your potentials won't wait for you. While you're dilly-dallying about discovering them, when you should have already done so a long time ago, the fact is that you may miss out on those opportunities. So, saddle your mind-colt, satchels packed and ready, and get to riding toward your destination. Don't procrastinate. The time is ticking.

Procrastination is the thief of all opportunities. It is very harmful, and if you fear nothing else, you need to be terrified about putting things off. In the words of Denzel Hayes Washington, the renowned American, actor, director, and producer, "I'd be more frightened by not using whatever abilities I'd been given. I'd be more frightened by procrastination and laziness." Avoid procrastination and laziness like a plague. Let me explain it to you in the next few points some of the things you stand to lose when you procrastinate instead of acting, either to unearth your potentials or abstracting its outputs from trade and profit through the process of refining:

YOU WILL MISS THE OPPORTUNITIES AVAILABLE TO YOU

The *first* thing you may stand to lose when you procrastinate instead of acting on the whim to unearth your potentials are *the opportunities those abilities may create for you.* As you should know by now, discovering your latent possibilities avails you the opportunity to develop new skills and gives you the ability to sharpen those that you already possess. These skills give you a certain level of appeal and unique distinction. The people who need a service in the area of your strengths notice you and start to engage you.

However, should you not see the urgency of unearthing your hidden abilities, many destiny-transforming opportunities that could greatly benefit you will continue to elude you. I stumbled on a story about *The Adventures of Marco Polo* from the May 2001 edition of the National Geographic magazine written by Michael Edwards. In 1260, when Marco was just six years of age, his father, Niccolò Polo, and uncle, Maffeo Polo, jewel merchants and adventurers, traveled to Mongolia (part of present-day China).

The Mongol emperor showed his interest in Christianity, asking the two merchant brothers to deliver a letter to the Pope, asking for as many as one hundred wise men or evangelists to spread the Gospel among his vassals. In 1271, Niccolò and Maffeo set out with Marco, who was 17, for their return trek. Did the Mongol emperor get his one hundred evangelists or wise men? Sadly, no.

The church saw it fit to send only two friars to satisfy the emperor's requests. Sadly, the two did not even make the trip, returning home shortly after the journey began. Could you imagine if his full demand was met? We could be reading a whole different history of China today. This was a destiny-transforming opportunity that eluded the church. What a dolor to

Christianity! Don't miss out on the chance of unearthing your latent potentials.

Do you have to go back to school? Then why wait for it? Register and start plugging away at it, while you've still got the chance. Do you need to gain professional certification? Get started on it. Hesiod, the Ancient Greek poet, once said, "The man who procrastinates is always struggling with misfortunes." Hence, *why linger? Why plague yourself with the woes, worries, and the weight of guilt that missing golden opportunities will lay on the hunchedback of your wailing-weary conscience?* Remember, *More act, less lag.* What do you have to do to get focused about prioritizing your potentials? Assess it, act on it, and adjust your scale of priorities to favor your unearthing process. You must get on it. There are countless opportunities that even the first step in the direction of unearthing your potentials would make a whole world of difference. It will afford you the privilege of taking it by the horns. However, first, *you will have to take that step.*

Some may be overwhelmed at the thought of embarking on this self-exploratory journey. Some may feel that the process is too cumbersome, or that it just has many parts to it. However, take some time and reflect on what you could become for the *small price* you would have to pay by doing the activities I have presented in this volume, all to unleash the potent gems locked up in the depths of your subliminal-self. Just think of the *littlest steps* you can take in that direction. It is an exercise you could practice right now.

For instance, *what strengths did you discover when you took the SWOT analysis test?* That could be the breadcrumbs you need to follow to your greater tomorrow. Take a step in that direction. Write those strengths down and think about the different things you will have to do to actively start on them. Don't make it a complicated process. Simplify it and start acting on them one at a time. Say you discovered your strength was in music, and possibly you are cut out to become a musician. Now, the question you should be asking yourself is, *What things do I need to do to become a professional musician?* Some of it could be writing the music, recording yourself singing to hear how you sound, singing to yourself and then in front of an audience—big or small, having a studio recording for a more professional feel to your music. Or, it could be as simple as uploading some of your content on social media (e.g., YouTube) and getting some feedback from your potential followers, etc. These are all practical steps that you can take.

Becoming a musician was just an analogy I chose to discuss some practical steps you could take to start doing something in the line of unearthing your potentials through your strengths. Activating your potentials and transforming them into practical steps could be done in any position of your strength and competitive advantage. Do something in line with your depths. You know the details of your inner powers that you itemized from going through the *Strength* (**S**) quadrant of your SWOT Analysis Matrix in Chapter 4. You are acquainted with what piques your interests and desires. Therefore, personalize this exercise to suit you when you do it. Act on your strengths. There is no better time to start than now. Put the PDCA cycle (i.e., **P**lan–**D**o–**C**heck–**A**ct or **A**djust) from Chapter 8 to work and establish a workable plan that allows you to work toward maximizing your potentials.

It is all about making sequential moves—step-by-step, precept-by-precept, sequence-after-sequence—toward discovering, refining, trading the outputs of your potentials, and sustaining your successful movements.

Coming back to our musician analogy, I reckon the most straightforward step the person in this illustration would have to do would be singing. Next could be writing their own lyrics. Next, perhaps recording a video of the song for social media. Next could be recording an album in a professional studio. The list goes on and on. However, what should ensue are practical steps toward unleashing potentials—whatever they may be—until they are completed. This significantly reduces the chance of being intimidated by the innate possibilities that you carry. As I mentioned, even the first few simple steps alone could open you to opportunities that you otherwise wouldn't have had. Don't miss out on the opportunities that come your way. Strive to leverage them all.

You Will Miss Out on Building Quality Relationships

The *second* thing you may stand to lose when you procrastinate instead of acting on pushing forward to unravel your intrinsic abilities is *the quality relationships you may miss out on.* Your potentials open doors of opportunities to you. Some of those opportunities could come in the guise of quality relationships as you network with others. You could leverage these relationships to assist you in your bid to unravel your potentials. However, the benefits need not be a one-way traffic street. They could involve a symbiotic effort where they too benefit from you. Hence, you stand to lose out on quality relationships that could help you advance the cause of releasing and maximizing your newfound potentials.

Back to our musician analogy, the person with the potential to hold a wide melodic vocal range who attempts to operate in those faculties—whether by social media or some other outlet—is bound to meet other people who share a mutual interest. Not only that, a music producer who's looking to sign up a new act is more likely to reach out to you when you are out there operating in the capacity of that potential, as opposed to some other person who is not currently working in those areas. Those portals of opportunities open, all because you have taken the cogent steps toward unearthing your innate abilities. Stay active in your pursuit. Plunge yourself into the mind-shafts of your subliminal-self. Shun being passive by not discovering your inherent possibilities.

People want to build a relationship with other people who share similar interests with them—that is a fact—people who will understand their strengths and celebrate with them. Therefore, when you discover what your depths are, like a magnet, you begin to attract the people in that space to yourself. As the famous idiom goes, *Birds of a feather flock together.* The process is organic and almost automatic. People of like mind always find a way to come together and connect through circles of common interest. Your potentials create value around your person. It opens the door to people who want to associate with you, all because of the *value* you offer.

People whose attention you desire will be more willing to give you an audience, especially when they know you are not just there to take advantage of them. Building a following is most feasible under the clouds of engagement when you can share an interactive experience with your target audience. For example, people these days hold celebrities in such high esteem that they too often forget they too are also human. They too desire to connect, instead of being constantly hounded by fans coveting an autograph, or by paparazzi who literally hunt them for the next best image to sell to gossip tabloids for the next big story. However, with your potential discovered, access becomes more natural with people of such status. You now speak the same value-lingua-franca. It's no more just a pursuit of superficiality. Talks, now, are more value-driven.

You May Be Waiting Forever

The *third* thing you may stand to lose, should you linger in unraveling your abilities, is that *you may end up waiting forever.* If, by any means, you hold thoughts of *tomorrow* in your head, as if tomorrow was guaranteed, then you just might end up waiting forever. Remember the idiom, *Make hay while the sun still shines.* Take advantage of the favorable conditions that you have today. Use them to your advantage to get ahead. Unearth your potentials, refine them, extract their outputs, trade with them, and sustain them. The best time to have started digging for your talents was yesterday, and the next best day is today. Make the most of an opportunity when it is available.

Why not start right now? Why continue to put off the actions that could transform your life and put you in a great place? Why barter the possibilities of a great tomorrow in exchange for sub parity? If there is nothing that stands in your way from getting started, then do yourself a favor and start right away. Harry Bernstein was fortunate enough to have lived up to his 90s, passing on at the ripe old age of 101 years. Could you estimate the number of your years? Could you tell me how long you are slated to be here on earth? You can't tell me with absolute certainty that you have all the whole time at your beck and call to do whatever you please and still have the chance of unearthing your potentials. Life is transient, and you cannot predict when you will be called to resign from your ephemeral walk.

Procrastination will keep you in the *Could-Have-Been Waiting Room of Regret. I could have unearthed my potentials, but I did not apply myself to dig into my subliminal-self. I could have been, but I am not.* Will these be your lamentations? Well, they will, if you keep giving yourself excuses to not start today in earnest to unearth your latent potentials. There is the likelihood you may run out of time and end up waiting forever. Remember that *time is the only resource that can never be replenished.* The seconds or minute it took you to read this paragraph are gone, and you can't reclaim it back. I trust the one minute it took you to read it is an excellent investment of your time because of its positive message. Don't put off delving into your subliminal-self. Don't postpone your destiny. Take the bulls of your fate by the horns and conquer it. In the words of Sam Levenson, "Don't watch the clock; do what it does. Keep going." Unearth your latent potentials.

Have some sense of urgency in this self-exploration expedition. Let that urgency drive you to pursue your potentials with full alacrity. Like that architectural blueprint earlier mentioned that becomes a building when constructed, make your efforts to unearth your inner powers and create something tangible. Don't wait forever to unearth those potentials.

You Risk Never Finding Fulfillment

The *fourth* thing you may stand to lose when you procrastinate instead of reaching for your inner powers is that you *risk never finding fulfillment* in life. One of the terrifying thoughts is going through life, never knowing what it means to be really fulfilled doing things that matter to you. The fault cannot be passed to anyone but yourself. It is your failure and shame to bear. We are all credited the same 31,556,926 seconds in a non-leap year to accomplish our goals and missions and fulfill our dreams. You don't have to go through a completely life-changing event in your life to see the importance of unearthing your potential—a process that often leads to fulfillment. Sometimes, it will come in the form of a book like this, nudging you to get out and discover yourself and all your inherent capabilities.

If you think procrastination is an easy option, think about the pain of spending the rest of your life without anything to give it color. The greatest regret you will ever experience in this life is knowing you could've been more. However, because of fearing the unknown, you never tried to take that leap of faith off the allegorical cliffs of possibilities to discover the hidden potential that could have ushered you into the arms of an all-round life-transforming success. And what is worse is you cannot silence the unrelenting nudge in your mind that you were made for more. As human beings, it is the one thing we are very aware of: the presence of potentials in us, even when we don't know what exactly they are. We are all carriers of possibilities. However, you will never know what you can achieve if you never try. So, stop putting off your dig, and start digging now.

Get uncomfortable with only desiring what you could become. Don't just wish, take the necessary first step, and start acting on your passions. Start unearthing, take the tools you have been given through this book, and hold on tight to them. Swing after every emblematic swing, break through the barrier rocks that separate you from the gems buried in your subconscious. Break through the unplowed grounds and depths of your subliminal-self, for it is time to unravel the best version of yourselves. Don't be so risk-averse that you rob yourself of the possibilities of your future fulfillment. Hold on tenaciously to the vision of who you see yourself becoming through the outputs of your newfound gifts. Hang onto the aspiration to become your best self. Don't stop reaching or seeking until you find that unique you. It will be the source of your fulfillment.

You Risk Operating Below Par

The *fifth* thing you may stand to lose when you defer discovering your subconscious skills is that *you risk operating below par.* Who wants to be mediocre in life? Everyone wants to be the focus of attention. When you are performing above par, you instantly become the toast of every occasion. Potentials are so powerful that they can be anything—the possibilities are just endless. There's no limit to how big they could get or the impact they'll have. Let us go back to the illustration of the architectural blueprint. On paper, you can hold the entire building with your two hands, and if you didn't know the equivalence of those measurements in real-time, it would just be the drawing of a beautiful structure that you think looks good but doesn't mean much else, after that. At best, an unconstructed architectonic blueprint is subpar to its full potential, a domicile built for habitation.

However, when the drawing is translated in real-time, through building construction and everything else required in the process, you will better appreciate the measurement of spaces typified in the 2-dimensional architectural drawing and space planning matrix. Standing in a 10×10 square foot (i.e., 3.04×3.04 square meters) standard-size bedroom takes on a whole new different meaning as you begin to experience the room 3-dimensionally than when you look at it on a 2-dimensional floor plan. That is how big potentials can get: from something as small as an idea to a life-size behemoth of an actualized idea gone live.

By procrastinating and holding yourself back, you remain that small, 2-dimensional floor plan drawn on the construction-drawing documents. You stay just a *potential,* not an *expressed-potential,* a *fraction* of a possible *whole.* You will remain unaccomplished and unfulfilled, just like that media that holds the drawing before it is transformed through construction into the actual building. Tell me, *do you want to remain just a drawing or plan of what you could become all your life?* Or, *do you want to grow into all your forms and become of lasting value?*

Regardless of what holds you back, let that truth ring in your ears: you are much more than what you are now. Don't let anyone lie to you by telling you that you are not worth much. Refuse to be less than all you can be. Don't be subpar. At the end of the day, it all remains a function of chance. If you take the opportunity to unearth your hidden skills, you have a chance of discovering them. If you don't, then it is what it is: an opportunity foregone. It is all your choice.

—~—

What are you waiting for? Begin your expedition to explore the many potentials that lie latent in you. Do something about it and be unapologetic about it. Don't just assimilate this knowledge without action. Practicalize it, and make it work for you. Take a chance on yourself and discover your potential. Let the world celebrate the genius you carry within you. Let them benefit from the true riches of that genius written in the DNA of your subconscious.

Be it the genius of excellent musical performance, exceptional athletic skills, great people leadership skills, intellectual wealth, great oratory powers, just to mention but a few.

Whatever it is, don't deny the world the brilliance of your one-in-a-million genius. Now, it might not feel that way at the beginning when it is still rusty and in need of dedicated deliberate practice. That's why it is a *potential.* That is something that can *become.* The characteristic traits are there recessively, waiting to be expressed.

Start where you are. Begin with your strengths, and put them to work. Rise with your courage, and give no room to cowardice. Commence with the resources available to you. *Half a loaf is better than none.* Nothing can stop the determined soul who presses forward toward the mark of their high-calling and distinction. Persevere through the process, just like miners searching the earth for minerals. They don't readily give up their relentless search. The knowledge that they are digging for something valuable is enough to inspire them to keep the dig alive.

The journey may not be all smooth-sailing at first. However, in discovering your potential, you are finding something that will be of great significance. The resplendent benefits will not be just for you, but also to the people who will be beneficiaries of its *products* and *by-products.* While there is a limit to what you can control life, this self-discovery process lies firmly in your hands. You choose whether to embark on the journey or not. It is a game of choices. If you do choose it, you stand a chance of a big win. If you don't, well, you may never know what you can attain. It is a responsibility to which you should step up.

Start probing now. Don't put it off till tomorrow. Remember, *tomorrow is not guaranteed. This very second, this very moment, is all you've got, so use it wisely*. Begin the journey toward *unearthing your latent potentials.* Make a date with destiny and start *discovering the gems of your subliminal-self.* Trade the outputs of your potentials to profit to your advantage. Enjoy the life your newfound possibilities create for you. Sustain your abilities through more discoveries. Make this process strategically cyclical. Your destiny is yours for the taking. So, *what will it be?*

CHAPTER 15

Let the Digging Begin!

FROM THE TIME THE EARTH has been in existence till date, many discoveries have been made. It is pertinent to say that with the astronomical rise in scientific innovations, there isn't much that can stand in the way of future discoveries. These discoveries are proof of the availability of potentials within the earth's paunch. Just think about the future of humanity and how these discoveries will continue to shape the way we live and the difference we make. We can say without any modicum of doubt that the human element is crucial in the existence of all things. The impacts are seen in the past, in the present, and in eons to come.

In the constitution of all things, elysian and ephemeral, you matter more than you think. In the changes and innovations we are experiencing, coming to us at astronomical speeds, you do matter. You are uniquely made to make a difference in this lifetime. You can enter the *Chronicles of Time,* being written by Lord Chronos, and be remembered for doing extraordinary things that changed the drift and reverberation of human existence. It's high time you discover the genius in you, unearth it, refine it, and unleash it. All of humanity is waiting for your *full* expression.

The goal of this book is to help you make your own discovery so that you, too, can contribute to the world.

You were not made to be just ordinary. You can become extraordinary by unearthing your hidden abilities. You were not made to be just common. You can become uncommon by unraveling the unique gems of your subliminal-self. You can become more. You can do more. You can become that force of innovation that transforms our today, writing and re-writing the unique ciphers of our tomorrow. Don't shortchange yourself and the destiny of humanity through self-doubt or fear. Believe that *you can* and *you will.* Spur yourself into action. In the words of Paul Harvey Aurandt, American broadcaster, "I've never seen a monument erected to a pessimist." Become optimistic that *you can* unearth your golden potentials and the monuments of your discoveries will grace the landscapes of the annals of time. Take that first step. Remember, as I have said many times before in this book, *More act, less lag.*

With this book, I hope you will be spurred toward the process of self-discovery. My sincere wish is to see you develop a deep-seated hunger in the innards of your soul that pushes you forward toward doing more. I desire to see you engulfed under the cloud canopies of the thought of, *What more can I become?*

I hope you will be motivated to embark on this explorative journey of self-discovery. I desire to see you discover your distinct voice waiting for expression. I want you to become the best version of yourself yet by *unearthing your latent potentials.* The gems of your subliminal-self are waiting for you to discover them. Don't hold yourself back. Start digging, today!

Build an ongoing relationship with this book. Each word is alive and actively seeking a relationship with you, the reader. This book's contents are quick and potent, and it will drill through the crusts of your subconscious to make kinetic the potential energies stored in the gems of your hidden abilities. The words are transformational. They will nudge you toward becoming more than you currently are, but only if you let them. The words you read seek to only help you gain an understanding and the discovery of your inner capacities.

We have come a long way through this book. We are in the final chapter of *Unearthing Your Latent Potentials.* Throughout this book, we have spoken to different subjects as it relates to unearthing your latent potentials (i.e., our abilities, gifts, skills, or talents).

In the *Preface* and *Introduction,* we started by laying the underpinning of the work and preparing our minds for the self-exploration journey. We looked at the process of unearthing your possibilities and likened it to extracting natural minerals like gold, crude oil, diamond, etc.

Next, in *Chapter 1,* we saw what potentials are.

We then moved on to *Chapter 2* to learn why our inner potentials could remain latent (i.e., dormant, hidden, inactive, or in a suspended state). We saw in elaborate ways of how *fear, self-doubt, procrastination, giving up prematurely,* and *laziness* could easily keep your potentials under. Avoid them.

In *Chapter 3,* we took some time and liberty to delve into some pre-activities (i.e., *the art of journaling, noting your patterns,* and *drawing up a vision for your life*) that would help you in your self-exploration expedition. *First,* as you interact with the book by reading it, you will start generating thoughts and ideas from its content. How best to record these thoughts than by writing them down? *Second,* as you read through this book, you will start noticing patterns in your life. Again, write them down. *Third,* with the new information you gain, start forging a vision for your life as you interact with this book. Once again, write them down.

From *Chapter 4* all the way to *Chapter 7,* we spent a considerable amount of time dissecting our strategic self-analysis tool of choice (i.e., the SWOT Analysis Matrix Tool) that we can use to unearth the rudiments of our *status quo* as we dug into our subliminal-self.

In *Chapter 4,* we took the liberty to look at how we could discover our *Strengths* (**S**). We looked at how you develop your strengths by investing in personal development, getting a mentor, being deliberate about acquiring new skills, engaging in constant practice, and taking on responsibilities, just to mention but a few. Our strengths are a clear signal that point us toward our potentials.

In *Chapter 5,* we saw how we could identify our *Weaknesses* (**W**) and the various reasons why we should not tolerate them. No one wants to be the weakest link in any scenario whatsoever. Allowing an infected wound will only make it deteriorate into gangrene. We harped on the need to *recognize* our weaknesses. A defect that we recognize is already half solved. Failure to see our weaknesses means they will continue to eat away at the fabric of us unearthing our innate potentials. We must utilize our strengths to help us mitigate, or preferably eliminate, our weaknesses.

In *Chapter 6,* we took an in-depth look at our *Opportunities* (**O**). Here, we saw the need to make the most of the *moments* that come to us as a chance to *shine.* We saw that opportunities mostly come like a flash, often not seen or recognized by many and often lost. Therefore, we need to become more perceptive at the instances of the opportunities coming our way. Look around you for chances to make an impact. Look at your competition to see if that motivates you to do more. Look for principal pain points that you can do something about. The principal factor here is for you to leverage most or all opportunities you encounter. Make sure you grab any once-in-a-lifetime chances whenever they come your way.

In *Chapter 7,* we discussed the *Threats* (**T**) we could face in our process of unearthing our potentials. It is *an element in the environment (i.e., external), or even internal, that can cause us damage, trouble, or some potential harm.* Today, we hear of all kinds of threats—security, nuclear, cyber, health, financial, ecological, environmental, etc. We are not to play around with fatal risks, and they must be dealt with decisively, whether it's your weakness that morphs into a hazard, an area of your life threatens other areas resulting from when equilibrium is lost, or your current skills losing relevancy in the now or future, etc. Whatever the threat, don't play around with it. Eliminate it immediately, or it will destroy you. There is no room for mercy. Be ruthless in eliminating your threats. It may seem harsh, *but it is literally kill, or be killed.*

While exploring this strategic self-analysis tool, (i.e., the SWOT Analysis Matrix) in *Chapter 4–7,* several cogent questions were asked as we surveyed each attribute. Asking probing questions is advantageous because it helps us dig deeper into areas of our lives that we don't want to bring to the spotlight areas that need better illumination and clarity or the discovery of necessary answers that can provoke a reaction toward our essential transformation. By answering these inquiries and journaling them, you begin to delve deeper into your subconscious self. We begin to excavate the dirt of our flaws and limitations as we start discovering the makeup of your *status quo.* Asking and answering these questions and more help you to begin generating the raw material gems that you can use to unleash the best versions of yourself yet.

In *Chapter 8,* we then saw a practical way that we could do this by using the continuous improvement model for carrying out change—the **P**lan-**D**o-**C**heck-**A**ct (PDCA) cycle. Here, we saw that by planning, doing, checking, acting, or adjusting, in consonance with the facts we obtained from the SWOT Analysis Matrix, we could practically commence the unearthing process. As the circle has no end but is continuous, so also is the PDCA cycle. Deploying it means we are thinking about sustainable terms toward preserving the continuity of what we have started.

In *Chapter 9,* we saw how we could refine or polish our potentials. To do so, we saw that extracting our possibilities is the first step to perfecting them. If you don't excavate those potentials, you will have nothing to polish. Next step in the refining process is distillation. Here, we learned how to *set a mindset,* meaning the removal of the chaotic and the elimination of the foreign, extraneous, or objectionable elements from the mind palace. Anything that does not add value should be eliminated. In the refining stage of this process, *first,* practice your way to perfection, and *second,* allow the heat of trials to shape you. *Third,* put your newfound potentials to the test. Try them out to determine their potency. When you hone and make the most of your potential, you become recognized by those around you.

In *Chapter 10,* we saw that the process of refining your newfound abilities gives you the chance to begin extracting the *products* and *by-products* that are produced. We saw that the *products* of our potentials could be *hard skills* or *soft skills.* We then looked at some possible *by-products* such as *skill expression, confidence, competence, passion and enthusiasm, valuable network, and service.* These outputs provide the means to trade our newfound potentials for the various benefits they offer.

In *Chapter 11,* we then proceeded to look at how we could trade the outputs of our newfound abilities. After all, *who wants to retain the inventory of products in any process?* In my career history, working as a manager and leader in the retail industry, one of the most significant sources of wastage that we always faced were direct results of excessive inventory levels. The most practical business sense is to get the products in the hands of the customers. Stocking them in your backrooms or warehouses for prolonged periods does not make the right business sense. The goal is to market your yields for profit, not to keep them. The same applies to the outputs of our potentials. Some of the ways we saw for trading the outputs of our newfound potentials were branding, product development, publicizing or advertising, training, entrepreneurship, volunteering, or by just adding value as an employee of an organization.

In *Chapter 12,* we saw that when you sell the outputs of the unearthing process of our potentials, we amass earnings or benefits from the process. We saw that the benefits could be monetary or non-monetary benefits. *Should you not enjoy the fruits of your labors?* In the words of Eileen Caddy, the late British writer, "Live and work but do not forget to play, to have fun in life and really enjoy it." Relish your work and make it a point of duty to find time to enjoy the benefits that your potentials create. There is nothing wrong with that notion at all.

In *Chapter 13,* we looked at the sustainability of our newfound potentials via the lens of several *sustainability bits* that I recommend you review from time to time. No one wants the lifespan of their success to be short-lived. We want the profits of our skills in action to be sustainable. We do so by keeping our self-exploration life processes alive and cyclical. As mentioned above, the PDCA cycle can help us do just that as we continue to improve and reinvent ourselves.

In *Chapter 14,* a clarion call is made, urging you, the reader, to begin your expedition toward unearthing your latent potentials. We addressed some of the dangers of procrastination like *missing out on vital opportunities available to you, missing out on quality relationships, waiting forever because of your inaction, never finding fulfillment,* and *operating subpar.* Don't procrastinate. It doesn't help you in any way. Do well and start your journey immediately. The best day to start was yesterday, and today is the next best day. Therefore, *just start.*

Now, here we are, in *Chapter 15,* where I am taking my last shot at the bullseye of your subconscious, my final gesture, and windup call as I nudge your debonair indulgence to let the digging begin in earnest. Remember, *Tempus fugit—Time flies.*

Once again, don't forget all the knowledge you have obtained going through this book. If you must review it repeatedly to gain mastery of its practical contents, do so. Combine your thoughts with its suggestions. Synergize with it.

Remember, *synergy is energy.*

—~—

There is a lot you are capable of that you probably don't know yet. There are a lot of potentials buried in the depths of your subconscious. A lot of us limit ourselves because we have not pushed past our limiting beliefs to give ourselves a chance to excel. Now, here is your golden opportunity to break through that mold.

The possibilities of your innate potential are extensive, and the limitations you experience are a direct product of your own imagination. You can be whatever you want to be if only you can recognize your hidden talents and make consistent efforts toward developing and applying them in meeting societal needs. Don't live a small-minded life. Challenge yourself to dig out those latent potentials and let them find full expression in your everyday living.

Don't go to the grave with all those potentials. Be determined to never let that become your story. The cemeteries are already filled with the unfulfilled possibilities of those who have passed on. Don't let yours go there too. Empty yourself out. Start unearthing your potentials, today.

Be excited at the possibilities of what you could become. Allow this book to be the catalyst that provokes you into action. Take the first step toward your best life ever. Motivate yourself to begin the journey of self-exploration today!

Do not procrastinate. The best day to start was yesterday, and today is the next best day.

Start *unearthing your latent potentials.* Start *discovering the gems of your subliminal-self* today.

Ije ọma! Bon voyage!

ACKNOWLEDGMENTS

In Africa, specifically in Nigeria, there is an Igbo and Yoruba adage that also exists in many other African languages and cultures: *It takes a village to raise a child.* Raising a child is not a *solo* effort. It takes a community to help raise a child into what they become in the future. The same can be said of this book. *It was not a solo effort.*

Writing a book is not an easy feat, to say the very least. It is a complicated process—right from the conceptualization stage to writing the last line of the manuscript. I have invested hundreds of hours bringing this book to fruition. I am very appreciative for the countless tangible and intangible contributions from friends and loved ones. For it all, I am very thankful.

The book *Unearthing Your Latent Potentials: Discovering the Gems of Your Subliminal-Self* bears testament to God who has given me the life and the years to be here today and the ability to pen this work down. My life, so far, has been nothing but exploratory—an exciting adventure into my subconscious depths. For the tacit knowledge I have gained from experience on this journey, I am eternally grateful, first to God, to whom I ascribe my ability to move and have my being.

Many thanks to the Omotoyes for standing solidly behind me through this process. Thank you, Mila, for your unflinching support and encouragements through this process. You have been a brother, indeed. To the Abrakas, I am not ungrateful. Allison, your assistance through this process has been pivotal. Your inputs were always full of erudition and always welcomed. Thank you for the acclaim. To the Anigilajes, many thanks to you. Rotimi, your prayers and support were nothing but golden.

I extend my appreciation to the Ibejis. Amara, thanks for your brotherliness, interest, support, and acclaim through this process. To Dawn Lovely, I appreciate the time you took out from your busy schedule to read my manuscript. Thank you for your acclaim. Thank you to Ogbonnaya Okorie. Your challenge to me made this work happen. Thanks for always checking in on my progress through the writing phase. Akin Okon, you surprised me with an expensive tactile keyboard, a kind gesture well appreciated. Thank you for your support. To Susan Aihe, your moral support and acclaim through this process have been fantastic. Thank you.

To Udo Nwankwo, my brother and friend, our many inspiring chats have been pivotal in making this happen. Thank you for your support, and many appreciations for also introducing me to Chinomso John Okebie, a friend indeed whom everyone should have on their team. Chinomso, you have been remarkable, supportive, inspirational, and a definite plus. Thank you for your acclaim, your IT altruism, and everything. Also, many thanks to all my in-laws for your prayers, support, and understanding.

Time will fail me as I give my many appreciations to all those who have been very supportive to me in this process. You are in my heart and can never be forgotten. In the spirit of my book title, *Unearthing Your Latent Potentials: Discovering the Gems of Your*

Subliminal-Self, you are all *gems* set on the tablet of my heart. To the *Obsidian,* the *Aventurines,* the *Onyxes,* the *Sunstones,* the *Lapis Lazuli,* the *Chrysoprase,* and the like, I say a warm and sincere thank you to all.

For the Illustrations in this book, I want to thank Natalia Bystrova (*www.neitdesign.com*), for the exciting infographics in this book. I also want to thank Rachel Reclam for designing and organizing the journal section of this book. Many thanks to the Amnet-Systems team for their work to ensure the line editing of this book, the cover design, typesetting, formatting for both paperback and eBook, and indexing came out superb with no hitches. I appreciate Murali Krishna and Udhayakumar Raja for making the communication with Amnet-Systems seamless and personal. Thank you to you and your team.

To my current and future fans who are reading this book, I say thank you for entrusting the hours of your life to me and this book. I have invested hundreds upon hundreds of hours in bringing this book to life. My goal is to see that your life does not remain the same. I hope reading this book has added some value to your life, and that the time you spent reading it has been beneficial, instructive, and full of learning and continuous improvement. Thank you to all my readers who saw value in this book. Thank you to those who trusted me and my work enough to also recommended it to others for them to purchase. I am forever grateful and indebted to you all. Thank you, again.

To my parents, HRH Ezeogo Elder Dr. and Lolo Agom-Eze, I owe a lot of thanks for setting an excellent example for me to look up to. This book is about the discovery of one's innate potentials and caught the passion for discovering possibilities by looking up to the examples of my father. Dad, thank you for your models and achievements. The process of discovery requires the attributes of *patience* and *passion*. These two qualities I got from my mother. Mum, thank you. Your love, care, your support, and fatherly and motherly compassions have been pivotal in instilling a will to become the best person I was created to become through the discovery of my various innate potentials.

I owe thanks most of all, though, to my family—my wife and kids. To Jaden, my first child and handsome prince, thank you for your care, for always asking me about how my day was and about my progress with my manuscript. To Zoe, my second child, and the beautiful princess, thank you for your caring to know about my writing process. To Jonathan, my third child, and the handsome prince. *You were my sidekick through this process*. Thanks for the many hours you behaved sitting by me at Starbucks while I plugged in many hours writing this book; for your discipline, patience, and understanding.

Finally, Kelechi, my wife, you have been *my rock* and *mainstay* through thick and thin, for better for worse, we rise. Challenges of the past came, and we conquered all with the help of God. We braved the *losses* of the past that rocked our boat as we sail together through life, together. Thank you for your love, patience, and understanding for the many days I was away toiling away—word-after-word, precept-after-precept—at Starbucks and in the home office, while you took care of the home front. You have been my backbone through this process. I love you, and I say thank you.

INDEX

ABOUT THE AUTHOR

OGBONNAYA AGOM-EZE IS THE AUTHOR of *Acorns of the Soul,* a compendium of poetry. He is the founder of the media organization www.scoopiforist.com, a U.S. based online media company and subsidiary of Scoopiforist, LLC, and other companies.

For more information about Ogbonnaya Agom-Eze, visit his website at *www.ogbonnayaagomeze.com.*

READING GROUP GUIDE

Unearthing Your Latent Potentials

Discovering The Gems of Your Subliminal-Self

Ogbonnaya Agom-Eze

A note to book clubs and discussion groups from the author of

UNEARTHING YOUR LATENT POTENTIALS

—∞—

MY GOAL OF WRITING *"UNEARTHING YOUR Latent Potentials: Discovering the Gems of Your Subliminal-Self,"* is to start a broader *discussion* on the topic of *"Potential."* I believe that every human being is created to become more. No one is designed to be mediocre. I want to see people on a broad scale delving deeper into the art of introspection. In so doing, people can unearth the great gems of potentials that are buried in their subconscious.

There is a power that is inherent in the sharing of ideas with others. Discussions allow us to rub our minds together. Group discussions allow for the diffusion of thoughts from the different participating members. In a group discussion (e.g., at a book club), more than one brain is thinking about the topic. As you discuss your gains and opinions about opinions that this book has spawned, be open to the views of your team members. Allow the analysis generated by the divergent thoughts that arise to help you discover or mold your potentials even better.

It is quite exciting that you and your team have chosen my book as the focus of a group discussion. I am humbled and most appreciative of this—thank you. Therefore, I have posited several questions that can allow your group to delve deeper into the concept of *potentials.* I hope that as you discuss this book, that it will help you become more self-aware as you take yourself to the next level of positive self-discovery.

Have a swell time reading this book.

QUESTIONS AND TOPICS FOR DISCUSSION

1. In your own words, *what are potentials*? Do you practice self-reflection as a way of searching out your hidden abilities? Share some of your thoughts and practices?

2. Think of the most recent skill you acquired. What was it? How long did it take you to master and become very efficient at its use? How beneficial has this discovered potential been in your life? Share some of your thoughts.

3. What limiters have you faced in your life that has barred you from achieving your dreams of unleashing your potentials? Was it fear, self-doubt, procrastination, giving up prematurely, laziness, or something else. Share some of your thoughts on these limiters and what you did to overcome them.

4. How do you record your thoughts and ideas? Do you journal? If yes, what medium do you love best? How beneficial is this art to you? Are you a paper-and-ink person, or do you record your thoughts digitally? How have you benefitted from this art?

5. Do you believe that a human is a composite organization of patterns? What are some of the prevailing models in your life? Are they beneficial, or do you need to change them? How have you benefitted from this art?

6. What is your thought concerning this phrase: *Vision guides?* Do you have a vision that guides you? What does it look like,

and what is it composed of? Do you feel like your vision keeps you grounded? If so, how?

7. What are your strengths? Are they dreams, hard or soft skills? What are you exceptionally good at? What privilege do you have that gives you leverage over others? What achievements are you most proud of? What values do you hold that puts you at a place of advantage? What do people commend you for recurrently? Seeded in such accolades could be your strengths—your potentials. Finally, what is that one thing you would like to do more of? Discuss these group of questions to help you unravel the depths of your strengths.

8. What are your weaknesses? What do you struggle to do? Is there an area of work you do that you don't enjoy? Do you have any values that you struggle with? Are there some skills of value that you should have but do not wish to acquire? What are some of your character flaws? Discuss these group of questions to help you uncover the depths of your weaknesses that need to be diminished, or preferably eliminated.

9. What are your opportunities which your inward strengths/ skills do I need to leverage? Are there particular skills you have overlooked? Which ones could immediately add value to you? Looking outward, what are some of the opportunities that surround you? What is your competition doing that motivates you to want to do more? Is there a principal pain point (i.e., a problem) that you can do something about? Give examples of how you have leveraged tech as an advantage?

10. In Chapter 6, I stated that *"Life is all about Weltanschauung—your perception about your world view."* That being said, what is your world view? Does your world perception govern your actions? How has it benefitted you?

11. What threats do you face in your journey to unearth your potentials? Do you have any significant concerns in your life impeding your progress? Is there any weakness in your life that could become a threat to your life vision? Is there any sense of disequilibrium in your life? Could such imbalance threaten your life, and your ability to unearth your potential? Is there any area of your life that is thriving while the others are suffering? Are your skills still relevant to the future? Are the acts of your competitors a threat to you?

12. Do you agree that the *Art of Questioning* can help you in digging deeper into your subconscious? Which of the questioning types (i.e., identifying, probing, outcome-seeking, and action questions) do you see yourself using most and why? How has this art been beneficial to you?

13. What are you doing to unearth your latent potentials? Have you discovered your strengths? If yes, what are they? Are you using them? If yes, how? What are you doing to develop yourself? Do you have a mentor? What skills have you deliberately acquired?

14. What are some of the practical things you are doing to refine your potentials? Are these actions that you are taking habitual?

15. What are some of the products and by-products of your potentials that you can visibly see in your life?

16. What are some of the skills *(hard skills or soft skills)* that you feel most competent at? How did you become competent and confident in the use of these skills? What was your process of mastery?

17. How are you trading these *products* and *by-products* of your potentials? Are they profitable for you?

18. You have discovered your potential! Now, how do you intend to sustain it? Which of the sustainability nuggets in Chapter 13 resonates most to you?

19. What have you missed by not unearthing your latent potentials? Have you missed opportunities, or on building quality relationships? Are you there chances you seem to have missed out on that launched you into a long waiting period of times of stagnancy?

20. The concept of potentials is panoramic at best. There are many concepts to discuss and discover in this introspective journey. Do you have any miscellaneous thoughts that you would love to share on this concept? (NB. As the author of this book, I would like to hear some of the different ideas from your book club or discussion group. Feel free to email me at author@ogbonnayaagomeze.com).

APPENDIX

MINI-WORKBOOK JOURNAL

Unearthing Your Latent Potentials

DISCOVERING THE GEMS OF YOUR SUBLIMINAL-SELF

OGBONNAYA AGOM-EZE

SWOT Analysis Matrix

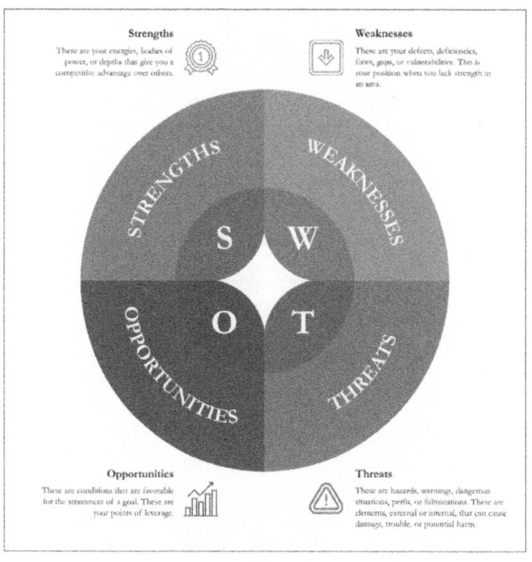

"The SWOT Analysis strategic assessment tool has been used for years by companies to drive productivity and increase organizational efficiency, effectiveness, and profitability. It is a reflective tool that allows the organization to look inwards, stipulating its status quo characteristics. What does the tool do? First, it allows your company to overcome challenges as it determined new leads to pursue. Second, it gives organizations the full knowledge of all the minute constituents involved in a decision. Therefore, this tool can be strategically used in the process of self-discovering and the unearthing of latent potentials in an individual. The core of this book is to take you through a self-auditing process using the SWOT Analysis tool. Hence, discover your hidden abilities. Write them down."— Ogbonnaya Agom-Eze

Miscellaneous Notes:

SWOT Analysis Matrix: Strengths (S)

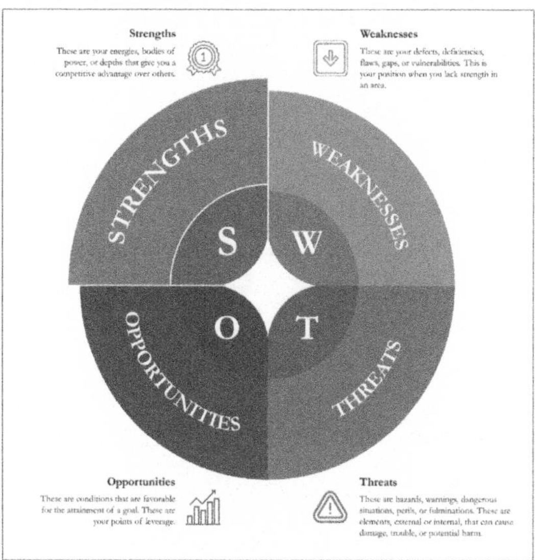

"Your strength is your inherent capacity to manifest energy or a body of powers in an area—or multiple areas—of your life that gives you a competitive advantage over others." — Ogbonnaya Agom-Eze

Questions

What are my dreams? ______________________________

____

____

____

____

____

____

What is my area of strength? ______________________________

____

____

____

____

What am I exceptionally good at? __________________________

____

____

____

____

What do people commend me for?___________________________

____

____

____

____

What is the one thing I would like to do more of?______________

____

____

____

____

What privilege do I have above other people?__________________

____

____

____

____

____

____

What achievements am I most proud of? ____________________

What are my values? ____________________

Miscellaneous Notes: ____________________

SWOT Analysis Matrix: Weaknesses (W)

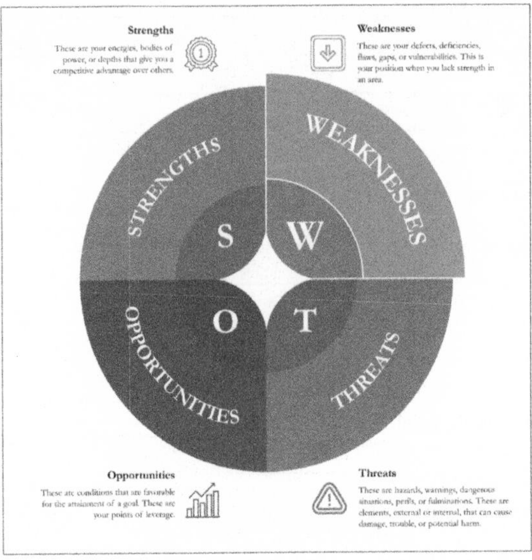

"Weakness (W) (i.e., defects, deficiencies, or gaps) is the lack of strength, firmness, vigor, or the like." — Ogbonnaya Agom-Eze

Questions

What do I struggle to do? ________________________________

____

____

____

____

____

____

____

____

What area of my work do I enjoy least of all? ________________

What values do I struggle with? ________________

What are some valuable skills I do not wish to acquire? ________________

What are some of my character flaws? ________________

Miscellaneous Notes: ________________

SWOT Analysis Matrix: Opportunities (O)

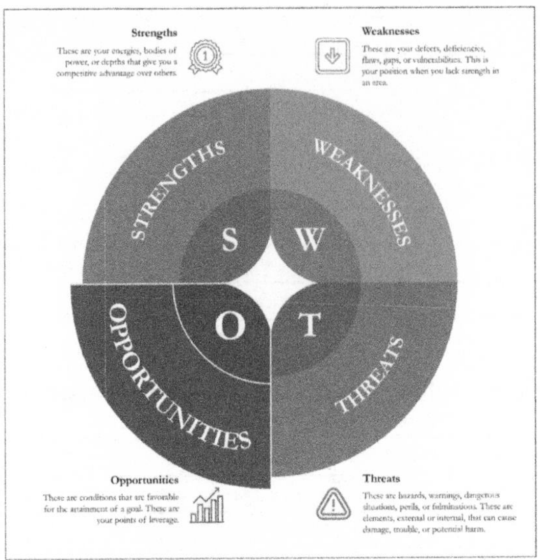

"An opportunity is a situation or condition favorable for the attainment of a goal. It is a good position, a chance, or prospect that channels you toward a protracted advancement or success."
— Ogbonnaya Agom-Eze

Looking Inward

Which of my inward strengths/skills do I need to leverage?

____

____

____

____

____

____

Which of my skills/abilities have I underplayed or overlooked?_

What skills can I learn that can be advantageous to me and help me add value?

Looking Outward

What immediate opportunities surround me?

What is the competition around me that motivates me to do more?

Is there a principal pain point that I can do something about?

How can I leverage technology in my life and career? ________

Miscellaneous Notes: ________

SWOT Analysis Matrix: Threats (T)

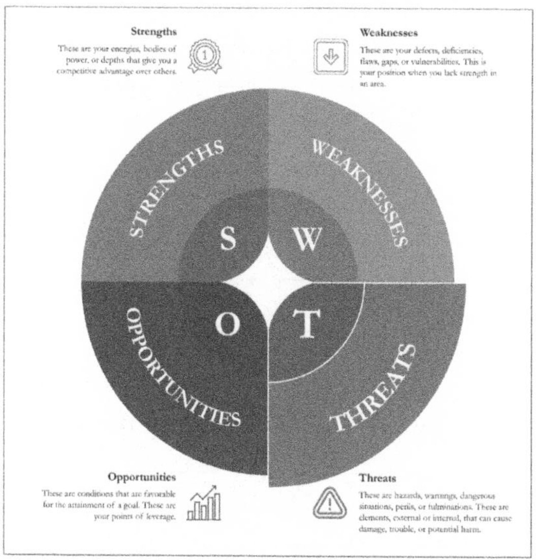

"Threat (i.e., hazard, warning, menace, or peril) is an element, internal or external, that can cause us damage, trouble, or some potential harm." — Ogbonnaya Agom-Eze

Questions

What are the major concerns in my life right now? ____________

____

____

____

____

____

____

____

Could any of my weaknesses be a threat to my life's vision? ____
____
____
____
____

What values do I struggle with? ____________________
____
____
____
____

Does any area of my life threaten another? If yes, how? ______
____
____
____
____

Are my current skills relevant to the future? ____________
____
____
____
____

What are your competitors doing? __________________
____
____
____
____
____
____

What achievements am I most proud of? ____________________

What are my values? ____________________

Miscellaneous Notes: ____________________

PDCA Cycle Tool

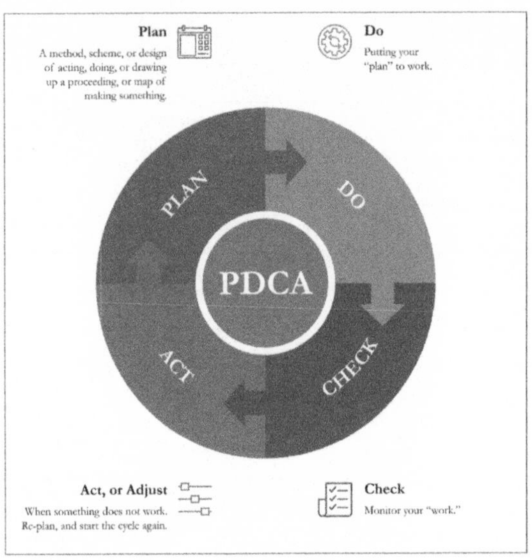

"The American Society for Quality (ASQ), the Plan–Do–Check–Act, or Plan–Do–Check–Adjust cycle (Deming or Shewhart cycle) is a four-step continuous improvement model for carrying out change by planning, doing, checking, and acting, or adjusting. It is beneficial for driving constant improvements to projects, processes, products, or services. Plan allows you to develop a framework to change a perceived need. Do lets you perform by putting the plan into action. Check helps you monitor your efforts to see what you've learned (i.e., what works and what does not work). Act or Adjust allows you to improve on what you have learned. Hence, successful activities are repeated with a broader scope. If unsuccessful, the plan is adjusted, and the process is repeated."— Ogbonnaya Agom-Eze

So, let is get to planning, doing, checking, acting, or adjusting!

Miscellaneous Notes: ______________________________

PDCA Cycle: Plan (P)

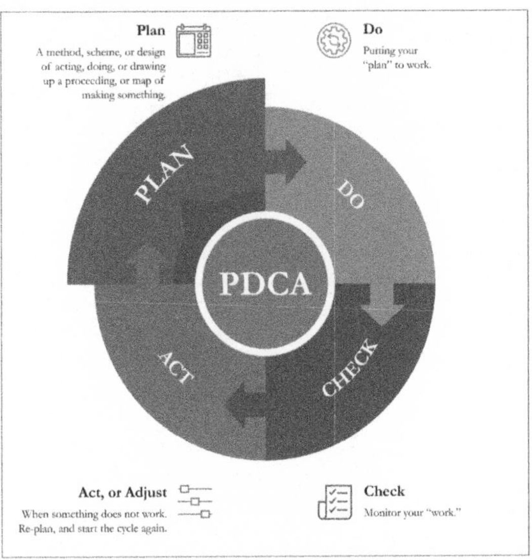

"Plan (P) (design, layout, or map, etc.) is a method of acting, doing, drawing up a proceeding, or a map for making something."— Ogbonnaya Agom-Eze

Questions

Have you gathered inputs using the SWOT Analysis tool to help you build a plan of action? (Circle one: Yes / No). Any other thoughts on this?______________________________

____

____

____

____

____

Do you have a vision of what to do with all the inputs you have gathered? If yes, what is it? ______________________________

What hurdles do you anticipate in this process of developing a plan? ______________________________

What means 'do you have' to deploy to achieve your vision? What resources 'do you need' to unearth your latent potentials? _____

What is your anticipated strategy to achieve your plan? What are the options you can utilize with your resources to reach your goals?______________________________

What time-bound and accountable steps do I need to take to unearth my hidden potentials? ______________________________
____
____
____
____

Re-Check your plan? Do you see any changes? What are they? __
____
____
____
____

Miscellaneous Notes: ____________________________________
____
____
____
____
____
____
____
____
____
____
____
____
____
____
____
____
____

PDCA Cycle: Do (D)

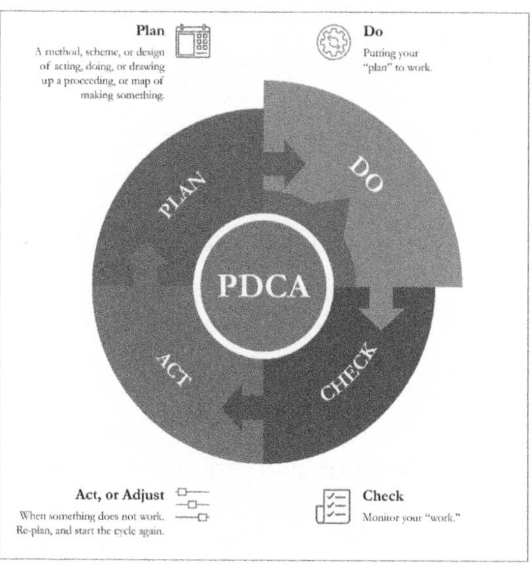

"The Do (D) phase is putting the plan into works." — Ogbonnaya Agom-Eze

Take actionable steps to achieve your goals.

Questions

Have you identified your strengths? If yes, are you working with them? How are you investing in personal development? _______

____

____

____

____

____

Do you have a mentor? If yes, who is he or she? If no, will you consider getting a mentor? ____________________________

____

____

____

____

What skills have you deliberately acquired? ________________

____

____

____

____

What skills have you practiced and perfected to the point of mastery?

____

____

____

____

____

What are some challenging responsibilities that you have recently embraced? ____________________________________

____

____

____

____

Miscellaneous Notes: _____________________________

____

____

____

PDCA Cycle: Check (C)

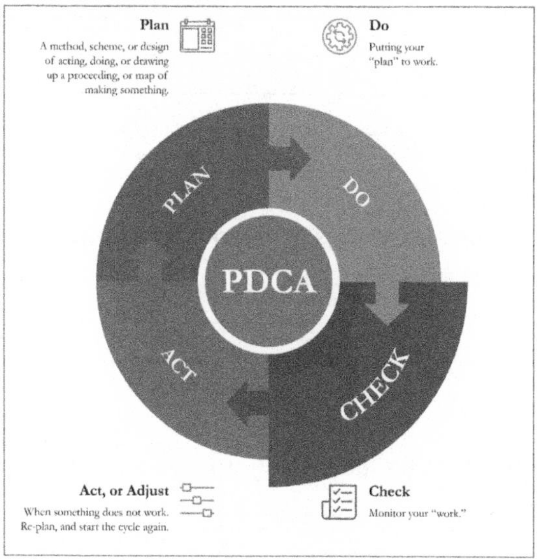

"Check (C) or monitoring phase allows you to observe your actions to ascertain what you have learned and any gaps that may have arisen during the process." — Ogbonnaya Agom-Eze.

Hence, take time to doublecheck yourself.

Questions

How is my digging coming along? ______________________

____

____

____

____

____

What progress am I making in discovering my hidden abilities? ___

What is working and what is not working in my process? ___

What do I need to change in order to make my action plan more efficient? ___

Miscellaneous Notes: ___

PDCA Cycle: Act or Adjust (A)

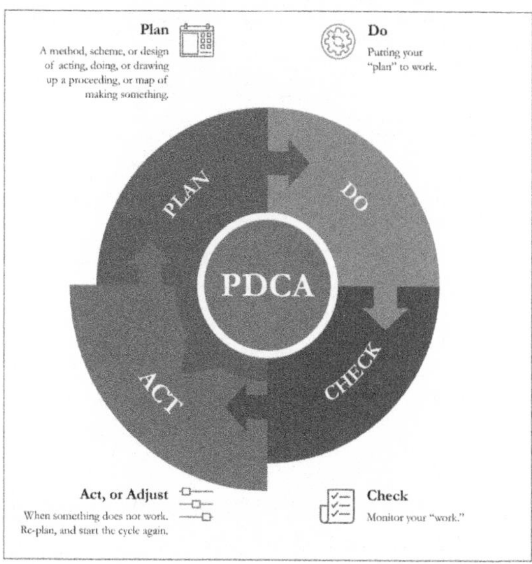

"Act or Adjust (A) phase gives us the chance to continue with a process going in the right direction (i.e., Act), or changing course if not (i.e., adjust)." — Ogbonnaya Agom-Eze.

Questions

Do you see the desired results from acting on your plans? If yes, what are they? ______________________________

____

____

____

____

____

____

Do you see any flaw as work on your plan? If yes, list them out?

What can you adjust in your plan to bring about the desired result?

After acting on your adjusted plan, was the result better than before? If yes, what was different?

As you repeat this step to get better results, what are some of the lessons you have gained in the process?

Miscellaneous Notes: ____________________________________

The Art of Journaling!

"Develop the Art of Journaling, as it is your pathway to exactness and sureness." — Ogbonnaya Agom-Eze

Write the Vision Down!

"Drawing up a vision for your life is like transferring— by journaling or taking note of exemplars—that mental vision from your subconscious to print. Write the vision (i.e., idea, concept, image, thought, or fantasy, etc.) down and make it visible to motivate yourself to start unearthing them."
— Ogbonnaya Agom-Eze

Capitalize on Opportunities!

"Opportunities come like shooting stars. You only have but a moment to catch a glimpse of it and then it is gone."
— Ogbonnaya Agom-Eze

Stay Determined!

"Determination today will lead to success tomorrow."
— Ogbonnaya Agom-Eze

Realize Your Potentials!

"With realization of one's own potential and self-confidence in one's ability, one can build a better world." — Dalai Lama

Get Out of Your Comfort Zone!

"I want to challenge you today to get out of your comfort zone. You have so much incredible potential on the inside. God has put gifts and talents in you that you probably don't know anything about." —Joel Osteen

Reach Your Full Potential!

"The will to win, the desire to succeed, the urge to reach your full potential... these are the keys that will unlock the door to personal excellence." — Confucius

You've Got Potential!

"You can be much more." — Ogbonnaya Agom-Eze

Be a Champion!

"I hated every minute of training, but I said, 'Don't quit. Suffer now and live the rest of your life as a champion."
— Muhammad Ali

You Can Do It!

"The mind is the limit. As long as the mind can envision the fact that you can do something, you can do it, as long as you really believe 100 percent." — Arnold Schwarzenegger